THE
PRESUMPTION
OF **GUILT**

ALSO BY CHARLES J. OGLETREE, JR.

All Deliberate Speed: Reflections on the
First Half-Century of Brown v. Board of Education (2004)

Beyond the Rodney King Story: An Investigation of
Police Conduct in Minority Communities
(with Mary Prosser, Abbe Smith and William Talley, Jr.) (1994)

EDITED COLLECTIONS

Life without Parole: America's New Death Penalty?
(edited with Austin Sarat; forthcoming 2012)

The Road to Abolition? The Future of Capital Punishment
in the United States (edited with Austin Sarat) (2009)

When Law Fails: Making Sense of Miscarriages of Justice
(edited with Austin Sarat) (2009)

From Lynch Mobs to the Killing State: Race and the
Death Penalty in America (edited with Austin Sarat) (2006)

Brown at 50: The Unfinished Legacy
(edited with Deborah L. Rhode) (2004)

THE PRESUMPTION OF GUILT

The Arrest of Henry Louis Gates Jr.
and
Race, Class, and Crime in America

CHARLES J. OGLETREE, JR.

palgrave
macmillan

This book is dedicated to my parents, Charles J. Ogletree Sr. and Willie Mae Ogletree, my wife, Pam Ogletree, my children, Charles Ogletree III and Rashida Ogletree, my daughter-in-law, Rachelle Ogletree, and my three granddaughters, Marquelle, Nia Mae, and Jamila Ogletree. Through them all, I'm blessed to do the work designed to promote justice and equality.

THE PRESUMPTION OF GUILT
Copyright © Charles Ogletree, 2010, 2012.
All rights reserved.

First published in hardcover in 2010 by PALGRAVE MACMILLAN® in the US—a division of St. Martin's Press LLC, 175 Fifth Avenue, New York, NY 10010.

Frontispiece photos: "Professor Henry Louis Gates arrest" by Bill Carter, © Demotix/Bill Carter; "Beer Summit," © Reuters/Jim Young/Landov. Reproduced by permission.

Where this book is distributed in the UK, Europe and the rest of the world, this is by Palgrave Macmillan, a division of Macmillan Publishers Limited, registered in England, company number 785998, of Houndmills, Basingstoke, Hampshire RG21 6XS.

Palgrave Macmillan is the global academic imprint of the above companies and has companies and representatives throughout the world.

Palgrave® and Macmillan® are registered trademarks in the United States, the United Kingdom, Europe and other countries.

ISBN: 978-0-230-12065-5

The Library of Congress has catalogued the hardcover edition as follows:
Ogletree, Charles J.
   The presumption of guilt : the arrest of Henry Louis Gates, Jr. and race, class and crime in America / Charles Ogletree.
      p.   cm.
   ISBN 978-0-230-10326-9 (hardback)
   1. Gates, Henry Louis. 2. Race relations—United States. 3. African Americans—Civil rights. I. Title.
E185.615O35   2010
810.9'896073—dc22
[B]
                                                                    2010017304

A catalogue record of the book is available from the British Library.

Design by Greg Collins

First PALGRAVE MACMILLAN paperback edition: April 2012

10 9 8 7 6 5 4 3 2 1

Printed in the United States of America.

CONTENTS

INTRODUCTION
The Cop and the Professor   9

CHAPTER 1
"Keep the Cars Coming." What Really Happened?   15

CHAPTER 2
"President Obama Doesn't Like White People."
The Public Reaction   41

CHAPTER 3
"Don't Tase Me, Bro!" How Far Have We Really Come?   65

CHAPTER 4
Fair Harvard? The Class Issue   77

CHAPTER 5
Driving while Black.
Fighting Back against Racial Profiling   101

CHAPTER 6
Race, Class, Justice, and Post-Racial America   115

AFTERWORD
Race Matters: The Struggle Continues   129

EPILOGUE
100 Ways to Look at a Black Man   145

ACKNOWLEDGEMENTS   263

NOTES   267

INDEX   277

THE
PRESUMPTION
OF **GUILT**

The Cop and the Professor

The presumption of innocence. These four words are echoed by judges in state and federal courts and by defense lawyers and prosecutors in their opening and closing arguments probably every day. The concept is understood by juries as the bedrock legal standard in our criminal justice system, and jurors are admonished to set aside any bias and to determine fairly the fate of an individual facing the possible loss of property, liberty, or life. It is a concept that is embedded in our law, and a foundation for protecting citizens from the awesome power of government.

For centuries the American people have aspired to create a system where the actions of courts, legislative bodies, and public officials are uniformly committed to the presumption of innocence. The essential point is that a person accused of a crime is presumed innocent until proven guilty. Whether arrested, charged, or indicted, the government must prove its case against the individual beyond a reasonable doubt. Suspicion by police, or witnesses, and an arrest based upon the reports of a victim or eyewitness are not enough. The legal standard requires that the presumption of innocence remain unless and until a judge or jury concludes that the person charged is actually guilty of a crime.

The presumption of guilt. These four words reveal their true meaning as events actually transpire. On July 16, 2009, at 17 Ware Street in Cambridge, Massachusetts, Professor Henry Louis Gates, Jr., Alphonse Fletcher University Professor at Harvard and world-renowned expert on issues of racial equality, found himself at once accused and presumed guilty of breaking into his own home by Cambridge Police Sgt. James Crowley.

On that day, Sgt. Crowley responded to a call about a possible break-in. The eyewitness informed a police dispatcher that one suspect might have been Hispanic but provided no information indicating that an African American was involved and even expressed some doubt as to whether a break-in was in fact occurring, speculating that perhaps a resident was simply struggling to open his own door. Professor Gates was approached by Sgt. Crowley shortly after entering his home. After informing the officer that he lived at 17 Ware Street and producing both his Harvard University identification and his Massachusetts driver's license with his photo and address on it, Gates was arrested. He was, to put it simply, presumed to be guilty of a crime rather than presumed to be a resident in his own home telling the truth about who he was. The obvious question is why.

While the presumption of innocence is fundamental to our system of government, it was clearly absent during this encounter. Again, the question is why.

In this book, I will review the statements, documents, and other important evidence pertaining to the arrest of Professor Henry Louis Gates on July 16 in order to answer these questions. Moreover, my central goal in *The Presumption of Guilt* is to ensure that, whatever point of view you might have about the events of that day, you will also understand that issues of race, class, and justice continue to challenge our nation. The incident was an eye-opener, and it presents us with an opportunity to reassess where we are today.

As Professor Gates' attorney, I am aware that I present one person's perspective on the matter. However, my vantage point as Professor Gates' attorney during the events addressed here is only a part of the story. My conclusions are also based on decades of experience in courtrooms, classrooms, and public and private forums. While a student at Harvard Law School in the criminal clinic, I represented indigent clients in criminal cases. When I graduated from law school, I worked for eight years as a criminal lawyer with the District of Columbia Public Defender Service. My clients were charged with a range of crimes from petty larceny to murder. Throughout my career I have addressed the topics of race, class, and justice with the view of proposing ways to generate more dialogue and understanding and less fear and instill more respect between citizens and law enforcement. My firmly felt goal is that when it comes to the relationships among minority communities, police, and other legal entities and institutions, there should be no conflict between the principles of security and liberty. They should be able to coexist fairly. My aim is not necessarily to change minds, although that would be beneficial, but to open minds to the reality of how problems of race, class, and justice collided (as they do routinely elsewhere) on an otherwise bright, sunny, and beautiful day in Cambridge, Massachusetts.

I will cover new ground, examining the full record of Professor Gates' arrest and information that Sgt. Crowley conveyed then, through police recordings and eyewitness accounts. This information presents a dramatically different scenario from what was originally reported about what happened that day and transforms the context of Gates' arrest. Furthermore, the exchanges between Sgt. Crowley, the eyewitness, the Cambridge police dispatcher, and Professor Gates will offer a new perspective on the confrontation and the charges and explain the quick dismissal of all charges against Professor Gates.

I will explore how the issues of race, class, and crime were ever present in this incident and in the national reactions to what happened. The arrest created a relentless tidal wave of perspectives on police accountability, racial profiling, and the responsibility of individual citizens to respect the role of police officers in preventing crime. Law enforcement experts and political pundits all had something to say about the event, and it set off a blistering series of exchanges on television, in newspapers, on radio shows and blogs. Perhaps the most surprising response came from none other than President Barack Obama, whose offhand comments during a press conference focused on the proposed health care debate offered support for his friend Professor Gates and accused the Cambridge Police Department of "acting stupidly" for arresting someone in their own home. The responses of President Obama and others are as significant as the event itself.

Professor Gates' encounter with the police was not unprecedented. I will examine other notable encounters between the Cambridge police and African American males, including Harvard faculty and students. I will also take a look back at the most significant recent conflict between African Americans and police, the Rodney King beating in 1991, by reexamining some relevant threads in the event that left dozens of people dead, millions of dollars in damage, and, sadly, little evidence of racial reconciliation when examined more than a decade and a half later. The important signs of a problem not fully pursued following the Rodney King beating and the obvious failure of society and institutions to learn lessons from it remind all of us of the unfinished work that lies ahead.

Finally, this book is about more than the arrest of one man. It is about how we need to examine our criminal justice system to ensure that fairness, not power, is the currency of our system. When we move from a presumption of innocence to a presumption of guilt, we diminish our sense of community and undermine our democratic ideals.

I examine the race and class dimensions of the Gates arrest by looking at how other successful, prosperous, and noteworthy African American men (who are by no means alone in experiencing problems of racial profiling) have grappled with a wide range of encounters not only with police but with countless everyday citizens and found themselves being judged by the color of their skin rather than "the content of their character." Ultimately, if we are to move forward as a nation, we must examine not only what happened to Professor Henry Louis Gates, Jr., on July 16, 2009, but we must also examine what we can and must do, individually and collectively, to develop a justice system that is truly committed to the presumption of innocence.

CHAPTER 1

"Keep the Cars Coming." What Really Happened?

Sgt. James Crowley is a Cambridge native who once worked for the Harvard University Police Department for three years as an officer on the graveyard shift.[1] Professor Henry Louis Gates, Jr., has been on the Harvard faculty for nearly two decades.[2] Yet their paths had not crossed formally (or, to their knowledge, informally) in that period of time. On July 16, 2009, Gates and Crowley, who was serving in his eleventh year in the Cambridge Police Department, found themselves on a collision course with history.[3] Their lives changed instantly, as the story of their meeting drew national and global attention. Ultimately, the Crowley/Gates affair itself may fade into history, but the events of that day and beyond will reverberate for some time, given the combustible ingredients of race, class, and crime.

The irony of the events as they unfolded is not only that Professor Gates and Sgt. Crowley are as different as day and night, left and right, and Black and White, but also that such an esteemed figure on the subjects of race and equality would find himself in any confrontation with the police. Professor Gates has received dozens of honorary degrees and national awards and has been hailed as one of the nation's leading intellectuals. He has been affiliated with the Institute of Advanced Studies at Princeton University, has taught at Duke and Yale, and, since 1991, has been the Alphonse Fletcher University Professor at Harvard University.[4] While Professor Gates is known widely for his role at Harvard University, he had traveled there literally and figuratively thousands of miles and many years away from his humble birthplace in West Virginia.

Gates was born in Keyser, West Virginia, on September 16, 1950.[5] While Gates was still in middle school, his parents learned that their son, a very active and outgoing child, had polio, necessitating several operations and extensive medical care throughout his childhood. One of the consequences of his early health problems is that one leg is shorter than the other, such that he needs a cane to get around.

Gates grew up in Piedmont, West Virginia, during a time when segregation was the norm, and every opportunity for African Americans to assert their racial pride was memorable for him. He shared stories in his best-selling memoir, *Colored People*, about the famous and infamous Black men and women who were celebrated and condemned in the Black section of Piedmont. Both proud of and at times disappointed in the Black cultural experiences in the town, he learned much and grew intellectually as a result of them. Gates attended the local Piedmont High School before going on to Yale for his BA, graduating *summa cum laude*, and to the University of Cambridge in England for his PhD in English Literature.[6]

James Crowley grew up in North Cambridge, a working-class community that also contained a rising middle-class population.[7]

Cambridge is affectionately known as the People's Republic of Cambridge for its progressive politics.[8] Despite the generally liberal ideology, residential segregation, based upon income and personal preferences (by Blacks and by Whites), was prevalent during Crowley's formative years.[9] Following the lead of his older brother, he attended the only public high school in Cambridge, known as CRLS, the Cambridge Rindge and Latin High School.[10] Crowley was a successful but not a star student and was well liked by his teachers, coaches, and classmates. He is well respected by his African American former coach at CRLS, George Greenidge. Coach Greenidge remembers Crowley's remarkable success in wrestling and tenacity on the football field. He speaks enthusiastically about Crowley and considers him one of the most disciplined athletes he has ever coached. Greenidge states that, to this day, he would swear by Crowley at a moment's notice.[11]

After graduating from high school, Crowley worked in several capacities as a police officer and ultimately followed in the path of his father and older brother by pursuing a career in law enforcement in Cambridge. As a result of his success as a police officer in Cambridge, Sgt. Crowley was able to move to Natick, a suburb of Boston, where he owns a comfortable, spacious home and resides with his young family.[12]

Professor Gates rents a comfortable home owned by Harvard in a predominately White neighborhood where residents expect police to investigate any suspicious behavior, prevent as many criminal acts as possible, and maintain the safety of the neighborhood.[13] Residents there have a very different sense of the police than residents of nearby Area IV.

Area IV has a significant African American and Latino presence.[14] Parents there often feel that their children are harassed by the police and that young men are routinely confronted with the misconception that every Black male wearing baggy pants, tennis shoes, and some kind of a baseball cap fits a profile.[15]

Living on Ware Street, fewer than two blocks away from Harvard University, it would seem clear that Professor Gates would be protected—not targeted—by law enforcement. The reality, however, turned out to be quite different. He would soon learn a lot about his own assumptions and understand firsthand the difference between the fundamental principle of the presumption of innocence and the practical application of the presumption of guilt.

July 16 was a bright summer day in Cambridge. Professor Gates was on his way home following a very successful business trip to China. Sgt. Crowley was halfway into his morning schedule, patrolling familiar territory near his old high school. Ms. Lucia Whalen, a circulation and fundraising manager for *Harvard Magazine,* was working at her desk at 7 Ware Street. The summer pace was a little slower because the next issue of the magazine would not be published until October.

Professor Gates was eager to get home after the grueling and long trip. He was not just exhausted but was also suffering from a nagging cold. Despite his exhaustion, Gates was happy to return home to begin editing the results of the genealogical research and interviews he had conducted in China for his *Faces of America* PBS series. He also knew that within days he would begin a relaxing summer at his home on Martha's Vineyard in Oak Bluffs, a community where, for hundreds of years, many African American families have spent the summer.

Professor Gates was met at Logan Airport by one of his favorite drivers, Mr. Driss Elghannaz, who worked for the Boston Car Service, and they went on their way. When Professor Gates arrived at his home in Cambridge at noon, he attempted to enter but discovered that his front door was jammed. He and his driver were able to open it by pressing against the door and forcing it open. Then they discovered that the lock was defective and needed to be replaced.

Professor Gates called Ms. Amanda Moore at the Harvard Real Estate Office to report the damage to his door. She arranged to have it repaired that afternoon. He was pleased that this matter was resolved and looked forward to a routine day. But as we all know, it would turn out to be anything but routine. The day would end with the accomplished professor under arrest, charged with disorderly conduct.

Why did Sgt. Crowley actually arrest Professor Gates, and what was the crime or, better yet, the motivation, for the arrest? The short answer is that neither of these men, who both worked in Cambridge, knew each other, and so presumptions ruled the progression of events. During their interaction, neither felt respected by the other and neither trusted the other. Despite the fact that Gates had the First Amendment right of freedom of speech in his own home and Crowley had the authority of law at the moment to make an arrest, the outcome was not inevitable. How much did race and class contribute to the results of that day?

Shortly after noon, there was a clash of absolutes: the man in his home demanding to be respected and understood, and the police officer investigating an alleged breaking and entering who was displeased with what he viewed as a hostile and uncooperative Black man. There would be trouble. A detailed analysis of an event that only lasted for a few minutes reveals both what happened and what did not happen. The threshold question is: What crime did Professor Gates commit, if any, that justified his arrest on the porch of his home?

Among the most significant factors in the arrest of Professor Henry Louis Gates, Jr., is the statute invoked by Sgt. James Crowley to justify the arrest and the officer's narrative of the six-minute encounter.

The Massachusetts statute invoked is generally entitled Crimes against Chastity, Morality, Decency, and Good Order. As defined, the relevant section (53) applies to: "Common night walkers, common street walkers, both male and female, common railers and brawlers, persons who with offensive and disorderly acts or language accost or annoy persons of the opposite sex, lewd, wanton and lascivious persons in speech or behavior, idle and disorderly persons, disturbers of the peace, keepers of noisy and disorderly houses, and persons guilty of indecent exposure."[16]

The penalty for a violation includes "imprisonment in a jail or house of correction for not more than six months, or by a fine of not more than two hundred dollars, or by both such fine and imprisonment."[17] A close examination of this statute reveals that it does not apply to Professor Gates' conduct in his home or on his porch. Yet it is by nature a broad statute that gives police officers virtually unfettered discretion in effecting an arrest.

Sgt. Crowley's police report tells a story that might appear to be difficult to challenge: a seamless discussion of an investigation into a reported crime. Crowley prepared the public document after the arrest, filing it with both the police department and the office which handles criminal matters in Cambridge, the Middlesex District Attorney's Office. All this before Gates appeared in court to defend himself on Friday, July 17, 2009.

Sgt. Crowley's report described the arrest as follows:

> On July 16, 2009 Henry Gates, Jr. (of Ware Street, Cambridge, MA) was placed under arrest at Ware Street, after being observed exhibiting loud and tumultuous behavior, in a public place, directed at a uniformed police officer who was present investigating a report of a crime in progress. These actions on the behalf of Gates served no legitimate purpose and caused citizens passing by this location to stop and take notice while appearing surprised and alarmed.
>
> At approximately 12:44 PM, I was operating my cruiser on Harvard Street near Ware Street. At that time, I overheard an ECC broadcast for a possible break[-in] in progress at—Ware Street. . . .
>
> When I arrived at—Ware Street I radioed ECC and asked that they have the caller meet me at the front door to this residence. I was told that the caller was already outside. As I was getting this information, I climbed the porch stairs toward the front door. As I reached the door, a female voice called out to me. I turned and looked in the direction of the voice and observed a white female, later identified as Whalen. Whalen, who was standing on the sidewalk in front of the residence, held a wireless telephone in her hand and told me that it was she who called. She went on to tell me that she observed what appeared to be two black males with backpacks on the porch of—Ware Street. She told me that her suspicions were aroused when she

observed one of the men wedging his shoulder into the door as if he was trying to force entry. Since I was the only police officer on location and had my back to the front door as I spoke with her, I asked that she wait for other responding officers while I investigated further.

As I turned and faced the door, I could see an older black male standing in the foyer of—Ware Street. I made this observation through the glass paned front door. As I stood in plain view of this man, later identified as Gates, I asked if he would step out onto the porch and speak with me. He replied "no I will not." He then demanded to know who I was. I told him that I was "Sgt. Crowley from the Cambridge Police" and that I was "investigating a report of a break[-in] in progress" at the residence. While I was making this statement, Gates opened the front door and exclaimed "why, because I'm a black man in America?" I then asked Gates if there was anyone else in the residence. While yelling, he told me that it was none of my business and accused me of being a racist police officer. I assured Gates that I was responding to a citizen's call to the Cambridge Police and that the caller was outside as we spoke. Gates seemed to ignore me and picked up a cordless telephone and dialed an unknown telephone number. As he did so, I radioed on channel 1 that I was off in the residence with someone who appeared to be a resident but very uncooperative. I then overheard Gates asking the person on the other end of his telephone call to "get the chief" and "what's the chief's name?" Gates was telling the person on the other end of the call that he was dealing with a racist police officer in his home. Gates then turned to me and told me that I had no idea who I was "messing" with and that I had not heard the last of it. While I was led to believe that Gates was lawfully in the residence, I was quite surprised and confused with the behavior he exhibited toward me. I asked Gates to provide me with photo identification so that I could verify that he resided at—Ware Street and so that I could radio my findings to ECC. Gates initially refused, demanding that I show him identification but then did supply me with a Harvard University identification card. Upon learning that Gates was affiliated with Harvard, I radioed and requested the presence of the Harvard University Police.

With the Harvard University identification in hand, I radioed my findings to ECC on channel two and prepared to leave. Gates again asked for my name which I began to provide. Gates began to yell over my spoken words by accusing me of being a racist police officer and leveling threats that he wasn't someone to mess with. At some point during this exchange, I became aware that Off. Carlos Figueroa was standing behind me. When Gates asked a third time for my name, I explained to him that I had provided it at his request two separate times. Gates continued to yell at me. I told Gates that I was leaving his residence and that if he had any other questions regarding the matter, I would speak with him outside of the residence.

As I began walking through the foyer toward the front door, I could hear Gates again demanding my name. I again told Gates that I would speak with him outside. My reason for wanting to leave the residence was that Gates was yelling very loud and the acoustics of the kitchen and foyer were making it difficult for me to transmit pertinent information to ECC or other responding units. His reply was "ya, I'll speak with your mama outside." When I left the residence, I noted that there were several Cambridge and Harvard University police officers assembled on the sidewalk in front of the residence. Additionally, the caller, Ms. Whalen[,] and at least seven unidentified passers-by were looking in the direction of Gates, who had followed me outside of the residence.

As I descended the stairs to the sidewalk, Gates continued to yell at me, accusing me of racial bias and continued to tell me that I had not heard the last of him. Due to the tumultuous manner Gates had exhibited in his residence as well as his continued tumultuous behavior outside the residence, in view of the public, I warned Gates that he was becoming disorderly. Gates ignored my warning and continued to yell, which drew the attention of both the police officers and citizens, who appeared surprised and alarmed by Gates's outburst. For a second time I warned Gates to calm down while I withdrew my department issued handcuffs from their carrying case. Gates again ignored my warning and continued to yell at me. It was at this time that I informed Gates that he was under arrest. I then stepped up the stairs, onto the porch and attempted to place handcuffs on Gates. Gates initially resisted my attempt to handcuff him, yelling that he was "disabled" and would fall without his cane. After the handcuffs were properly applied, Gates complained that they were too tight. I ordered Off. Ivey, who was among the responding officers, to handcuff Gates with his arms in front of him for his comfort while I secured a cane for Gates from within the residence. I then asked Gates if he would like an officer to take possession of his house key and secure his front door, which he left wide open. Gates told me that the door was unable to be secured due to a previous break [-in] attempt at the residence. Shortly thereafter, a Harvard University maintenance person arrived on scene and appeared familiar with Gates. I asked Gates if he was comfortable with this Harvard University maintenance person securing his residence. He told me that he was.

After a brief consultation with Sgt. Lashley and upon Gates' request, he was transported to 125 6th Street in a police cruiser (Car 1, Off.'s Graham and Ivey) where he was booked and processed by Off. J.P. Crowley.[18]

Officer Carlos Figueroa, to whom Sgt. Crowley refers, arrived on the scene and filed his own short report. Interestingly, while it supports Crowley's report to a large extent, it mistakenly states that Gates had refused to show his ID. It would seem that Officer Figueroa had his own doubts about Gates' right to be in the house. The Figueroa report reads in full as follows:

On July 16, 2009 at approximately 12:44 PM, I Officer Figueroa #509 responded to an ECC broadcast for a possible break at Ware St. When I arrived, I stepped into the residence and Sgt. Crowley had already entered and was speaking to a black male.

As I stepped in, I heard Sgt. Crowley ask for the gentleman's information which he stated "NO I WILL NOT!". The gentleman was shouting out to the Sgt that the Sgt. was a racist and yelled that "THIS IS WHAT HAPPENS TO BLACK MEN IN AMERICA!" As the Sgt. was trying to calm the gentleman, the gentleman shouted "You don't know who you are messing with!"

I stepped out to gather the information from the reporting person, WHALEN, LUCIA. Ms. Whalen stated to me that she saw a man wedging his shoulder into the front door as to pry the door open. As I returned to the residence, a group of onlookers were now on the scene. The Sgt., along with the gentleman, were now on the porch of Ware St. and again he was shouting, now to the onlookers (about seven), "THIS IS WHAT HAPPENS TO BLACK MEN IN AMERICA!" The gentleman refused to listen to as to why the Cambridge Police were there. While on the porch, the gentleman refused to be cooperative and continued shouting that the Sgt. is [a] racist police officer.

Certain facts are indisputable in this case. It is indisputable that a 911 caller had observed two men attempting to enter 17 Ware Street. It is indisputable that the caller believed that the two men could be working or living at 17 Ware Street and therefore attempting to enter the residence lawfully. It is indisputable that the caller never raised the issue of race until prompted by the police dispatcher, and then only mentioned the race of a possible Hispanic person. What is arguable is the description of events and conduct as articulated by Sgt. James Crowley. It is his interpretation of those facts that deeply influenced the way this case unfolded, and resulted in the arrest.

A review of Sgt. Crowley's own words and actions and supporting documents has led many experts to conclude that not only was the arrest illegal and the charge of disorderly conduct unproven, but also that Sgt. Crowley's report is inconsistent with both what the eyewitness told him and what the police dispatcher reported. Ultimately, his rendition is incompatible with reality. Sgt. Crowley was unpersuaded by any of Professor Gates' pleadings and presumed his guilt—guilty of being elitist, defiant, arrogant, angry, and unrepentant, and, finally, guilty of being a trespasser in his own home.

The eyewitness in this case—publicly identified by her lawyer, prominent Massachusetts criminal defense attorney and Northeastern University Law School professor Wendy Murphy, and in public documents—is Ms. Lucia Whalen, who, as mentioned earlier, is employed by *Harvard Magazine* and worked on Ware Street. Shortly after noon on July 16, a senior citizen in the neighborhood approached Ms. Whalen, saying that she saw someone apparently breaking and entering at a house. Ms. Whalen's actual transcript of her conversation with the police when she called 911, which is reported below, is starkly different from the written report provided by Sgt. Crowley on the same date. Ms. Whalen's call to the police is straightforward about whether any crimes were being committed. Her description of what she saw and doubts about whether an actual crime was in progress could not be clearer. The transcript not only reinforces the point that Ms. Whalen *never* identified two African Americans, but also that she never stated that they had backpacks. To this date, the only person ever to suggest that two African Americans with backpacks were involved is Officer 52 in this transcription, who is identified as Sgt. James Crowley:

911 Call

Dispatcher: Tell me exactly what happened.

Caller [Ms. Whalen]: Umm, I don't know what's happening. I just have an elder woman, uh, standing here, and she had noticed two gentlemen trying to get in a house at that number, 17 Ware St., and they kind of had to barge in. And they broke the screen door and they finally got in, and when I had looked, I went further, closer to the house a little bit, after the gentlemen were already in the house, I noticed two suitcases, so I'm not sure if these are two individuals who actually work there, I mean who live there.

Dispatcher: You think they might've been breaking . . .

[Ms. Whalen]: I don't know, 'cause I have no idea, I just noticed. . . .

Dispatcher: So you think the possibility might have been there or . . . ? What do you mean by barged in? Did they kick the door in or . . . ?

[Ms. Whalen]: No they were pushing the door in, like uhhh, like the screen part of the front door was kind of like cut.

Dispatcher: How did they open the door itself, the lock?

[Ms. Whalen]: I didn't see a key or anything 'cause I was a little bit away from the door. But I did notice that they pushed their . . .

Dispatcher: And what did the suitcases have to do with anything?

[Ms. Whalen]: I don't know. I'm just saying that's what I saw. I just [inaudible].

Dispatcher: Do you know what apartment they broke into?

[Ms. Whalen]: No, just the first floor. I don't even think that it's an apartment. It's 17 Ware St. It's a house. It's a yellow house. Number 17. I don't know if they live there and they just had a hard time with their key, but I did notice that they had to use their shoulder to try to barge in and they got in. I don't know if they had a key or not 'cause I couldn't see from my angle. . . .

Dispatcher: [inaudible] black or Hispanic? Are they still in the house?

[Ms. Whalen]: They're still in the house I believe, yeah.

Dispatcher: Are they white, black, or Hispanic?

[Ms. Whalen]: Umm, well there were two larger men, one looked kind of Hispanic, but I'm not really sure. And the other one entered, and I didn't see what he looked like at all. I just saw it from a distance, and this older woman was worried, thinking someone's breaking in someone's house. They've been barging in, and she interrupted me, and that's when I had noticed. Otherwise, I probably wouldn't have noticed it at all, to be honest with you. So I was just calling 'cause she was a concerned neighbor, I guess. . . .

Dispatcher: All right, well, police are on the way, you can meet them when they get there.[19]

Police Transmissions

Female dispatcher: Respond to 17 Ware Street for a possible B and E in progress. Two SPs [suspicious persons] barged their way into the home, they have suitcases. R-P 5-SP. Stand by, trying to get further.

Officer 52 [Sgt. James Crowley]: 52. Ware Street right now, 17?

Dispatcher: 17 Ware Street . . . both SPs are still in the house, unknown on race. One may be a Hispanic male, not sure. . . .

[Sgt. James Crowley]: Stand by. Can you have the caller come to the front door? . . .

Dispatcher: It's not her house, she doesn't live there. She's a witness in this.

Officer 13: C-13 to patrol I'm on Broadway (inaudible).

Dispatcher: Received. . . .

[Sgt. James Crowley]: I'm up with a gentleman who says he resides here (background voice) but uncooperative. But uh, keep the cars coming.

Male patrol 1: Copy.

[Sgt. James Crowley]: Can you also send the Harvard University police this way?

Male patrol 1: We can send 'em in. . . .

[Sgt. James Crowley]: He gave me the name of the resident of Henry Louis Gates Jr. (background voice) on Harvard property. . . .

Officer 2: (inaudible) to patrol. Do we have a wagon coming through to the location?

Male patrol 3: Patrol to wagon.

Wagon: Wagon.

Male patrol 3: 17 Ware Street.

Wagon: Copy.[20]

As the actual 911 call reveals, Ms. Whalen gave a candid assessment of the events as she observed them that day. In her 911 call to

police, she made clear that she'd seen some individuals but never identified anyone as African American. Indeed, the only identification that
she gave during her call was that there were two gentlemen, one Hispanic, who were trying to open a door. She also explained that it wasn't clear to her that a crime was going on. An important point is that
she suggested to the police dispatcher that there may have been a
problem with the key. In the context of these comments, Sgt. Crowley's report seems incomplete.

Sgt. Crowley's report of the incident reflects his presumption that
a criminal act was taking place and reflects his skepticism about
Professor Gates' actual identity. What is clear from the official
transmissions is that no one had indicated that African Americans
were involved in the alleged breaking and entering and no one
stated that backpacks were being used. Even more breathtaking
from my point of view is the confirmation that Professor Henry
Louis Gates not only produced proof of his identity while in his
own home but he also asked Sgt. Crowley to call Chief Bud Riley,
the chief of the Harvard police, and pleaded with him to confirm
that he was telling the truth about being in his own home—a fact
that could be confirmed by a simple call to the Harvard University
Police Department:

[Sgt. James Crowley]: I'm up with a gentleman who says he
    resides here (background voice) but uncooperative. But uh,
    keep the cars coming.
Male patrol 1: Copy.
[Sgt. James Crowley]: Can you also send the Harvard University police this way?

Male patrol 1: We can send 'em in. . . .

[Sgt. James Crowley]: He gave me the name of the resident of
Henry Louis Gates Jr. (background voice) on Harvard
property.

An examination of Sgt. Crowley's entire report tells a story of the type of clash that occurs when a police officer believes, perhaps because of his prejudices, that a crime is being committed and an innocent person believes that he is being unfairly profiled by a police officer. It is clear that this clash reflects both Sgt. Crowley's skepticism about Professor Gates' identity as an innocent resident and Professor Gates' outrage that a police officer does not believe that he is actually lawfully in his own home.

It is also clear that from the moment Sgt. Crowley entered Professor Gates' home, without express permission, he assumed that Gates was an SP, or suspicious person, and not legally permitted to be at 17 Ware Street.

What actually happened was that at the moment Sgt. Crowley appeared on the porch of Professor Gates' home, Gates was talking on the phone to the Harvard employee about his door. Professor Gates was surprised to see a police officer on his porch so soon after he'd reported the incident of the damaged door to the Harvard University real estate office, and Sgt. Crowley seemed surprised that the person he assumed was an intruder was talking on a portable house phone. Before he ended his conversation with Ms. Moore about his damaged door, Professor Gates seemed to recognize that Sgt. Crowley wasn't there to help him. In the ensuing conversation, Professor Gates observed that Sgt. Crowley had a very unfriendly attitude and insisted that the professor come outside. Professor Gates chose not to go outside but simply asked the officer why he was there and what he was doing. The conversation continued with Sgt. Crowley insisting that Professor Gates step outside. Gates' decision to stay in his house rather than step out on the porch at the point of the initial exchange may have been quite fortunate for him. A key element of disorderly conduct is that the disturbance must be likely to affect the public.[21] As their discussion continued, Sgt. Crowley asked Professor Gates for identification. When Professor Gates provided it, little appeared to change in Sgt. Crowley's actions. He still appeared to believe he had a suspect in a burglary at 17 Ware Street, even though Professor Gates didn't fit the description given by the eyewitness or the details provided by the dispatcher.

One of the important parts of the chronology of events is that when asked to produce identification, neither man disagrees that Gates complied. In response to Sgt. Crowley's request, Professor Gates turned around to walk to a nearby table to get his Harvard ID and his Massachusetts driver's license. At that moment, to Gates' surprise, Crowley followed him into his home. In fact, the officer was standing directly in front of Gates as he gave him his Harvard identification and his Massachusetts driver's license. These two documents contained Gates' photograph, listed his home address as 17 Ware Street, and confirmed he was a Harvard University employee. It is telling that, at that critical moment, Sgt. Crowley acted as if he doubted that Gates was who he claimed to be and was where he belonged.

Sgt. Crowley's transmissions with the Cambridge police dispatcher reveal his skepticism about Gates' identity and his reaction to Gates' anger at not being believed to be a lawful occupant of the home. In

Crowley's recorded conversations with the dispatcher while in Professor Gates' home, the sergeant reported, "I'm up with the gentleman who says he resides here . . . but uncooperative. But, uh, keep the cars coming." And after Professor Gates pleaded with Sgt. Crowley to "Call the chief," meaning Chief Bud Riley of the Harvard University Police Department, an acquaintance of Gates, Crowley never called the chief but urged the dispatchers to notify the Harvard University police to come to the scene.[22] From all of the reports provided that day, Crowley never spoke with Chief Riley, nor did he seek to confirm Gates' identity by simply speaking to any of the Harvard University police who arrived on the scene. Sgt. Crowley's next comments were "Can you also send the Harvard University police this way?" and the male patrol officer said he would. Crowley then reported shortly thereafter, appearing to still doubt that Professor Gates was indeed the resident of the house: "He gave me the ID of a Henry Louis Gates. . . . He gave me the name of the resident of Henry Louis Gates Jr. on Harvard property." It is clear that even while producing his ID, Professor Gates could not persuade Sgt. Crowley that he was lawfully in his own home. As the police report indicates, Sgt. Crowley then stated that he had been called names of a racial nature by Professor Gates, which precipitated further action. In his report, the sergeant stated that he asked Gates to step out onto the porch, and Gates refused, and then Gates demanded to know who he was. Crowley indicates that he identified himself as Sgt. Crowley from the Cambridge Police Department.

What this exchange most clearly illustrates is that this investigation had gone awry, and as a result of it, Professor Gates was arrested after having been persuaded to step out on his porch to improve the acoustics. But many experts, who have spent a fair time on matters of this nature, tell a different story regarding the motivating factors behind this unfortunate encounter between the professor and the cop. My colleague and friend Walter Prince, Esq., appeared in court with Professor Gates to represent him on the charge of disorderly conduct. Although Professor Gates was arrested and booked on Thursday, July 16, and was clearly outraged about his treatment by Sgt. Crowley, he followed my legal advice to keep the matter quiet until after the charges were dealt with in court on Friday, July 17, and subsequently dismissed by the district attorney on Tuesday, July 21, 2009.

The day before the charges were dismissed, the first mention of Professor Gates' arrest came from the *Harvard Crimson,* the student newspaper at the university. The headline reported "Renowned African-American Professor Gates Arrested for Disorderly Conduct," but the subtitle noted the incredible circumstance of Professor Gates being arrested in his own home and Gates' view of Sgt. Crowley's actions: "Gates, who was trying to enter his own home, reportedly accused police of being racist."[23]

As the events of July 16 became national news there were numerous comments concerning Sgt. Crowley and Professor Gates. John Payton, a graduate of Harvard Law School and a former classmate and close friend of mine, is a celebrated civil rights lawyer and currently serves as the director-counsel and president for the NAACP Legal Defense and Education Fund in New York City. After learning of the Crowley/Gates encounter, he wrote a commentary on Gates' decision not to go outside when initially approached by Sgt. Crowley while standing in his house. In short, Payton wrote that it was perfectly legal for Gates to remain in his home, and it was permissible to express his disagreement with Sgt. Crowley when the officer entered his home.[24]

In addition to John Payton's view that Professor Gates acted appropriately, retired Judge Andrew Napolitano, a regular judicial analyst and commentator on legal issues on Fox News, weighed in on Sgt. Crowley's decision to enter Gates' home and the lack of evidence supporting the professor's arrest. Napolitano's point was that even if the police were investigating the report of a potential crime, such a report was not just cause to trigger the use of government power and violate a resident's constitutionally protected rights.[25] He noted that armed only with a third-party account, the officer could not lawfully enter the premises either.

Offering his written analysis of Professor Gates' arrest, Professor John Banzhaf III of George Washington University Law School in Washington, DC, encouraged Gates to pursue legal action against Sgt. Crowley and the Cambridge Police Department, citing the illegality of the arrest and defending Gates' First Amendment right to make even disrespectful statements to a police officer. Professor Banzhaf thought it was important for the public to understand why Crowley's decision to arrest Gates was wrong and why Gates' anger was legal. In defending Gates' behavior and the legitimacy of a lawsuit, Banzhaf highlighted the law in Massachusetts as it applies to the Crowley/ Gates incident: "The law in Massachusetts, as well as elsewhere, is clear: people cannot be arrested simply for being disrespectful to or shouting at the police, even to the point of shouting insults at them in public. Yet the practice is so common that the alleged crime has been given the name 'contempt of cop.'"[26]

Time magazine ran a story on the arrest of Professor Gates, with experts on both sides of the debate questioning and approving the decision of Sgt. Crowley to make an arrest under the circumstances as reported in the arrest report. The *Time* magazine article by Bonnie Rochman highlights the difficulties in determining when arrests for disorderly conduct are justified, particularly given the broad discretion that state statutes give to individual officers.[27]

Also commenting was Jon Shane, a former police officer and currently a professor at John Jay College of Criminal Justice in New York City. Professor Shane's opinion was that, if anything, Gates was guilty of "contempt of cop," noting that "you get loud and nasty and show scorn for a law-enforcement officer, but a police officer can't go out and lock you up for disorderly conduct because you were disrespectful toward them."[28]

The alleged crime of contempt of cop becomes even more complex when race conflicts are at play, such as when a law enforcement officer feels disrespected by an individual who is African American. In his commentary, Payton explains how Professor Gates' race played a critical role in Sgt. Crowley's decision to arrest him following his refusal to step outside on the porch:

> Clearly, a key to this puzzle is race. Skip Gates is not just a prominent member of the Harvard University faculty; he is also an African American. If we want to understand the Skip Gates incident, there is no way to leave race out of it. If the officer had found a white male, standing in his home, at about 12:45 pm in the afternoon, talking on the phone when he

knocked on the front door and asked if the person would step outside onto the front porch, would that refusal have generated the same resentment from the officer? We all know the answer.[29]

Banzhaf also addressed the impact of Gates' class and the potential to use the events of July 16 to create change for other African Americans faced with unwarranted confrontations with the police. He emphasized that Gates has greater resources than most other Black men who are arrested without legal justification.

As Bonnie Rochman reports in *Time* magazine, no matter how you look at it, it is hard to conceive of Gates' comments alone as criminal or as the basis for an arrest.[30] The article cites several authorities on racial profiling indicating their suspicion as to the validity of Professor Gates' arrest, noting, among other things, that Sgt. Crowley's report describes Gates' conduct as "loud and tumultuous behavior, in a public place" that "caused citizens passing by this location to stop and take notice while appearing surprised and alarmed," and that this raises the question of whether or not Gates was in a public place and whether or not his behavior constituted a disturbance.[31]

This point of view is supported by Massachusetts jury instructions that list the following elements of the crime of disorderly conduct:

1. The defendant engaged in fighting or threatening, or engaged in violent or tumultuous behavior, or created a hazardous or physically offensive condition by an act that served no legitimate purpose, AND 2. The defendant's actions were reasonably likely to affect the public, AND 3. The defendant either

intended to cause public inconvenience, annoyance or alarm, or recklessly created a risk of public inconvenience, annoyance or alarm.[32]

Although Professor Gates repeatedly insisted that he lived at 17 Ware Street and produced identification confirming that in fact he was a professor at Harvard University, Sgt. Crowley requested that the dispatcher "keep the cars coming." This entire encounter, which lasted less than six minutes, illustrated that Professor Gates' actions had angered Sgt. Crowley, and the one power he had, on the scene, was to arrest him. As Sgt. Crowley indicated in his report, the acoustics in Gates' house were poor, so Crowley asked Gates to step outside so he could both hear and address Gates' concerns. The first thing that Sgt. Crowley said, according to Gates, was: "Thank you for honoring my request. You are under arrest."

There are lessons to be learned from both Crowley's and Gates' actions. Sgt. Crowley could have waited for the Harvard police to arrive, verified that Professor Gates was lawfully in his home, and listened to Professor Gates' explanation of the problems with his jammed door. In that Sgt. Crowley requested that the Cambridge police dispatcher call the Harvard police, there was no urgency in seeking an arrest, and Gates did not appear to be a threat to him. If he had been a threat, Sgt. Crowley could have arrested the professor in his home and attempted to explain it later. At the same time, Professor Gates had the right to object to Sgt. Crowley's unwillingness to believe who he said he was, particularly after he presented both his official Harvard identification with his photograph on it and his Massachusetts driver's license with his 17 Ware Street address on it. When Crowley refused to accept these efforts, Gates had the right to object, even in strong terms. In my 20 years of teaching about individual confrontations between police and law students, I have advised my students and others of the following approach: quiet observance of an officer's name and badge number and making a mental note of any information you can glean during the encounter is a far better and safer way to protect your rights. Asking an officer for a name and badge number, or revealing your intent to file a complaint for harassment, is certainly legal but generally unproductive and perhaps unhealthy (to say the least), under the circumstances.

A telling event occurred the next morning, a Friday. When Attorney Walter Prince appeared in court on behalf of Professor Gates, the Middlesex County assistant district attorney, legally responsible for prosecuting Professor Gates, did not file any charges, but instead requested a continuance of the case until Tuesday, July 21. Over the next several days, Attorney Prince and I consulted with the Cambridge city manager, the district attorney, and the Cambridge police commissioner. After our discussions, there was a joint public statement announcing the dismissal of all charges against Professor Gates. The arrest and subsequent dismissal of charges against Professor Gates raised profound questions about police discretion and citizens' rights. While there are laws explaining when there is probable cause to arrest a suspect, the guided discretion allowed police officers is the key ingredient in determining what should occur in circumstances like those encountered by Sgt. Crowley, especially because discretion is influenced by an individual's presumptions.

CHAPTER 2

"President Obama Doesn't Like White People."
The Public Reaction

On July 22, 2009, President Obama held a public address focused on health care and was asked to assess what Professor Gates' arrest says about race relations in America. President Obama made an offhand comment that "the Cambridge police acted stupidly."[1] By making this brief, unscripted comment, President Obama unwittingly exposed a racial divide in the country. The president's characterization of the police's actions as stupid shocked many. However, it was a genuine reaction to the irony of the arrest of one of the country's most esteemed scholars on issues of race and a somewhat flawed attempt to show support for his dear friend "Skip" Gates.

Five years earlier, in July of 2004, just a few days after giving a stunning address at the Democratic National Convention, then senatorial candidate Barack Obama was invited to Martha's Vineyard to spend some time with longtime friend and campaign supporter Valerie Jarrett. I had the honor of serving as a mentor to both Michelle Robinson, who arrived at Harvard Law School in 1985 and graduated in June 1988, and Barack Obama, who entered Harvard Law School in the fall of 1988 and graduated in June 1991, before they met for the first time in Chicago. While on Martha's Vineyard, I called my former student and asked if he would stop by the Whaling Church in Edgartown for an annual discussion about race and social justice hosted by me and Professor Gates. Although I must admit I didn't give Senate candidate Barack Obama a clear sense of what to expect, he did stop by and was pleasantly surprised by the packed auditorium and loud applause as he entered the room. While he was only expected to stop by to say hello and then return to his brief vacation with his wife and children, he actually took time to speak to members of the audience, shake hands, take photographs, sign autographs, and meet old and new friends.

Professor Gates suggested that I invite Obama to his summer home. Gates wanted to welcome Barack and Michelle to the island and introduce them to some of the Vineyard's most prominent summer residents. Barack readily agreed, and he and Michelle came to Professor Gates' house two nights later. Gates' "White House" is where I first formally introduced Gates and Obama. The crowd was the usual collection of Martha's Vineyard guests, including Spike and Tonya Lewis Lee and Andrea Taylor and her mother, Della Brown Hardman, a legendary writer for the *Vineyard Gazette* who covered the social events that were central to the thriving Black community in Oak Bluffs.

At that event, I first introduced Michelle, a brilliant woman, as our next leader. Everyone thought I was talking about Barack except him. He knew me and knew that I was giving due praise to Michelle, who would then introduce him. My brother Richard and his family were in town and had a chance to meet Barack. They also had the chance to meet one of Professor Gates' dear friends, Chris Tucker. It was a merry time, and everyone considered Senate candidate Obama on the chart for success. In Martha's Vineyard, Obama and Gates sealed a friendship that continues to this day.

President Obama's decision to intercede on behalf of his friend is not at all surprising if you know both men. The friendship Henry Louis Gates and Barack Obama began developing six years ago is only part of what connects them. A natural affinity as a result of the similar formative years that sparked their fates likely had a larger impact than idle conversations at social gatherings over the years. Both men learned a lot about race, and racism, from their mothers at a young age. Both men had close relationships with their mothers, and the wisdom imparted by their mothers has influenced both men's writings and lives. Professor Gates' mother, Pauline Augusta Coleman Gates, was a Black woman who grew up in the segregated South. President Obama's mother, Stanley Ann Dunham, was a White woman who was born and raised in Kansas and later moved to Hawaii to attend school and married an African man. Despite their outward differences, both women were deeply influenced by the practice of racial segregation and made it their business to teach their sons about the history of American race relations.

Professor Gates' mother raised her two sons, Paul and Skip, in Piedmont, West Virginia, where only 350 people out of the total population of roughly 22,000 were African American. Gates speaks of the proud, but segregated, Black community during his childhood in Piedmont. His mother was, in all respects, a proud woman and wanted her sons to appreciate who they were and from where they came. Even at a young age, Gates would watch her demonstrate her racial pride while also breaking down barriers for Black people, and particularly Black women, in West Virginia. Mrs. Gates never went to college, sacrificing her opportunity to do so and choosing to raise her two sons and assist in raising her younger siblings. In his memoir, *Colored People*, Gates is reminded of a disparaging comment made by his daughter about his aging mother, and it triggered warm memories of his mother's strength in the face of adversity: "I found myself wishing, too, that Maggie could have seen my mother when she was young and Mama and I would go to a funeral and she'd stand up to read the dead person's eulogy. She made the ignorant and ugly sound like scholars and movie stars, turned the mean and evil into saints and angels. She knew what people had meant to be in their hearts, not what the world had forced them to become."[2]

Gates went on to lament that his daughter would never witness the values his mother exhibited while he was a child: "If only Maggie could have seen Mama when she'd stand up to read the minutes of the previous meeting of the PTA. Because in 1957, Mama was elected the first colored secretary of the PTA. . . . Before Mama started reading the minutes, colored people never joined the PTA."[3] Gates watched as his mother celebrated Black progress and strength during the height of racial tension in America and as leaders emerged to speak on behalf of the race: "[W]hen I was nine, Mike Wallace and CBS aired a documentary about Black Muslims. It was called 'The Hate That Hate Produced,' and these were just about the scariest black people I'd ever seen. Black people who talked right into the faces of white people, telling them off without even blinking. . . . 'Amen' she said, quietly at first. 'All right now' she continued, much more heatedly."[4] Gates further observed: "The same thing would happen several

years later when the Martin Luther King riots were shown on television. The first colored secretary of the Piedmont PTA watched the
flames with dancing eyes. But Mama was practical as well as proud.
Her attitude was that she and Daddy would provide the best for us, so
that no White person could put us down."[5]

Barack Obama was born in 1961 and was raised largely by his
mother and grandparents. Obama speaks of the diversity but lack of
Black families as he grew up in Honolulu, Hawaii. The very title of
President Obama's first book, *Dreams from My Father: A Story of Race
and Inheritance,* is largely about issues surrounding race. The book
describes his upbringing in Hawaii, his formative years in Indonesia,
his high school and college studies, and even beyond, and the theme
of race is never too far from his analysis. In his book, Barack Obama
speaks freely and fluidly about his earliest experiences in being told
by his mother of his Black heritage. His mother talked glowingly of
his father's culture and how much young Obama would have to learn
about race as an American-born child whose father was of African
descent. In a critical discussion of his understanding about race as a
young boy, Obama describes how his mother instilled a sense of race
consciousness in him early on, to make him proud of his absent father and of his racial heritage: "Increasingly, she would remind me of
his story, how he had grown up poor, in a poor country, in a poor
continent; how his life had been hard. . . . He was diligent and honest, no matter what it cost him. . . . I would follow his example, my
mother decided. I had no choice. It was in the genes."[6] She informed
Obama: "You have me to thank for your eyebrows . . . your father has
these little wispy eyebrows that don't amount to much. But your
brains, your character, you got from him."[7]

Stanley Ann wanted Obama to appreciate his history and heritage, and, like Gates' mother, she urged her son to celebrate his Blackness: "Her message came to embrace black people generally. She would come home with books on the civil rights movement, the recordings of Mahalia Jackson, the speeches of Dr. King. When she told me stories of school children in the South who were forced to read books handed down from wealthier white schools but who went on to become doctors and lawyers and scientists, I felt chastened by my reluctance to wake up and study in the morning."[8] When he was young, Barack Obama's mother taught him that, historically, being Black was the source of unique burdens and blessings: "Every black man was Thurgood Marshall or Sidney Poitier; every black woman was Fannie Lou Hamer or Lena Horne. To be black was to be the beneficiary of a great inheritance, a special destiny, glorious burdens that only we were strong enough to bear."[9] Those lessons would prove pivotal as he grew older and became more comfortable discussing race matters. When Obama was elected as the first African American president of the *Harvard Law Review*, he talked about the historic election and hoped that it was a barometer of progress in the academic achievements to be expected in the future for other African Americans. However, he expressed concern that some might see his achievement as a sign that racial progress had been completely achieved when he believed it was too early to draw such a conclusion. Also as a student, Obama gave a little-known introduction of Professor Derrick Bell, the first African American professor at Harvard Law School, who left the school to protest the absence of diversity in the hiring of women. Obama introduced Professor Bell as the Rosa Parks of the legal profession.[10] After he completed his education at Harvard Law School,

Obama declined more profitable opportunities in order to represent largely African American women and men as a community organizer. Later, as a state senator, Obama supported efforts to address racial profiling in Illinois.

In their own subtle and direct ways, the sons of Pauline and Stanley Ann grew up with an appreciation of who they were and of their inheritance. It is noteworthy that these two African American men were close to their mothers and learned a great deal from them about race and race relations and that, decades later, those early experiences would be revisited in the context of twenty-first-century racial profiling.

On July 16, 2009, President Obama was in New York giving the keynote address at a convention commemorating the hundredth anniversary of the NAACP. Little did he know that, as he spoke, his friend of five years was returning home after having been arrested for disorderly conduct.

Attending the Hundredth-Anniversary NAACP Convention in New York City was a priority for President Obama. The convention was an opportunity for him to give thanks to the founders of the NAACP for paving the way for his 2008 election. It also provided the president a platform to remind the NAACP of what he was doing for the African American community and to implore the organization to assume some responsibility for addressing that community's need to overcome economic, educational, and social problems.

President Obama delivered a moving and powerful speech. He encouraged, admonished, and preached to the largely African American audience. He addressed America's history of lynchings and Jim

Crow laws and the current challenges facing African Americans, including criminal justice issues, educational priorities, and jobs. It was
the most specific address ever given on the government's obligation to
address pressing needs in the African American community. The July
16, 2009, NAACP speech was a homecoming for President Obama,
and an acknowledgment of his commitment to the Black community:

> It was in this America where an Atlanta scholar named W. E. B.
> Du Bois—(applause)—a man of towering intellect and a fierce
> passion for justice, sparked what became known as the Niagara
> movement; where reformers united, not by color, but by cause;
> where an association was born that would, as its charter says,
> promote equality and eradicate prejudice among citizens of the
> United States.
>
> From the beginning, these founders understood how change
> would come—just as King and all the civil rights giants did
> later. They understood that unjust laws needed to be over-
> turned; that legislation needed to be passed; and that Presidents
> needed to be pressured into action. They knew that the stain of
> slavery and the sin of segregation had to be lifted in the court-
> room, and in the legislature, and in the hearts and the minds of
> Americans.
>
> They also knew that here, in America, change would have
> to come from the people. It would come from people protest-
> ing lynchings, rallying against violence, all those women who
> decided to walk instead of taking the bus, even though they
> were tired after a long day of doing somebody else's laundry,
> looking after somebody else's children. (Applause.) It would

THE PRESUMPTION OF GUILT

come from men and women of every age and faith, and every race and region—taking Greyhounds on Freedom Rides; sitting down at Greensboro lunch counters; registering voters in rural Mississippi, knowing they would be harassed, knowing they would be beaten, knowing that some of them might never return.

Because of what they did, we are a more perfect union. Because Jim Crow laws were overturned, black CEOs today run Fortune 500 companies. (Applause.) Because civil rights laws were passed, black mayors, black governors, and members of Congress served in places where they might once have been able [sic] not just to vote but even take a sip of water. And because ordinary people did such extraordinary things, because they made the civil rights movement their own, even though there may not be a plaque or their names might not be in the history books—because of their efforts I made a little trip to Springfield, Illinois, a couple years ago—(applause)—where Lincoln once lived, and race riots once raged—and began the journey that has led me to be here tonight as the 44th President of the United States of America. (Applause.)

Because of them I stand here tonight, on the shoulders of giants. And I'm here to say thank you to those pioneers and thank you to the NAACP. (Applause.)[11]

President Obama went on to address his concerns about racism and structural barriers in America (which turned out to be prescient a week later, when he called the treatment of Professor Gates a form of discrimination):

The first thing we need to do is make real the words of the NAACP charter and eradicate prejudice, bigotry, and discrimination among citizens of the United States. (Applause.) I understand there may be a temptation among some to think that discrimination is no longer a problem in 2009. And I believe that overall, there probably has never been less discrimination in America than there is today. I think we can say that.

But make no mistake: The pain of discrimination is still felt in America. (Applause.) By African American women paid less for doing the same work as colleagues of a different color and a different gender. (Laughter.) By Latinos made to feel unwelcome in their own country. (Applause.) By Muslim Americans viewed with suspicion simply because they kneel down to pray to their God. (Applause.) By our gay brothers and sisters, still taunted, still attacked, still denied their rights. (Applause.)

On the 45th anniversary of the Civil Rights Act, discrimination cannot stand—not on account of color or gender; how you worship or who you love. Prejudice has no place in the United States of America. That's what the NAACP stands for. That's what the NAACP will continue to fight for as long as it takes. (Applause.)[12]

President Obama left New York after delivering this triumphant formal address on race. A week later, it was his brief unscripted comments about the Crowley/Gates incident that focused the nation's attention on race and created a debate largely split along racial lines. On July 22, 2009, President Obama held a public address to answer questions about health care. The very last question was asked by Lynn Sweet of the *Chicago Sun-Times:* "Recently, Professor Henry Louis Gates, Jr. was arrested at his home in Cambridge. What does that incident say to you, and what does it say about race relations in America?"[13] President Obama's response, which surprised some and stunned many, was as follows:

> Well, I should say at the outset that Skip Gates is a friend, so I may be a little biased here. I don't know all the facts. What's been reported, though, is that the guy forgot his keys. Jimmied his way to get into the house. There was a report called into the police station that there might be a burglary taking place. So far so good. Right? I mean, if I was trying to jigger in—well, I guess this is my house now so it probably wouldn't happen. Let's say my old house in Chicago. Here I'd get shot. But so far so good. They're reporting, the police are doing what they should. There's a call. They go investigate what happens. My understanding is at that point Professor Gates is already in his house. The police officer comes in. I'm sure there's some exchange of words but my understanding is that Professor Gates then shows his I.D. to show that this is his house. And at that point he gets arrested for disorderly conduct, charges which are later dropped. Now, I don't know, not having been there and not seeing all the facts what role race played in that, but I think it's fair to say, number one, any of us would be pretty angry. Number two, that the Cambridge police acted stupidly in arresting somebody when there was already proof that they were

in their own home and, number three, what I think we know separate and apart from this incident is that there is a long history in this country of African-Americans and Latinos being stopped by law enforcement disproportionately. And that's just a fact.

As you know, Lynn, when I was in the state legislature in Illinois we worked on a racial profiling bill because there was indisputable evidence that blacks and Hispanics were being stopped disproportionately. And that is a sign, an example of how, you know, race remains a factor in this society. That doesn't lessen the incredible progress that has been made. I am standing here as testimony to the progress that's been made.

And yet, the fact of the matter is that, you know, this still haunts us. And even when there are honest misunderstandings, the fact that blacks and Hispanics are picked up more frequently and often time for no cause casts suspicion even when there is good cause, and that's why I think the more that we're working with local law enforcement to improve policing techniques so that we're eliminating potential bias, the safer everybody's going to be.[14]

The president's remarks at the end of an otherwise successful national address on his priorities in the increasingly antagonistic health care debate initiated a firestorm. These comments, given without preparation—and, as President Obama mentioned, without knowing all the facts—were designed simply to affirm his support for one of his dear friends, but they had unintended and far-reaching effects. His comments generated responses throughout the world and became fodder for conversations in barbershops and beauty parlors as well as in executive offices and churches and on the street. President Obama's efforts to promote health care reform were completely sidetracked, and health care was off the front page of the newspapers for more than a week.

President Obama's remarks about his friend and fellow African American, Henry Louis Gates, Jr., were enthusiastically embraced by many Blacks and Latinos. Not only did the president talk about how unfortunate Gates' arrest was, but he went on to discuss the "long history in this country of African-Americans and Latinos being stopped by law enforcement disproportionately."[15] For the first time since the campaign, President Obama had spoken forcefully and personally about the issue of racial profiling, generating an enormous public response from African Americans, who thought he had been much too cautious in addressing issues of race and racial injustice in the past.

On the other hand, President Obama's comment that the police acted "stupidly" resulted in the public eruption of an otherwise underground torrent of racism directed at him. Glenn Beck, a conservative commentator on Fox News, expressed indignation at Obama's criticism of a White police officer who was just doing his job by arresting a resistant suspect. In short, Beck claimed that President Obama doesn't like White people, and he's a racist, too. Among Beck's comments were these:

Okay. So here you go. Here is the latest on the Gates thing. This whole nightmare with the president, I personally believe the president has real race issues. He has a real problem. I mean, he called his own grandmother the typical white person. I mean, what does that even mean, she's a typical white person, she tenses up around black people.[16]

Beck was both admonished and praised for his very explicit views on President Obama's intervention. A number of Beck's sponsors decided to withdraw their sponsorship in light of his remarks.[17] On the other hand, Glenn Beck's popularity as a conservative commentator sky-rocketed. His criticism of Barack Obama actually moved the conservative agenda forward. The president's intervention in the Crowley/Gates matter had the unintended impact of increasing conservative support of Glenn Beck and expanding the forum for direct criticism of the president along race lines.

There was also significant criticism of both Gates and Obama by some members of the law enforcement community, including some African American police officers. Two of Crowley's colleagues, Sgt. Leon Lashley, who was present when Professor Gates was arrested, and Officer Kelly King, defended his actions and criticized Professor Gates' motives in characterizing the arrest as racist. Sgt. Lashley acknowledged that there have been situations in which arrests have been racially motivated, but he denied that Gates' arrest was one of them: "It happened to be a white officer on a black man, and the common cause, call, a lot of times is to call it a racist situation. . . . Don't get me wrong, it does happen. It has happened here in Cambridge. And I can't say it will not ever happen again in Cambridge. This situation, right here, was not a racial[ly] motivated situation."[18]

Officer King went further and criticized Obama for his comments on the incident: "It's unfortunate. I supported [Obama], I voted for him, I will not again. . . . He should have stepped back. And he should have said, 'I support my friend, but I don't have all the facts. I won't weigh in yet.'"[19]

President Obama's comment that the Cambridge police had acted "stupidly" generated a rash of criticism from many White people, who saw the steady and deliberate Obama all of a sudden take a strong stance on a racially charged issue. In short, President Obama's two-minute response to what seemed an innocuous question had the unanticipated effect of *blackening* him.

While Obama has long embraced his race, as demonstrated by his writings in *Dreams from My Father: A Story of Race and Inheritance,* he has also, on occasion, rejected its relevance. In 2004, Obama first addressed issues of race on a national level when he was selected by Senator John Kerry to give the keynote address at the Democratic National Convention in Boston, Massachusetts. It was on that world stage that the nation first caught a glimpse of then Senate candidate Barack Obama, and soon fell in love with him. Obama said with great eloquence and force that Americans should not be defined or divided by race or politics:

> Now even as we speak, there are those who are preparing to divide us—the spin masters, the negative ad peddlers who embrace the politics of "anything goes." Well, I say to them tonight, there is not a liberal America and a conservative America—there is the United States of America. There is not

a Black America and a White America and Latino America
and Asian America—there's the United States of America.[20]

His message was well received around the nation and the world, and
he became an instant star. Nevertheless, there would be milestones
and setbacks over his nearly two-year campaign for the presidency,
and, all too often, the issue of race would prove to be a consistent bar-
rier to progress in winning the Democratic nomination and ultimately
the presidency.

Four years after Obama's speech questioning the relevance of race
in national politics, Senator Obama was forced to address race head
on when his relationship with the Reverend Jeremiah Wright became the subject of controversy. The Reverend Wright was the pastor who baptized Obama, persuaded him to join Trinity United
Church of Christ in Chicago, married him and Michelle, and baptized their children. Fox News began to examine a few of the reverend's comments and played very widely some of the strong
language he used in addressing his congregation. Conservatives
spliced together the Reverend Wright's comments in a way that
made a caricature of a very complex and sophisticated expert on
Black theology. The national media and mainstream America soon
embraced what many believed to be an effort by the conservative
Fox News to label the Reverend Wright as racist, homophobic, and
anti-Semitic. It was the biggest challenge Obama experienced in his
entire campaign. Many deemed it inappropriate that a candidate
ready to bring all of America together would be so closely associated with someone who had such explicit views on the issues of race
and religion and was so divisive.

Obama refused to respond directly to each controversial statement made by Reverend Wright. Instead, on March 18, 2008, Obama appeared in front of the Philadelphia Constitution Center and gave one of the most important discussions on race in our nation's history. He talked about his humble beginnings and his heritage, as the son of an African man from Kenya and a White woman from Kansas. He talked at great length about the lessons he'd learned traveling across the country and trying to deal with issues of race. His most emphatic comments were about Reverend Wright, and he made clear that he had not been present during any of the sermons that had been labeled bombastic, racist, and anti-Semitic at the United Church of Christ. He went further, though, to make clear that he was not going to disown his pastor in light of these remarks. Candidate Obama's speech provided significant insight into how race is viewed through different lenses:

> I can no more disown him than I can disown the black community. I can no more disown him than I can my white grandmother—a woman who helped raise me, a woman who sacrificed again and again for me, a woman who loves me as much as she loves anything in this world, but a woman who once confessed her fear of black men who passed by her on the street, and who on more than one occasion has uttered racial or ethnic stereotypes that made me cringe.[21]

But presidential candidate Obama went even further. In perhaps his most enlightening comments that day, from my point of view, he also made it clear that he understood how White Americans might view themselves as being treated unfairly in our system:

Most working- and middle-class white Americans don't feel that they have been particularly privileged by their race. Their experience is the immigrant experience—as far as they're concerned, no one's handed them anything, they've built it from scratch. They've worked hard all their lives, many times only to see their jobs shipped overseas or their pension dumped after a lifetime of labor. They are anxious about their futures, and feel their dreams slipping away; in an era of stagnant wages and global competition, opportunity comes to be seen as a zero sum game, in which your dreams come at my expense. So when they are told to bus their children to a school across town; when they hear that an African American is getting an advantage in landing a good job or a spot in a good college because of an injustice that they themselves never committed; when they're told that their fears about crime in urban neighborhoods are somehow prejudiced, resentment builds over time.[22]

Obama's speech was applauded by many in the mainstream media, including the *New York Times*. The *Times* editorial reported that the moment was extraordinary, especially in a country where racial mistrust has deep roots and is often hidden beneath the surface. The reporter compared the speech to other great presidential speeches, from Lincoln to Kennedy.[23] The Wright issue that temporarily staggered the Obama campaign erupted again after more divisive public comments by the reverend, and presidential candidate Barack Obama eventually resigned from the church and condemned the pastor:

THE PRESUMPTION OF GUILT

I am outraged by the comments that were made and saddened over the spectacle that we saw yesterday.

You know, I have been a member of Trinity United Church of Christ since 1992. I have known Reverend Wright for almost 20 years. The person I saw yesterday was not the person that I met 20 years ago. His comments were not only divisive and destructive, but I believe that they end up giving comfort to those who prey on hate and I believe that they do not portray accurately the perspective of the black church. . . .

I want to be very clear that moving forward, Reverend Wright does not speak for me. He does not speak for our campaign. I cannot prevent him from continuing to make these outrageous remarks.[24]

Barack Obama's earlier attempts to move beyond race—through his 2004 speech before the DNC, his 2008 speech on race, and his eventual denunciation of the Reverend Wright—were ultimately undermined by his brief, unscripted comments about the Gates arrest. The polls consistently revealed that the loser in this dispute was President Obama, with a majority of those polls concluding that his claim that the "Cambridge Police acted stupidly" was wrong and that a greater racial divide on racial profiling emerged. The racial divide in response to the president's comments is quite stark: 63 percent of Whites but only 26 percent of Blacks questioned in a CNN poll agreed with the statement that Obama acted stupidly when commenting on the arrest.[25] Additionally, 61 percent of Blacks interviewed sympathized with Professor Gates, compared to only 29 percent of

Whites, and 45 percent of Whites sympathized with Sgt. Crowley, compared to 19 percent of Blacks.[26] A Rasmussen Reports national telephone survey found that 78 percent of Blacks believed that Obama did an excellent or a good job handling the Gates incident, while only 23 percent of Whites agreed with such an assessment. Indeed, 50 percent of Whites surveyed believed that Obama handled the situation poorly.[27]

In order to move forward on his efforts to promote health care reform and move away from the Crowley/Gates dispute, President Obama invited both men to the White House for an informal meeting over beer. The meeting was deemed the "beer summit" by the media. President Obama also appeared, unannounced, at the White House Press Room and issued measured remarks indicating that both Crowley and Gates could have acted differently to prevent the incident on July 16: "I continue to believe, based on what I have heard, that there was an overreaction in pulling Professor Gates out of his home to the station. I also continue to believe, based on what I heard, that Professor Gates probably overreacted as well."[28]

Not everyone agreed that the president's proposed beer summit was a good idea. Indeed, some found that his remarks and his involvement further strained race relations rather than creating opportunities for more unity and cooperation. *Washington Post* columnist Colbert King, an African American, urged Professor Gates to use the beer summit as an occasion to talk about racial profiling and wrote that the failure to do so was a lost opportunity. King also acknowledged that while President Obama's decision to sit down with Gates and Crowley may have been a political success, the president did not take advantage of, to use his own words, a "teachable moment" to inform the "American people about the First Amendment, police powers, and citizens' rights."[29] King criticized Obama for "sending a message of racial harmony when, in fact, race and law enforcement are sores on the body politic."[30]

As Professor Gates' counsel, I encouraged him to attend the beer summit, and I traveled to Washington with him; his father, Henry Louis Gates, Sr., who is 97 years old; his brother, Dr. Paul Gates; his fiancée, Angela Deleon; his two daughters, Elizabeth and Maggie Gates; and Glenn Hutchins, his friend and chairman of the board of the Du Bois Institute. Sgt. Crowley came with his wife, his twin son and daughter, and his older daughter. Sgt. Crowley was understandably nervous about the White House beer summit, because President Obama had publicly stated that Gates was his friend, which might make a dialogue among the three men uncomfortable. To assuage the situation, two members of the Cambridge Police Union joined Sgt. Crowley at the White House.

During that meeting at the White House, I had the chance to speak with Sgt. Crowley for nearly an hour, and we talked about our own upbringings, the fact that he and my children had both attended Cambridge Rindge and Latin High School, and how surprised he was to learn, hours after he had arrested Professor Gates, that Gates was a highly regarded and well-known member of the Harvard community. This was a surprise to Sgt. Crowley because he had worked at Harvard University for three years, albeit on the night shift, and had never encountered Professor Gates.

President Obama handled the beer summit deftly, even dragging the vice president into the photo op with Gates, him, and Crowley, with Biden having a beer mug in front of him (with nonalcoholic beer, as Biden does not drink alcohol). This photo of four guys, two White and two Black, two with sleeves rolled up on the hot July day, as though they were lifelong friends enjoying a brewski, was published throughout the world. Ultimately, the beer summit saved the day, and, for the moment, it helped shift the public dialogue from race relations to health care.

The president's initial comment about the Gates incident was unfortunate and quite unusual for him. He likely regrets having made this particular statement, even though his words accurately captured the persistent problem of racial profiling in America. President Obama, perhaps unintentionally, also touched on the issue of class by emphasizing that Professor Gates was arrested after providing proof that he was in his own home. It is often young African American males, walking, standing, or even driving on the street, who are deemed suspicious based solely on their dress or location or the time of day, when in fact many are engaged in lawful and appropriate conduct. These young men often find themselves unjustly confronted by police officers, Black or White. Gates, a neatly dressed 59-year-old professor inside his own home in the middle of the day, is not the typical African American who one would imagine would be subject to racial profiling. Therefore it is not surprising that the arrest of Professor Henry Louis Gates, Jr., would generate an enormous discussion about race in America and race in a neighborhood that is only five minutes away from Harvard University. The unprecedented episode of the president of the United States being involved in a public debate about the arrest of a friend would soon subside, but the larger problem of the Harvard professor's arrest would serve as a reminder of a persistent problem.

CHAPTER 3

"Don't Tase Me, Bro!" How Far Have We Really Come?

The Gates arrest was one more striking reminder in a long series of painful reminders that little has changed since the infamous Rodney King beating in 1991. In some respects, the arrest of one of the country's most prominent scholars in the comfort of his upscale Harvard University home was as egregious in the hearts and minds of some members of the African American community as the blatant, brutal beating of King. It suggested that there was no place in America where African Americans could receive what the law guarantees to its White citizens: a presumption of innocence. Gates' arrest sadly reminded us that African Americans still bear the burden of a presumption of guilt and are disproportionately subjected to an arbitrary use of police force and abuse of power, even when they are accomplished, law-abiding citizens.

The Rodney King case put a glaring spotlight on police abuse and misconduct, confirming the Black community's long-standing grievances about law enforcement. It also illuminated the Black community's mistrust of law enforcement and justified its hypersensitivity to police misconduct and abuse. Gates' arrest was born out of that context—law enforcement prone to be biased against African Americans and an African American community conditioned to be mistrustful and fearful of law enforcement.

Andrew Meyer understood that context well. On September 17, 2007, Meyer had a lot on his mind and wanted to ask Senator John Kerry, the unsuccessful candidate for president in 2004, some burning questions. The University of Florida student attended a campaign rally and wanted to address his belief that Kerry won the 2004 presidential election by actually having more votes than Bush. He also wanted to comment on the disenfranchisement of voters. When the University police came to remove him from the auditorium because he would not leave the question podium, in an event that was captured on television cameras and cell phones, Meyer would become an instant celebrity by shouting out four now-famous words to the police, "Don't tase me, bro!"[1]

After a few days of silence, Meyer discussed his arrest by the Florida University police and apologized for his behavior. Meyer's pleading, "Don't tase me, bro!" resonated with many in the African American community, harkening back to the most notorious tasing incident of the twentieth century: the beating, kicking, and tasing of Rodney King.

It is now part of history that Rodney King committed a series of crimes on March 2, 1991, and the case sparked a national discussion about race and the criminal justice system.[2] He was under the influence of alcohol, well above California's legal blood-alcohol level. He was driving at an excessive speed, above the legal limit, and placing innocent citizens and police officers at risk of serious bodily injury or death and potentially catastrophic property damage. He refused to respond to multiple efforts by the police to stop his speeding vehicle and surrender himself to authorities. He failed to follow the lead of the other two occupants of the car that night, his friends "Pooh" Allen and Freddie Helms, who cooperated with police after the stop and throughout the ensuing questioning. Rodney King broke the law that night, but George Holliday's video of his brutal beating by police provided the nation and the world with evidence illustrating the conduct of some members of the Los Angeles Police Department (LAPD) and only reinforced views firmly held both by supporters and opponents of police officers.

The King incident influenced the way the concept of excessive force is now considered and prompted endless calls for reform not only of police conduct, but also the use of tasers as a nondeadly police tool. Rodney King's arrest and beating was a defining moment in furthering the divide between law enforcement officials and members of the civil rights community.

The true hero in this tragic incident was George Holliday, who happened to be in the area where the LA police officers were questioning King and instinctively turned on his camera to videotape the beating, tasing, and arrest of King. Holliday, a manager of a local plumbing company at the time, went to the window of his bedroom terrace apartment after hearing helicopters and police cars and seeing flashing lights about 100 feet away on the streets. His video depicted several officers striking King on his body, kicking and stomping him, and beating him on his face with metal batons. The officers also used an electronic stun gun to try to subdue King, and the video reveals that it was used several times. None of the officers was aware that their conduct was being videotaped. The conversations among the police after King was arrested reveal how much they enjoyed beating him. The officers communicated to each other saying such things as "U just had a big time use of force. Tased and beat the suspect of CHP [California Highway Patrol] pursuit."[3] One stated, "I haven't beaten anyone this bad in a long time."[4] Another compared the incident to *Gorillas in the Mist*,[5] a 1988 film based upon the book written by Dian Fossey depicting the violent poaching of gorillas in Rwanda.

It would prove to be an embarrassing event for the LA police and for the city, including Tom Bradley, its African American mayor. Mayor Bradley not only called for the resignation of LAPD chief Daryl Gates (which Gates refused) but acknowledged the racial element in the arrest and stated publicly: "There appears to be a dangerous trend of racially motivated incidents running through at least some segments of the [Los Angeles] Police Department."[6]

Surprisingly, Rodney King was released the next day, and none of the charges against him were pursued. There was a clamor throughout LA and the nation to prosecute the officers involved in the incident. The key officers in the attack were quickly suspended from their jobs and soon after indicted on a number of charges. The district attorney, Ira Reiner, indicted the four officers who played a central role in the arrest, and they retained lawyers. The turning point in the case occurred when the defense lawyers moved to transfer the case from LA, given the enormous amount of negative pretrial publicity that would prejudice the opportunity for the police to select an unbiased jury. Their request led the trial judge, Stanley Weisberg, to transfer the case more than an hour away from Los Angeles, to Simi Valley, in Ventura County. Simi Valley was far less ethnically diverse than Los Angeles County and was considered much more conservative and police friendly. A number of LA police officers lived in Simi Valley, and some veterans had retired there. The most significant procedural step taken by one of the police officers' lawyers was to use a peremptory strike to remove the only African American juror who actually made it to the jury box. At the same time, other African Americans sought to avoid sitting on a jury that would have both national and racial repercussions.

After weeks of testimony, the repeated showing of the videotaped beating, and an effective justification by the police officers' defense expert of all 56 of the baton blows used to subdue Rodney King, the jury deliberated for seven days. The prosecutor, Mr. Terry White, an African American lawyer, did not call King as a witness and was little match for the more experienced lawyers hired to defend the police officers.

On April 29, 1992, one year and one month after King's March 2, 1991, beating, the jury refused to convict any of the four defendants of any of the charges.[7] Los Angeles exploded in a matter of minutes, and the toll over the next two days was substantial: 7,000 arrests, 54 deaths, and over $1 billion in damages.[8] Mayor Bradley might have added fuel to the subsequent flames when he expressed his raw feelings following the verdicts: "Today, the jury told the world that what we all saw with our own eyes was not a crime."[9] African Americans, in particular, took to the streets and pulled innocent White residents, like truck driver Reginald Denny, from their vehicles. In Denny's case, they knocked him unconscious with a cement brick and fractured his head in over 90 places. Others looted department stores throughout LA, and still others targeted Korean-owned grocers. After looting one Korean grocery store, a riot participant was captured on camera saying: "This is for Rodney King!"[10]

While the LA riots were an enraged response to the jury's acquittal of the officers who beat Rodney King on March 2, they were also a response to pent-up frustrations as a result of what many considered a largely unreported killing that occurred in South Central LA involving a 15-year-old African American girl and a 49-year-old Korean woman working at a Korean liquor store. Exactly two weeks after Rodney King's beating, Latasha Harlins, a student at Westchester High School in LA, visited the South Central LA liquor store Empire Liquor, owned and managed by Billy Heung Ki Du, when his wife, Soon Ja Du, was behind the counter. Latasha picked up a bottle of orange juice to purchase and put it in the top of her backpack. The orange juice cost less than two dollars. Latasha had the money for the purchase in her hands. While Ms. Du later reported that Latasha was stealing the orange juice and that she acted in self-defense, two eyewitnesses in the store and the store's video camera revealed that, in fact, Latasha was attempting to purchase the juice.[11] As Latasha approached the counter, Ms. Du grabbed the girl's sweater and backpack. Latasha responded by striking Ms. Du three times and knocking her to the floor. Latasha then picked up the orange juice, which had fallen out of her backpack, placed it on the counter, and turned to walk out of the store. Ms. Du grabbed a shotgun from behind the counter and shot Latasha Harlins in the back of the head. Harlins died as a result of the shooting.

Weeks later, Ms. Du was indicted, tried in Los Angeles, and convicted of voluntary manslaughter with a potential penalty of life imprisonment.[12] The jury recommended a sentence of 16 years, which the trial judge could accept, increase, or reduce. The judge, Joyce Karlin, determined that, because this was Ms. Du's first offense and in light of the difficulty that her family experienced operating their store in South Central Los Angeles, she deserved a minimal punishment and imposed a sentence of five years of probation rather than incarceration. Judge Karlin also sentenced Ms. Du to 400 hours of community service and imposed a $500 fine, which outraged those who felt that greater punishment was warranted.[13]

While the Rodney King jury deliberated, the festering anger over Ms. Du's sentence lingered in the air in Los Angeles. It was little surprise that the African American outburst following the acquittal of the four officers indicted for beating King resulted in the targeting of Korean grocers and Korean citizens in South Central LA rather than law enforcement officers. The damage was extensive, and represented targeted attacks and random acts of violence. Many of those who died were Korean, and a lot of the property damage occurred in Koreatown. The Latasha Harlins murder, the sentencing of Ms. Du to probation, the Rodney King beating, and the acquittal of the four LAPD defendants created a combustible mixture with elements of race, class, culture, and crime in Los Angeles. In hindsight, it is worth asking the plaintive question raised by Rodney King in a public plea, to end the riots when he asked, "Can we all get along?"[14] That question is, regrettably, still worthy of answer nearly two decades later.

One of the more significant outcomes of the Rodney King beating was the decision by the Department of Justice, urged by President

George H. W. Bush, to pursue federal charges against three of the LA police officers. The case resulted in acquittals for two of the officers and convictions and 30-month sentences of incarceration for Officer Laurence Powell and Sgt. Stacey Koon. There were no riots, burnings, lootings, or deaths after the second trial in the Rodney King case. Shortly thereafter, King filed a civil lawsuit against the City of Los Angeles and recovered $3.8 million.

To ensure that the city would use the occasion of King's beating as a teachable moment, Mayor Bradley enlisted the support of a Los Angeles friend, Attorney Warren Christopher (who would later serve as secretary of state in the Clinton administration), to investigate the incident and to offer findings and recommendations to prevent something similar from happening in the future. The Report of the Independent Commission on the Los Angeles Police Department (1991), popularly known as the Christopher Commission Report, laid the groundwork for reform in the LAPD, but the question of whether the rest of the nation had woken up would remain.

At the same time, Judge Benjamin Hooks, the executive director of the national NAACP, initiated a series of public hearings, starting on July 9, 1991, in select cities throughout the United States, to focus on police conduct and its impact on minority communities. These hearings were recorded and, in early 1992, the NAACP enlisted the support of the Criminal Justice Institute at Harvard Law School and the William Monroe Trotter Institute of the University of Massachusetts in Boston to review testimony from the hearings and to issue findings and recommendations to be published in a report in March 1993. I was the founding director of the Criminal Justice Institute at the time.

The Northeastern University Press deemed the report compelling and published it in a book I co-authored called *Beyond the Rodney King Story: An Investigation of Police Conduct in Minority Communities.*[15]

In the book we published about the Rodney King beating, we made a number of recommendations designed to offer what we thought needed to be done and what we thought would stem the tide of police brutality and racial profiling. Essentially, we asked for a transformation of the way police officers are trained and the way they examine issues of race, and that they be willing to become familiar with the communities within which they serve. We firmly believed that community policing is a model that is essential to effective policing and would create an opportunity for law enforcement and the African American community, in particular, to have a much more cordial, collaborative, and respectful relationship.

While there is evidence that, in some jurisdictions, there is effective community policing and more trust between police and minority communities, far too many examples of conflict between police and African Americans reinforce the fact that we still have a long way to go in achieving racial justice. It only takes a few examples to reinforce this point clearly.

In 1997, for example, Abner Louima, an immigrant from Haiti, was physically tortured by police in a precedent-setting case.[16] As a result of the work of a group of lawyers led by Johnnie L. Cochran, Jr., Barry Scheck, and Peter Neufeld, not only was Louima able to receive a substantial settlement in the case, but changes were implemented in the practices of the New York Police Department in handling the investigation of claims of misconduct.

In 1998, in a case that drew national attention as an example of driving while Black, four young African American men were pulled over on the New Jersey Turnpike when police thought they were involved in gang activity. Shots were fired by the police, injuring some of the unarmed men. Fortunately for the four young men, they were represented by Johnnie Cochran and were awarded $12.95 million in a civil suit. The case resulted in reforms in the practices of the New Jersey Police Department.[17]

In 1999 Amadou Diallo, a native of Guinea working in New York, was outside his home when he was approached by several police in the Street Crimes Unit of the NYPD.[18] When Diallo reached for his identification in his wallet, the police officers responded by shooting at him 41 times, hitting him 19. Diallo died shortly thereafter. Despite a tide of vocal protests in New York and beyond, a jury acquitted the officers of all charges. This acquittal left many members of the African and African American communities in New York fearing that if Amadou Diallo, an innocent man who simply raised his wallet to identify himself, could be gunned down so viciously, progress in the relationship between African Americans and the police will be impossible.

As recently as 2008, the NYPD was involved in another fatal shooting, this time of Sean Bell, the night before he was scheduled to be married to Nicole Paultre.[19] Again, this is a case where several police officers, believing they were at risk, fired multiple shots that fatally struck an unarmed suspect. There were massive demonstrations in New York and a vigilant focus on the trial of the officers. The Reverend Al Sharpton led protests in New York City and other venues.

After the jury deliberated for three days on the charges of assault, reckless endangerment, and manslaughter, the officers involved were acquitted of all charges. In that same year Congressman Charles Rangel held a public hearing of members of Congress in New York to assess the impact of Bell's death.

Such events were not limited to the East Coast. Oscar Grant, a young African American, was fatally shot by a police officer working in the Metro system in Oakland, California, on January 1, 2009. The police officer, Johannes Mehserle, resigned before he was indicted for the killing. A settlement of $1.5 million was awarded to Grant's daughter.[20]

Fifteen years after our book on Rodney King was published, it is ironic that while confrontations between citizens and police continue, the proposals articulated in the book have yet to be enacted. Deep-seated concern about police conduct in minority communities continues without concrete evidence of either cultural or attitudinal changes in either camp.

The realities of racial disparity in the criminal justice system continue even today. Reports released by the Pew Center on the States, the Department of Justice, and the Sentencing Project all indicate the alarming prevalence of racial disparity in the Criminal Justice System. A 2008 report from the Pew Center, citing data provided by the Department of Justice, reveals that: "one in every 15 black males aged 18 or older is in prison or jail," versus one in every 36 men for Hispanic males and one in every 106 White males.[21] A 2003 report from the Department of Justice found that the lifetime risk of incarceration for a child born in 2001 is 1 in 3 for black males, 1 in 6 for

Latino males, and 1 in 17 for white males.[22] And a 2009 report from the Sentencing Project concluded that "one of every three black males born today will go to prison in his lifetime, as will one of every six Latino males."[23]

And while this data works to support the notion of racial disparity in the criminal justice system, what it does not always show is the compounding effects such disparities can have on the system. In *Reducing Racial Disparity in the Criminal Justice System: A Manual for Practitioners and Policymakers,* first published in 2000 and updated in 2008, The Sentencing Project, an organization founded to offer defense lawyers sentencing advocacy training, provides a powerful example: "if bail practices result in minorities being detained before trial at greater rates than similarly situated whites, they will also be disadvantaged at trial and sentencing by having reduced access to defense counsel, community resources, and treatment options."[24] The imprint of racial disparity snowballs as negative treatment on one level leads to greater consequences on the next level, which in turn further entrenches minority defendants into the criminal justice system. Thus, what originally begins as a *de minimis* imbalance can quickly spiral into significantly different (racial) treatment in the justice system.

These cases and the data illustrate that we have yet to solve the national problem of the relationship between law enforcement and communities of color, particularly African Americans. It would be a mistake to minimize the significance of Gates' arrest. Although his class afforded him protection against the more extreme reactions of law enforcement officers during confrontations with African American men, his arrest tells us that the underlying presumption of guilt makes such injustices possible.

CHAPTER 4

Fair Harvard? The Class Issue

arvard University is located in Cambridge, Massachusetts, and holds an esteemed place in American culture as the nation's oldest college. Originally known as the New College, it was "established in 1636 by vote of the Great and General Court of the Massachusetts Bay Colony," according to the Harvard University website. In was renamed on March 13, 1639, after its first benefactor, John Harvard, a clergyman from the London borough of Southwark and a graduate of Emanuel College at the University of Cambridge. At Harvard, tradition still matters. The traditional Harvard University commencement hymn, "Fair Harvard," tells a story of optimism and endless hope that is infused in the university's ideals:

> Fair Harvard! we join in thy Jubilee throng,
> And with blessings surrender thee o'er
> By these festival rites, from the age that is past,
> To the age that is waiting before.
> O relic and type of our ancestors' worth
> That hast long kept their memory warm,

First flow'r of their wilderness! Star of their night!

Calm rising thro' change and thro' storm.

To thy bow'rs we were led in the bloom of our youth,

From the home of our infantile years,

When our fathers had warn'd, and our mothers had pray'd,

And our sisters had blest thro' their tears.

Thou then wert our parent, the nurse of our soul;

We were molded to manhood by thee,

Till freighted with treasure thoughts, friendships and hopes,

Thou didst launch us on Destiny's sea.

When as pilgrims we come to revisit thy halls,

To what kindlings the season gives birth!

Thy shades are more soothing, thy sunlight more dear,

Than descend on less privileged earth.

For the good and the great, in their beautiful prime,

Thro' thy precincts have musingly trod,

As they girded their spirits or deepen'd the streams

That make glad the fair city of God.

Farewell! be thy destinies onward and bright!

To thy children the lesson still give,

With freedom to think, and with patience to bear,

And for right ever bravely to live.

Let not moss-covered error moor thee at its side,

As the world on truth's current glides by

Be the herald of light, and the bearer of love,

Till the stock of the Puritans die.[1]

The song proudly boasts that those associated with the university are "molded to manhood" by "Fair Harvard!" The song, whatever its intended meaning, offers a much more complex set of mixed messages today. Rather than being followed by an exclamation point, some African American men who have studied, taught, or traveled through the hallowed grounds of Harvard might ask whether the first phrase should be followed by a question mark. African American men associated with the university have indeed been molded, enriched, and taught critical lessons by their Harvard experiences, but not all of those lessons have been positive.

Members of the Harvard community have experienced treatment quite inconsistent with the message and theme of not just this song but the aims of the university overall. The five men discussed below are graduates of Harvard Law School, residents of Cambridge, or serve on the Harvard University faculty.

While each story is a compelling reminder of the problems experienced at Harvard University by African American men, it is clear that Harvard is simply a microcosm of a much larger and more troubling problem of race, class, and crime in America. The experience at Harvard is an example, but not the only example, of a societal problem causing African Americans to find themselves confronted with unfair suspicion, detention, and even arrest. Each of the following Harvard-located events is part of a larger discussion of why the problems of profiling African Americans persist and why the criminal justice system not only permits but often encourages such practices.

Dr. S. Allen Counter is a distinguished member of the Harvard University faculty and a noted scientist. Rory Morton is the dean of the upper school at Buckingham, Brown and Nichols in Cambridge and grew up in the city. Victor Bolden, James M. Jones, Jr., and Louis Sterling are all graduates of Harvard Law School. These five gentlemen have never met each other. They each have their own life successes and challenges, but a common denominator has influenced all of them: each has had the unfortunate experience of being presumed guilty, for crimes that they never committed, by either the Harvard University police or the Cambridge police—officers sworn to protect and serve the very communities they were racially profiling.

These African American men never thought that their Harvard experiences would challenge the themes embraced in "Fair Harvard." Yet each person mentioned herein was detained and questioned, when all he had done was appear in public as a Black man; these dual facts—being Black and appearing in public—were all it took to generate suspicion by the Cambridge or Harvard University police. Each man was a victim of teaching while Black, walking while Black, studying while Black, or being in the wrong place at the wrong time while Black.

What sets Dr. Allen Counter, Rory Morton, Victor Bolden, James M. Jones, Jr., and Louis Sterling apart from most other victims of racial profiling is that they have not only succeeded but excelled in attaining many of the privileges that are available to those who are academically and financially successful. Yet despite their respective success stories, each found himself in a position where it appeared that race trumps class. Their success did little to moderate the conduct of police prone to see them as suspected criminals because of the color of their skin.

It is a sobering story of how racial profiling is alive and well, and how African American and other victims of such profiling have little, if any, recourse when faced with being targeted because of the color of their skin. Their accounts are not only true and regrettable but are also a sad commentary on how far we have to travel in eliminating racial profiling from our legal lexicon.

———————

Dr. Allen Counter is a native of Americus, Georgia, and a graduate of Tennessee State University and Harvard University. He is a prominent neurobiologist who is best known for his remarkable discovery while on an expedition in northern Greenland to trace the history of the Henson family. The journey would become the basis for his best-selling book, *North Pole Legacy: Black, White, and Eskimo.*[2] Dr. Counter offers a compelling story of Matthew Henson and his role in the treacherous journey to the North Pole. Counter is also chair of the Harvard Foundation, having been asked to head that program by former Harvard University president Derek Bok. During his more than 20 years in that post, Dr. Counter has invited many prominent individuals, from Denzel Washington to Chesley Sullenberger, to Harvard to meet and interact with students and to offer some aspects of how their lives have been shaped by remarkable events.

Dr. Counter also has been active in his lab and research, and he has created an extraordinary relationship with the Nobel Prize Committee, traveling to Oslo, Norway, each year when the coveted awards are given to extraordinary individuals. As a neurophysiologist, Dr. Counter's work focuses on both clinical and lab research on nerve and muscle physiology, and he has also researched the effects of neurobiological lead and mercury exposure on the brain.

Despite all of his remarkable accomplishments, he was nevertheless viewed as a suspect one day when walking through Harvard Yard. In 2004, Dr. Counter was engaged in discussion with several of his students in planning future events for the Harvard Foundation, often leaving the foundation offices to attend a faculty meeting. While walking through campus, as he has done hundreds of times, he was stopped and questioned by two uniformed members of the Harvard University police. Dr. Counter was told that he was a suspect in a bank robbery that had occurred earlier that day. Not only did he have an alibi, having been meeting with his students that day, but he also was dressed in his customary Brooks Brothers suit and tie and had proof that he belonged at Harvard, although he had left his Harvard identification in the foundation office. The Harvard police insisted that the students produce it and vouch for Dr. Counter. They did. The person who was a suspect in the robbery had no resemblance to Dr. Counter, other than being identified as a Black male. When the university learned of this incident, the dean of students and other university officials apologized to Dr. Counter. To this day, however, he has never received an apology or an explanation from the Harvard police.

Rory Morton grew up in Boston. As a high school student, he worked in Harvard Square. His father died tragically when Rory was a teenager, and he began to spend more time with his high school friend, Elon Dershowitz, who also lived in Cambridge. Elon's father, Professor Alan Dershowitz, is a colleague of mine at Harvard Law School. During a class on police practices and racial profiling, Professor Dershowitz reflected on a series of incidents involving Rory and the Cambridge police. The story that he told years ago, and which Rory recently confirmed, was an eye-opener for our class of first-year Harvard Law students.

The Dershowitz family lived off Brattle Street, and Rory was encouraged to spend as many evenings there as he wished. Brattle Street is home to Cambridge's most prominent residents, but Rory had a problem. Very few African Americans lived on Brattle Street, and as he walked to the Dershowitzes' home late at night he would often be stopped and questioned by the Cambridge police. He did not "fit" in that neighborhood, especially during evening hours. Ostensibly, that only increased the police officers' suspicion that Rory did not belong.

In an effort to respond to the situation, Professor Dershowitz, who was more upset than Rory, decided to personally take Rory down to the Cambridge Police Department, introduce him to the officers who would be working in the Brattle Street area, and urge them to recognize Rory's face so that he would not be stopped again while traveling to and from the Dershowitz home. He not only asked the officers to take a good look at him but also gave them a photograph of the young man. He wanted the Cambridge police to know that Rory now lived with them on Brattle Street and had a right to walk to and from their home. This worked for Rory, and his day-to-day life was made easier, but the story raises a larger question concerning special privileges for some and not others, who happen to be Black, to be in certain places at certain times. Rory became the exception to the rule. But, alas, the rule remained: being Black in a wealthy white neighborhood was not acceptable. He was the Black youth allowed to walk, undeterred, on Brattle Street. The situation remains unchanged for other Black men who may not have the equivalent of a Professor Dershowitz in their corner, making special anti-profiling arrangements.

Victor Bolden's Harvard profiling experience occurred during his first year at Harvard Law School, in the fall of 1986. Victor was born in New York City in 1965 and grew up living with his father, mother, and two siblings in the Dyckman Housing Projects in Manhattan, then a racially mixed community.[3] Their apartment was a modest two-bedroom unit, in which he and his two siblings shared a bedroom. He attended an elementary school that was within walking distance of his home until fourth grade, when his parents were able to purchase a four-bedroom ranch-style home in Medford, Long Island. Victor recalls that the community, known as Twelve Pines Development, included about 800 modestly priced homes. It was an integrated neighborhood. Victor went on to attend Patrick Medford High School, a predominantly White and working-class school, where Black students constituted less than 10 percent of the student body. Although Victor recalls about 1,000 students in his freshman class, there was a significant dropout rate, resulting in a graduating class three years later of only 500 to 600 students.

Victor did well in high school and was a popular student, president of the Honor Society and the Future Business Leaders of America Club. He took advanced placement courses and excelled academically. In his senior year, he applied for early decision to Columbia University—the only school he applied to—and was accepted, enrolling in the fall of 1982.

A pre-law advisor at Columbia encouraged Victor to apply to Harvard Law School. He had the opportunity to receive a Robeson Scholarship if he attended Columbia Law School, but he chose Harvard instead. It was a tough financial decision for him and his parents. The cost of Harvard, he estimates, meant that in his first year of law school, he would be borrowing more money than he would have needed for four years at Columbia. Among other reasons, Victor chose Harvard because he wanted to broaden his experience and, for the first time, venture outside of New York.

Victor could never have imagined that getting outside of New York and broadening his experiences would mean a frightening encounter with the Cambridge police. Until that time, race had factored in his life only in indirect and subtle ways. But that changed when he entered Harvard Law School.

Victor Bolden was in his first year at Harvard when he, too, became a suspect. Needing a study break and craving something to munch on, he left his dorm room and walked north on Massachusetts Avenue with his friend James M. Jones, Jr. They were planning to buy chips and soda at Montrose Spa, a convenience store in close proximity to the campus that is usually open until 11 P.M. As they approached the store, the lights appeared on but the door seemed locked. Victor peered through the window and did not see anyone. Naturally, he assumed that he had missed his opportunity to get something to eat close to the dorm, so he and James left. Still hungry, they decided to head south to Harvard Square, knowing there was a 24-hour store that would have snacks. As they walked toward Cambridge Common on Massachusetts Avenue, several Cambridge police officers jumped out of cars.

Victor's memory of events that happened some 20 years ago is still vivid:

> James and I were walking toward Harvard Square at the time. The police handled this in like a SWAT team mentality. It was like four of them. We noticed after a while that we were being followed, but what we didn't know was that there were others following us as well. These were Cambridge Police. Afterwards at a meeting, they said they were looking for two Black men, between 5'3" and 6'3", weighing between 135 lbs and 235 lbs.

That's a broad description that a lot of Black people are going to fit. They said they had this list of a series of robberies and incidents that had allegedly been committed by these two men.

They wanted to know what we were doing. I was pissed and said, "You guys must be really bored tonight." Then one of them spouted something about seeing us casing some joint. At that point I got quiet and was nervous, because the guy had manufactured a lie pretty quickly. They already created their fact pattern to justify the stop.

The officers surrounded them and demanded their identification. Both Victor and James presented their Harvard University identification cards to the police. The students recall that one of the officers told them that the IDs were insufficient and requested that they both produce driver's licenses. After examining their driver's licenses, the officers left without any further explanation for the stop or an apology for their obvious and inappropriate profiling.

Victor remembers feeling "very powerless and very angry." Reflecting on the experience more than 20 years later, he commented:

> I had never had any difficulty with the police at any point in my life. I had never done anything that put me in jeopardy of being accused of criminal behavior. So to find myself accused simply for walking was difficult and left me emotionally scarred in a way. There's nothing you can do to change the situation.
>
> I sort of find it hard not to have thought about race, being Black, that is. I recall when I was 13 and the *Bakke* decision came out. I had been aware of Thurgood Marshall and King,

and I remember staying with an aunt in Harlem. I remember the news flash talking about the decision. I remember this aunt, Vivian Beasley, who didn't have a high school diploma, but understood the meaning of *Bakke,* and basically thought that it was going to set us back. Being there watching the television and news, you hear the talk, and obviously I couldn't understand all of the ramifications, but I knew that this was a change in the direction of how people talked about race. Growing up in the projects, you were always keenly aware that life was divided in particular ways racially.

It did not take James and Victor long to share their story with faculty and students at Harvard Law School.

Following Victor Bolden and James Jones' confrontation with the Cambridge police at Cambridge Common, they complained to me, the Harvard Black Law Students Association faculty advisor, and to Professor Phil Heymann, their criminal law professor. They also notified Professor Martha Minow, who is now the dean of Harvard Law School and was then their civil procedure professor. Professor Heymann arranged for the Cambridge police chief and the officers involved to attend a meeting at Harvard Law School to discuss what the African American students described as unwarranted racial profiling.

Drake Colley, a 1989 African American graduate of Harvard Law School and classmate of James Jones, Jr., and Victor Bolden, was present at that meeting. Drake currently serves as senior counsel at the New York City Law Department and argues many of the appellate cases on behalf of the city. He affectionately describes James and Victor as ministers' sons, good boys, and teetotalers. Although the incident occurred during a big homecoming weekend at Harvard, Drake was certain that neither James nor Victor would have been heading out to any celebratory parties. He recalls them as the two students least likely to be involved with the police.

Drake vividly remembers an exchange between him and the chief of the Cambridge Police Department at the meeting. Drake clearly recalls the chief saying: "When I see someone where they don't belong. . . ." That was all he needed to hear. The rest of the meeting was a lively and serious debate between the Harvard students and the Cambridge police. Drake was acutely aware that African Americans had been attending Harvard Law School since the 1860s and, as reported to me, refused to let the police chief's assertion go unanswered.

> Well, that pushed my buttons and I told him that I was born in this country, and my parents were born here, and their parents, and their parents. I told him I started working as a teenager and that I started paying taxes as soon as I was making enough to be responsible to pay taxes. I told him that I was a veteran of the U.S. Army with an honorable discharge. I told him that I was a summa cum laude graduate of Fordham University and that I was a student at what I am told is one of the more prestigious law schools in the country. And so given all of these things, I would like to know where precisely it is I don't belong. And so he said, "Well, if I see you in my backyard." And I said, "Well, if I see you in my backyard, but we're not talking about private property. We were talking about two students that were walking on a public sidewalk in Cambridge Common." That I

will never forget, because that might have been the first time I
spoke voluntarily at the school. I don't know a single Black male
that escaped an incident with the police.

Drake was not alone in his frustration, as it permeated the life of
Victor Bolden as well. And yet Victor transformed that frustration
into a very successful legal career. Since graduating from law school,
Victor Bolden has served as counsel to the NAACP Legal Defense
and Education Fund, Inc., and has been a lecturer on civil rights and
civil liberties issues since 1990. He is married and has a young son.
Fatherhood has caused him to reflect on the incident in new ways. In
1986, he was accused of a crime by the police. In 2009, he is the corporate counsel for the City of New Haven, Connecticut, and counsels
the police department in that city. He is bemused by the irony of his
new job. At the same time, he is ever mindful of how his past and
present experiences will, of necessity, require him to have many talks
with his son about race.

About a week or two after he was hired as the corporate counsel,
Victor was stopped by the New Haven police. His reaction to that incident, occurring more than two decades after his stop a few blocks
from Harvard Square, reflects his deepening understanding of the intersection of race, class, and power. Rather than feeling victimized,
Victor became the inquisitor, asking questions and seeking answers,
ultimately in order to help the police officers in the future and to prevent profiling from occurring when it can be avoided. Victor was
stopped while driving in a crime-ridden urban area. The officers
stopped him for a broken taillight. As their questions increased about

other matters unrelated to the taillight, he spoke up. As he recalls the
incident:

> About a week or two after I started this job, I was stopped by
> the New Haven Police. I thought back over the incident at
> Harvard 20 years ago, and it was because I knew who I was and
> secure in who I was that I was more inquisitive. And after the
> officer found out who I was, he was very nervous, because I was
> asking what this is all about, what's going on. I wanted to know
> exactly what it is they were doing. You know, there's this dual
> context where on the one hand I'm concerned because I'm
> being stopped, but on the other hand I also have this responsi-
> bility as the chief legal advisor to figure out how to minimize
> the city's liability. So I'm concerned in numerous ways because
> I don't need people engaging in activities that are going to re-
> sult in unnecessary litigations. But the way I felt in that car was
> entirely different than the way I did as a law student being sur-
> rounded by police and being powerless.

Victor's reflections suggest that the impact of racial profiling de-
pends upon the victim's sense of being included or excluded by the
larger society when confronted by those in authority. At the same time,
he is ever conscious of how race matters to his six-year-old son and
how he must both understand his son's curiosity about race and protect him from assuming that class will always trump race. He tells of
his son's positive identity with race and how he has to be aware when
that might change at any given moment:

It's funny how race permeates in ways that people don't really appreciate. Often I think people who are not of color don't fully appreciate how people of color recognize how life is coded in certain ways. Ezra Keats has these books for children, and one of them is called *A Snowy Day*. It's got an African American boy in it named Peter, and my son's name is Caleb. He identified with the character and wanted the character to be called Caleb, not Peter. So this was a book about a Black boy, and he identified himself in that book. We weren't talking to him about race, but he could see the differences in pigmentation, and he could see the differences between the characters in this book and characters in others. So there is a sense where the racial exclusivity of the world becomes understood by kids in ways that people sometimes don't appreciate, and try to wipe away or talk away. That was fascinating for me as a parent to see. And I think as a kid I was very conscious of that.

When I was sworn in as the corporate counsel here, Caleb came to my ceremony when the mayor swore me in, and there was the chief of police. So he got to meet the chief of police, which is an entirely different experience than most Black boys get to have. He also knows that I work for the mayor and that I'm the mayor's lawyer. So he understands that by virtue of my position, his understanding and relationship to power is different. He doesn't see city hall as the other, because of me, and that makes a difference. He understands that if he has a problem, he can be confident that it will be resolved, because of his context, because he has the connections.[4]

———————

Louis Sterling is the youngest of the five men discussed here, and yet he is as amazed as anyone that these practices, seemingly a thing of the past, would engulf him, the valedictorian of his college class at Howard University and a joint law school/business school graduate of Harvard University. What Louis experienced less than five years ago was the harsh reality that none of his degrees, education, or record of distinction mattered when the police viewed him wrongly as a criminal. It was the biting understanding that the police would not relent, even once it was established that he was wrongfully suspected of committing a crime. That bitter recognition began on an otherwise calm day for a young man at the top of his game.

Louis was born on July 20, 1978, on the West Side of Chicago and lived on the city's South Side. His father is a native Chicagoan and his mother was born in Costa Rica. He attended Whitney Young Magnet High School (the same high school Michelle Obama attended). Whitney Young is one of the most diverse public high schools in the city. Louis attended Howard University and, as a student, served on the university's board of trustees. He graduated from Howard Business School's undergraduate program as the valedictorian with a 4.0 grade point average.

Louis was inspired by his parents, who both stressed education as the vehicle to advance in life. After graduating from Howard University, advanced degrees in business and law at Harvard were his next goal. Little did he anticipate that four years of educational challenge and success would be tarnished by an incident that would alter his life in permanent ways.

As he describes it, "When I arrived in Cambridge, I was basically not thinking about race, but I recognized it in the sense that I'm an

African American male from the South Side of Chicago, but I've always treated others with open arms, embracing all races and people."

During his final year at Harvard, when he was taking both law and business classes, Louis was walking through Harvard Square carrying his laundry, when he was approached by two White gentleman who he later learned were Cambridge police officers in plain clothing. They detained him and questioned him about being a suspect in a domestic violence dispute. Louis was shocked to be detained and questioned, because he knew he was the wrong person and could not understand why the police would stop him without any evidence of his having done anything wrong. The police had an alleged victim come up to identify Louis, but she indicated that he was not the person she was seeking. In fact, the police were looking for the boyfriend of the victim of the domestic matter. As the photos of the individual and Louis Sterling subsequently revealed, the two men look nothing alike. Nevertheless, that didn't stop the police from questioning and detaining Louis Sterling in Harvard Square that day.

Louis reflects upon the experience by noting that it was the first time that he had seriously thought about race: "Never in my life—and I've lived in Chicago, DC, New York, LA—have I experienced such hostile treatment from the police department. That experience that day really was a dark cloud over my experience at Harvard. It's really unfortunate that it came about two months prior to graduating in June of 2006."

While the false suspicion by the police and their initial rejection of his claim of innocence troubled Louis, for him it was hardly the worst of the encounter. What really troubles him to this day is the failure of the officers or their superiors, including the chief of police, to admit that they were wrong or, upon reflection after knowing all of the facts, to offer any form of an apology. In his mind—and regrettably in theirs—he was just another Black man who might have committed a crime, and their error did not persuade them to clear up their false claims before moving on to other matters.

Louis painfully recalls:

> There was never an apology issued to me. Keep in mind that I was holding a bag of clothes when I walked across the street. These were not exigent circumstances where I was looking to flee or something. He [the officer who questioned me] didn't introduce himself, he didn't say he was a detective, he didn't say "I'm looking for an individual, can I ask you a couple of questions." That to me is proper protocol. When we [later] met . . . to discuss this incident, there was never an apology. I think he has always believed that he did nothing wrong, and for someone in his position to have been called to a meeting of this nature, and these were not frivolous complaints, he never acknowledged that he made a mistake, acted inappropriately, out of character or offensive. He never apologized in any way. That makes me think that in his mind he never made a mistake.

Despite this experience, Louis has his heart set on being a public servant, and his dream career would be to serve as a federal prosecutor. It probably never crossed the mind of the detective that day that, at some point in his career, he may be appearing in a prosecutor's office, asking Louis to issue a warrant for suspicion of crime, oblivious to the fact that his own actions years earlier might raise serious questions about his professionalism.

All five of the individuals just mentioned present compelling examples of how the Harvard and Cambridge police have interacted with African American males. Of course, these five men are not the only African American males who have experienced such incidents with the police in and around Harvard's campus. As Drake Colley recalled about his time at Harvard, "I don't know a single black male that escaped an incident with the police." Even if this is an exaggeration, it is enough to establish that Louis' and the other men's experiences were not rare.

Eventually, the university took notice. In August 2008, Harvard president Drew Gilpin Faust appointed a committee "to consider how best to assure the strongest possible relations and mutual understanding between the Harvard University Police Department (HUPD) and Harvard's highly diverse community."[5] In April 2009, the committee released its report, and the university announced its efforts to implement the committee's recommendations in August of that year.[6] The report, while acknowledging the police department's "well-earned reputation . . . for responsiveness and restraint," also declared that "both HUPD and the broader University community have work to do in order to achieve the shared goal of a welcoming, safe, and open environment."[7]

Notable university changes spurred by the report include establishment of a University Safety Advisory Committee, a deepening implementation of an "account management" model at HUPD (whereby officers have long-term assignments to specific geographic areas of the campus in an effort to increase familiarity and positive interaction from all parties), expansion of the role of the HUPD diversity and community liaison, and creation of a public safety ombudsman function within the University Ombudsman Office.

These efforts may help to provide more positive experiences for future generations of Harvard students and can serve as an example for similar university communities. But the broader issues surrounding these experiences remain. They created in these remarkable men not only unmistakable bitterness regarding their treatment as suspects of crimes but also this question: If they were not beneath such a prestigious umbrella, would justice actually happen? It is surprising that these kinds of encounters between law enforcement and African American students continue at places like Harvard University; time does not seem to cure this practice in any meaningful way. Should there be any distinction between African Americans who attend a place like Harvard University and those who live in urban centers outside of Cambridge when it comes to racial profiling? In other words, should it matter, if you are Black and male, whether you have a home in Cambridge or in such urban communities as Roxbury, Dorchester, or Mattapan? Should you be treated differently if you are Black and male and have a place on the Harvard faculty or multiple degrees from Harvard or are looking for a job in a depressed economy and take the train from Roxbury to Harvard Square to interview for a job in a retail store?

One of the central questions posed by the experiences in this chapter is clear: Should there be a special classification—privilege, or "a path," as Professor Dershowitz described it—that allows Rory Morton to travel back and forth to Brattle Street but does not apply to any other African American walking on Brattle Street? Should there be some special ID that African American Harvard faculty and students carry so that they can get a "pass" when law enforcement officials suspect them of conduct that might be attributable to others? Might officers treat them differently if they realize that they are Harvard students who are validly in Harvard Square, on the Harvard campus, or walking the streets of Cambridge, and not presumed to be the usual suspects from the predominantly African American communities of Roxbury, Dorchester, and Mattapan?

Clearly, the issues of race and class are not confined to Harvard or Cambridge, Massachusetts; rather, these stories illustrate that even in the most progressive of cities and the hallowed halls of Harvard University, race trumps class. African Americans have been attending Harvard College and Harvard Law School since the 1860s. In light of this relationship that dates back 150 years, the broader question is: Does class even matter? What is the value of hard work and academic achievement over a lifetime that allows you, on your merits, to be a Harvard faculty member, student, or alumnus? When can an African American say that he or she has "arrived" at the pinnacle of success and should be viewed as a bona fide member of the upper class? Will that ever happen?

Much of the dilemma that African American men at Harvard and beyond face has to do with the expectation that with success comes certain privileges. These include the privilege to go where your achievements take you, the privilege to dress in a fashion in which you feel comfortable, the privilege to drive a car that may be viewed as a luxury car, and the privilege to live in a neighborhood that is considered exclusive. However, under the scenarios just described, the privileges these men asked for were even more modest. They simply wanted the privilege of being left alone and the privilege of being presumed innocent. Dr. Counter wanted to be respected as the legendary scientist, doctor, and public servant that he had worked hard to become. Rory Morton wanted to be able to walk the streets of the city he loves and not have to prove that, as an African American, he belongs there. Victor Bolden and James Jones wanted to be able to go to Harvard Square and buy some ice cream without being accused of committing a robbery. Louis Sterling wanted to be able to take his laundry to the cleaners in Harvard Square and not be accused of being a suspect in a case of domestic violence. They wanted to have their Harvard identification mean something, and it is not hard to understand their emotional response when it did not.

In order to afford these accomplished men this modest privilege, should we create a special place, or special protection, for what W. E. B. Du Bois described as the "Talented Tenth"? How would we isolate those who are successful? Do we give them a badge? Do they live only in certain neighborhoods? Do they wear a certain kind of clothing? Do they speak in a "non-Negro dialect"? Does it matter if they are light-skinned? Does it matter if they have gone to Ivy League schools or work in major corporate law firms or other prominent institutions?

Most important, what about the millions of other Black males who do not have a degree or a teaching position or a connection with Harvard? What about everyday working-class Black men who are stopped, questioned, searched, or even arrested and, in some cases, prosecuted, convicted, and sentenced to death, based on an honest but mistaken identification, coerced confession, lying informant, or false report of a crime? When we create this exceptionalism, what do we say about the million Black men who are incarcerated? Do they deserve any deference, any respect, any opportunity to be treated fairly? Will we permit police to continue to employ the same tactics to assume the guilt of those who have not achieved these successes?

The answer in this struggle between class and race is not a simple one, and there are no easy answers. How do we get beyond it? More importantly, can we get beyond it? There are serious questions as to whether African Americans who have succeeded should be treated differently. Of course, they feel that they've earned it. They've worked hard to overcome the lack of education and impoverishment and have found prominent jobs, and yet this success does not mean that everyone believes that they are entitled to be treated differently. If we say that class trumps race, we also create a greater problem for the many individuals who are not wealthy, not well educated, who don't have a good job or live in a good neighborhood, and are not criminals, but nevertheless find themselves suspects. Creating a class exception will, inevitably, make things worse, not better, for African American men in general. Believing that they've earned the right to be treated differently does not, in and of itself, justify a special status for a class of African American men at the expense of every other person still facing suspicion and demeaning presumptions.

The solution of treating prominent middle- and upper-class African Americans differently from poor African Americans may be too great a cost for our community to bear. Indeed, it may have just the opposite impact, leading us to ignore that injustice and inequality in

CHAPTER 5

Driving while Black. Fighting Back against Racial Profiling

The frustrations that people like Dr. Allen Counter, Rory Morton, James Jones, Jr., Victor Bolden, and Louis Sterling have experienced in and around Harvard from the 1980s well into the twenty-first century exemplify the frustrations felt by all African American men who are falsely accused and detained by police and who never receive apologies. In each of the cases described in the last chapter, it is clear both that the police felt that they had their man or men, and that the African American men knew that they had done nothing to violate the law. In each case, the police were confident that they were doing their job in trying to prevent crime or address it after it occurred, and the African American men were wondering why, after all of their blood, sweat, and tears to become gifted members of the African American community, they were still viewed as everyday criminals and still had difficulty in persuading police officers that they were anything other than suspects. While these cases helped open the door for dialogue between Harvard faculty, students, and law enforcement, the larger problem of profiling, detention, and arrest of African American men across the country persists. In fact, the long term favorable resolution of cases of racial profiling are the exception rather than the rule. In most instances, victims like the ones discussed in chapter 4 go on to tell their stories of encounters with police to their children, grandchildren, and friends. And yet these victims feel an emptiness due to the lack of a meaningful relationship between the police and members of the African American community.

On some rare occasions, the victim of racial profiling can prevail and actually change the way the police conduct their work. One case in point occurred a year after the Rodney King beating. It was 3,000 miles away, on a highway in Maryland. The incident changed Robert Wilkins' life and led to meaningful reforms in police practices in the state of Maryland.

Robert Wilkins, an African American lawyer in Washington, DC, was born in Muncie, Indiana, at Ball Memorial Hospital. He grew up in the Midwest and he and his brother were principally raised by his mother. Robert's father lived in Chicago.

Robert graduated from Muncie Northside High School tied for number one in his class with a 4.0 GPA. He attended the Rose-Hulman Institute of Technology in Indiana. Eventually his interest shifted from engineering as a career to law. He was admitted to many law schools but ultimately chose Harvard.

While a student at Harvard, Wilkins served as the president of the Harvard Law School Black Law Students Association (HBLSA) and worked in a student criminal law clinic during his final year. After graduation, he received the job he had hoped for: he was hired as an attorney with the District of Columbia Public Defender Service. And yet all his preparation at Harvard Law School and his experiences as a public defender could not have prepared him for a fateful encounter with the police years later.

It was a somber day in May of 1992 when Robert Wilkins learned that his maternal grandfather had passed away. He and several relatives decided to travel by car from the Washington, DC, area to Chicago for the funeral. His grandfather was an accomplished man. There was a large gathering at his funeral at the church, and the obituary proclaimed his commitment to the struggle for progress for all African Americans. The songs for that day told a story about hopefulness, faith, and a life well lived.

Robert and his family members from the DC area stayed longer than expected in Chicago and decided to make the 12-hour drive from Chicago to Washington without stopping for an extended period of time. They were about an hour away from home, driving in a steady rain through Maryland, on the morning of May 8, 1992, when Robert Wilkins' life would change forever. Just before 6 A.M. Robert's cousin, Norman Scott Wilkins, was driving. They were eastbound on Interstate 68 coming through downtown Cumberland, Maryland, with Robert in the passenger's seat. They saw flashing lights behind them. A Maryland state police officer pulled them over, stepped out of his car, and came to the driver's side of their car. Officer V. W. Hughes told Scott that he had "paced him . . . doing 60 mph in a 40 mph zone."[1] Officer Hughes asked Scott for his license and registration. Since the family was in a rented Cadillac, Scott gave him the rental car contract. Officer Hughes returned to the car five minutes later asking Scott to step out of the car. After a brief discussion with the officer,

Scott leaned into the car and told his father and Robert, "They want to search the car."[2]

At that moment, Robert's instincts kicked in. Robert was stunned that this officer would use a traffic stop as an excuse to search the car. Using the knowledge he had attained as a defense lawyer and recognizing that many citizens have their rights taken away if they don't assert them, he and his uncle agreed that there was no basis to search the car, and they both urged their cousin not to sign the "Consent to Search" form that Officer Hughes presented to Scott. Scott did not sign it, and Robert went on to inform the officer that as he understood the law, there could be no search without an arrest, and furthermore, Scott had done nothing to create probable cause for a search. The officer's response, which startled Robert, was, "If [you have] nothing to hide, then what [is] the problem?"[3] Robert's response was that the problem is the law that says you have nothing to search for if you don't have probable cause that we've committed a crime.

Robert and his family refused to consent to the search. The officer told them that they would have to wait until a dog came to sniff the car and that he would not let them go. After nearly 30 minutes, the officer also told them that they would have to get out of the car for the search. Again Robert resisted, but the officer told them that they had no choice. Robert then tried to explain that they had just come from the funeral of his grandfather, the late G. R. Wilkins, Sr., in Chicago, and they had been driving all night so that Robert could appear in court that morning. He also offered to show Officer Hughes a copy of the obituary. The response, according to Wilkins, was that "he did not want to see any obituary, he wanted to search the car."[4]

After they waited some more, another officer, named Syracuse, came to the scene. Finally a third officer, a Sgt. Brown from the Allegany County Sheriff's Department arrived with a dog trained in the detection of narcotics. The officers insisted that Robert and his relatives get out of the car in the rain, and they proceeded to allow the dog to sniff throughout the car. The German shepherd sniffed everything inside and outside the car and of course found no indication of any contraband, drugs, or anything else. After this embarrassing and humiliating procedure ended, Sgt. Brown and the others finally told Robert and his family that they could get back in their car.[5]

This was a stinging moment for Robert. He was still experiencing the pain of losing his grandfather and was exhausted both emotionally and physically. The idea of being stopped by Maryland police and then being sniffed by a dog for contraband as cars passed by taking a peek at "the African Americans in trouble" added more humiliation and insult to the circumstances. Robert could not believe what he was going through; his objections as a lawyer and the citation of legal precedent had no impact on the officers. At that moment, the law did not protect him from an unwarranted search by a German shepherd.

Eventually, Robert and his family were allowed to leave, but a bitter taste remained in his mouth from this experience. All of the years that Robert had been a law student and a lawyer had not prepared him for being the client rather than counsel for those who found themselves in challenging legal circumstances.

The incident was not the end but rather the beginning of this story. After returning to work and finding that he was too late for his court appearance, Robert thought more and more about the episode. Ultimately, he was determined to take some action, and his family members supported him. When the American Civil Liberties Union (ACLU) agreed to take the case, Robert stated that he wanted to file a lawsuit against the Maryland state police for profiling; the ACLU wanted to examine the legal basis for the stop and ways to keep it from happening to other innocent citizens.[6] As a result of the filing of the lawsuit, Robert and his counsel ultimately received the criminal intelligence report for the Maryland state police. According to Robert, the report discussed the problem of crack cocaine in the Cumberland, Maryland, area and advised Maryland troopers that traffickers "were predominately black males and black females." The report indicated that "these dangerous armed traffickers generally traveled early in the morning or late at night along interstate 68, and that they favored rental cars with Virginia registration."[7] Having traveled on I-68 early in the morning, in a Virginia rental car, Robert and his family fit this broad profile. The problem, of course, is that no one in the car was dangerous, and certainly no one had any drugs or weapons.

This story illustrates how police power and the abuse of that power can deeply impact the lives of individuals and also damage the morale of a community. It tells how police officers without adequate training, and with presumptions about criminality based upon race, have made unfounded, unjustified, and ultimately illegal stops, yet very few have been taken to task. However, Robert was different. He was not going to allow himself or his family to be the victims of this harassment.

The matter was litigated in the Maryland courts, and ultimately in January 1995 there was an agreement to settle Robert's lawsuit. The family received a settlement of $50,000 in damages, and the State of

Maryland agreed to pay $46,000 in attorney's fees for the three years of litigation involved in this case.[8] The state also agreed to no longer use race-based drug courier profiles as law enforcement tools. The new Maryland state police policy would prohibit race as a factor in determining whom to stop, detain, or search without further evidence. The state also agreed that it would train all new and previously hired Maryland state police about this policy and would maintain computer records of all traffic stops in which consent to search is given and drug-sniffing dogs are used. Under this new policy, the Maryland state police agreed to prevent the "consideration of race as a factor [in developing] policies for stopping, detaining, or searching motorists."[9] Officers would also have to track the reason for traffic stops and the race of the person stopped. This information could then be used by a federal judge to monitor the future conduct of the Maryland state police.

Robert Wilkins was happy that the case was settled favorably but, at the same time, startled by the statistics the lawsuit uncovered. In the state of Maryland, the police reports indicated that 70 to 75 percent of people searched on I-95 were African American, even though African Americans represented only 17 percent of those driving on the highway and only 17 percent of traffic violators. By the same token, the Maryland state police would search over 400 African Americans compared to 100 Whites to find similar numbers of individuals with drugs or other contraband. It was clear that a disproportionate number of African Americans were stopped and searched without any valid basis.[10]

The actions of the Maryland state police and Robert Wilkins' quick and thoughtful response to challenge it led to an agreement that would be monitored for years and was designed to stop the practice of indiscriminately stopping people. Despite the settlement and the new training procedures that the Maryland state police agreed to implement, an examination of traffic stops after the Wilkins family's detention revealed a continuing pattern of disparities in stopping African Americans on the Maryland highways, even though, according to Wilkins, there was no increase in finding drugs being transported by African Americans, compared to whites.[11]

More than a decade after his encounter with the police, Robert Wilkins again brought suit against the Maryland state police, asserting that the practices of racial profiling continued and that court intervention was warranted to change these persistent discriminatory practices. Wilkins learned that although 100 complaints had been filed by African Americans against the Maryland state police, not a single one had been upheld. Wilkins and his lawyers sought to review the records; the Maryland state police opposed access to them, claiming that they were "personnel records" and could not be reviewed without violating the "privacy rights" of the police officers involved. In a stunning opinion, the Maryland Court of Special Appeals ruled against the Maryland state police privacy claim, stating:

> The main issue to be resolved is whether about ten-thousand documents that constitute the Maryland State Police's internal affairs files relating to allegations of illegal racial profiling are "personnel records of an individual" within the meaning of that term as used in the Maryland Public Information Act ("the Act"). We shall hold that the Circuit Court for Baltimore County erred when it concluded that the records withheld by

the MSP were "personnel records" within the meaning of the
Act. Therefore, the records must be produced for inspection
and copying by the NAACP. [12]

As a result, the Maryland ACLU and the NAACP can now examine
these records and determine whether other violations of the rights of
African Americans have occurred. This is an encouraging sign of
progress in the effort to stem the practice of racial profiling and to
make the Maryland Police Department more accountable to the
African American citizens who drive on the interstate daily and
should not be stopped on unconfirmed hunches based upon their race.

The lessons from the detention of Robert Wilkins are numerous
and stand as an example of how police, often eager—perhaps overea-
ger—to stem the flow of drugs into our neighborhoods, sometimes go
beyond the limits of the law and suspect individuals of drug trafficking on the slimmest of reasons, not based upon anything reaching the
level of due cause. When is it acceptable to stop a rental car, on the
highways of America, when the occupants are Black, simply because
you believe that you might find drugs? If you routinely stopped every
tenth car on any highway, the random and indiscriminate actions would
be legally acceptable but highly criticized by innocent victims of such
police practices. By the same token, when African Americans believe
that they are routinely stopped on interstate highways simply because
they fit a racial profile, it raises the concern of discrimination, and leads
to the belief that race, and race alone, is the only reason police ever stop
anyone on the highway. Not crime. Not suspicion. Not drugs.

This belief, albeit controversial, is widespread and has been the
subject of several studies and reports. The *New York Times* op-ed

columnist Charles M. Blow referenced a CBS/*New York Times* poll that asked: "Have you ever felt you were stopped by the police just because of your race or ethnic background?" Sixty-six percent of Black men responded yes to this question, whereas only 9 percent of White men responded affirmatively.[13] In addition, the agency that investigates complaints against New York Police Department officers, the Civilian Complaint Review Board, revealed that African Americans filed nearly six times as many complaints regarding street stops as did Whites. Eighty percent of the complaints filed in the past decade were by people of color. Blacks were 12 times more likely than Whites to have been stopped with physical force and 40 times more likely to be stopped by having a gun drawn on them by a police officer.[14]

A report prepared for the ACLU of Southern California found similarly troubling data revealing racially disparate outcomes in pedestrian and motor vehicle stops by the Los Angeles Police Department from July 2003 to June 2004. The report cites "prima facie evidence that African Americans and Hispanics are over-stopped, over-frisked, over-searched, and over-arrested."[15] These key statistics were found:

- Per 10,000 residents, the Black stop rate is 3,400 stops higher than the White stop rate, and the Hispanic stop rate is almost 360 stops higher.
- Relative to stopped Whites, stopped Blacks are 127% more likely and stopped Hispanics are 43% more likely to be frisked.
- Relative to stopped Whites, stopped Blacks are 76% more likely and stopped Hispanics are 16% more likely to be searched.

- Relative to stopped Whites, stopped Blacks are 29% more likely and stopped Hispanics are 32% more likely to be arrested.
- Frisked African Americans are 42.3% less likely to be found with a weapon than frisked Whites, and frisked Hispanics are 31.8% less likely to have a weapon than frisked non-Hispanic Whites.
- Consensual searches of Blacks are 37.0% less likely to uncover weapons, 23.7% less likely to uncover drugs, and 25.4% less likely to uncover anything else.
- Consensual searches of Hispanics similarly are 32.8% less likely to uncover weapons, 34.3% less likely to uncover drugs, and 12.3% less likely to uncover anything else.[16]

These statistics, when viewed in isolation, provide documented instances of racial profiling. But when viewed together, the data paint a much darker, more troubling picture of a criminal justice system teeming with racial imbalance. With such disparities entrenched in the system—and firmly perceived in the minds of the public—the situation quickly becomes even more dire. Marc Mauer, executive director of The Sentencing Project, wrote of this situation in his essay "Two-Tiered System of Justice." He juxtaposes incredible strides—the *Brown v. Board of Education* decision, the election of Barack Obama—with a quiet reality of lingering segregation in American institutions, particularly the criminal justice system. "Despite a specter of integration, certain policies, like the ones employed by the Maryland police when they stopped Robert Wilkins, have been implemented that work—directly and indirectly—to leave

Blacks incarcerated at disproportionate rates. The explosion of the U.S. prison population, the use of segregation tactics in controlling that population, and the ineffective use of the criminal justice system to address social issues have left communities, particularly Black communities, reeling." From this perspective, the story of Robert Wilkins only begins to scrape the surface of a much broader issue.[17]

Robert Wilkins' successful litigation of the issue of racial profiling might have changed a few practices, but changing police officers' minds in terms of what is probable cause to stop and search a car is a long way away from reality. The police motto of protecting and defending citizens must apply with equal force to African Americans, who today do not see police as their protectors but rather as members of a state-operated institution that criminalizes race.

After 18 years of toiling in the local and state courts of Maryland, testifying before Congress, appearing before forums in the United States and globally, Robert Wilkins can finally say that his issues have been addressed. He takes no solace in the fact that his victory stands as a small step toward forwarding the rights of so many people who have faced situations very much like his. Robert Wilkins is amazed by the fact that by turning over every leaf, examining Maryland's state police regulations with the eye of a litigator who did legal defense work, cajoling members of the legislature to rethink state policy about police practices, and testifying before Congress to show that the problem was not one of criminals but often of innocent people caught in the dragnet of police profiling, he was able to make a difference.[18]

Even though Robert Wilkins' victory in the Maryland Court of Special Appeals is a significant one, it in no way will change the hearts and minds of police officers who think that they are protecting the public by making these stops, by pursuing these investigations, by looking for drugs and trying to prevent the interstate transport of illegal substances in Maryland. Their ambition to stop crime is laudable, even though in their very broad scope and unrefined efforts they often stop people who are not criminals. The lesson from the Robert Wilkins case is that persistence and vigilance is essential but also costly in terms of money, professional time, and emotional capital, and that it is unlikely to succeed routinely.

Rather than focus on the Wilkins victory as a high water mark in addressing the issue of police conduct in minority communities, it is imperative that we as a society look more broadly at what we need to give police and citizens to ensure that no one is subjected to racial profiling and that police vigilantly pursue their jobs with enthusiasm and a focus on preventing and addressing crimes in our communities. The solution is not simple, and it will require an enormous amount of training, tolerance, execution, and acceptance on the part of police departments at local, state, and federal levels. It will also require that a community that has been subject to police profiling receive some relief when the police recognize that weak evidence, false reports, and mistaken identifications are inconsistent with truly fighting crime. There also needs to be a process of, at a minimum, public apology if not actual financial payment for mistakes, since many people will accept such steps as an acknowledgment of errors by police. Finally, the community must be involved in the effort to help police root out crime before it occurs and to build a relationship of trust and confidence in those who are sworn to serve and protect the community.

While Robert Wilkins' successful lawsuit must be applauded because of its significance, it took years of litigation and unprecedented rulings by courts before a modest settlement was received. At the same time, the need to monitor allegations of racial profiling has not ended and will continue indefinitely. Robert Wilkins was able to achieve success in Maryland by using every tool he had learned, but he is not alone in being stopped on the highways of America, suspected without proof of transporting drugs, and being asked to consent to a search by a canine unit. Building on his success is a formidable task, but if it takes litigation, legislation, public opinion, and a rethinking of the enormous costs of racial profiling, then it is a task that we must pursue with great urgency. To do otherwise is to allow the status quo to continue unabated.

CHAPTER 6

Race, Class, Justice, and Post-Racial America

I f the arrest of Professor Henry Louis Gates, Jr., proves anything, it is that America has not achieved its goal of being a post-racial society. Indeed, the arrest reinforces the fact that, as much progress as we have made with the election of an African American as president, we still have a long way to go to address the issue of racial injustice, particularly in the criminal justice system.

The lessons from the Rodney King beating apparently have had little lasting effect in LA and have not spread nationwide. While King's beating was captured on tape and led to a national public outcry, many episodes occur where no cameras, audio recordings, or eyewitnesses are around. In these circumstances, the outcome is not based on what justice requires, but rather on who is more believable, the police officer or the person profiled. It is exceedingly difficult for people to win the credibility contest when officers swear that they acted appropriately and have other officers, and often reports, to back up their claims.

In the cases of both Rodney King and Professor Gates, the police could have found other ways to address the situation. Our tendency to use force and violence as the response to disturbances runs counter to the law and the American way. In fact, it only reinforces mistrust and creates fear on both sides. If we can reduce the fear and increase the trust between police and community members, we will go a long way toward addressing the basic problems of liberty and security in our communities.

The presumption of guilt can have an insidious presence beyond an individual's interaction with police. We can imagine how this bias can affect juries, judges, the strength of a defense, and the outcome of a trial as well as a prescribed sentence. We can imagine that well-meaning, well-regarded individuals perform their daily roles unaware of their preconceived biases and their eventual effects.

One of the most remarkable ironies to contend with is the fact that as we think about Professor Gates' arrest, President Obama's intervention, the public reaction, and the broader issues of race, class, and crime, we find ourselves at a critical juncture in history. We must rejoice in the fact that Americans were able to put aside race and elect the person they thought was the most qualified individual to serve as president. This celebration echoed from California to Massachusetts, from Florida to Virginia, from North Carolina to Ohio. While this is an important sign of racial progress, it belies the fact that we are still a long way away from achieving Dr. King's dream of a society in which all people are judged by the content of their character, not by the color of their skin.

If America can elect an African American president, the thinking goes, how can we be accused of having a racially discriminatory society? The mistaken assumption is that since we have achieved so much racial progress, we should discontinue all the efforts to address racial discrimination in the twenty-first century. Those who believe that we are in a post-racial environment are naive at best or racially insensitive at worst.

The Reverend Eugene Rivers, a feisty African American minister in Boston and one of the founders of the Ten Point Coalition, a group of black ministers who fought to reduce violence and crime among young offenders in Boston in the 1980s, has spent most of his professional life working with young Black men involved in gangs and seeking to stem the violence in urban communities. In August 2009, Rivers participated in a public forum on Martha's Vineyard, hosted by the Charles Hamilton Houston Institute for Race and Justice and sponsored by the national law firm of Bingham McCutcheon, as a member of a panel entitled "Striking the Right Balance: Addressing Our Individual and Collective Responsibilities to Families and Communities." He said that he was worried by those who viewed the overexuberant celebration of Obama's election as a manifestation of the arrival of a post-racial America. Rivers implored those assembled that day to not be too quick to assume Obama's election solves our race problem. While Rivers admitted the value of Obama's election, and that it was wonderful to behold the nation embracing Obama, he said that we should not be too eager to claim a victory over racism. Reverend Rivers also reminded us of how little progress we have really made: "There is one black man in the White House and a million black men in prison."[1] The reverend's timely statement reminds us that we have much more work to do to overcome the barriers of class and race in our criminal justice system.

While this book has identified instances in which conflicts between police and members of the African American community have led to strong feelings of bias, the range of complaints concerning racial bias in the criminal justice system today is much larger. At nearly every stage in the system, we find disparities in punishment, in the provision of adequate defense counsel, and in policies and laws, as well as other forms of bias experienced by African Americans. Marc Mauer, president of the criminal justice advocacy group The Sentencing Project, recently noted that, "in the most profound betrayal of the promise of integration and opportunity, the United States has created a world-record prison population fueled by policies that have exposed substantial portions of African Americans to the life-changing consequences of the criminal justice system."[2]

What Mauer describes as a continuing legacy of slavery places far too many African Americans in jeopardy. That legacy is seen in the increasing disparities in our society. Marian Wright Edelman, president of the Children's Defense Fund, notes in her new study on disparities involving children, "America's Cradle to Prison Pipeline," that disparities start early and continue throughout African Americans' lives. Edelman describes many instances in which children are pushed out of school, given no meaningful alternatives, and soon find themselves in the criminal justice system as adults.[3] Furthermore, the criminal justice system compounds the problem by continually punishing race more than crime.

One of the greatest ironies in the criminal justice system is the propensity of prosecutors to strike Blacks from juries, not because of evidence of a potential juror's actual bias, but presumptions of racial bias. It is a practice that regrettably legitimizes perceived biases of prosecutors while presuming actual bias on the part of potential African American jurors. In several decisions the Supreme Court has chastised prosecutors for removing otherwise qualified African Americans from jury service because of their race. In *Batson v. Kentucky*, Justice Lewis Powell, writing for the majority, reversed a conviction of an African American defendant because the prosecutor had struck all of the potential Black jurors.[4] While the Supreme Court reversed Batson's conviction, Justice Thurgood Marshall might have had the best idea for ending discrimination in jury selection when he concluded that the appropriate solution would be to eliminate the use of peremptory challenges altogether.[5]

Prosecutors' use of peremptory challenges were also held unconstitutional in another Supreme Court case. In *Miller-El v. Dretke* Justice David Souter, writing for the majority, carefully scrutinized the entire record in the case and concluded that there were repeated instances of racial discrimination in striking African Americans as potential jurors.[6] Following the lead of Justice Thurgood Marshall nearly two decades earlier in the *Batson* case, Justice Stephen Breyer, in a concurring opinion, suggested that the use of peremptory challenges should end.

As federal district court Judge Reggie Walton has ominously stated, the disparate sentences received by African American defendants in drug cases will cause other African Americans to doubt the legitimacies of the criminal justice system. "African-American defendants sentenced for cocaine offenses wind up serving prison terms that are greater than those served by other cocaine defendants. I have a concern that the disparate impact of crack sentencing on African-American communities shapes social attitudes. When large segments of the African-American population believe that our criminal justice system is in any way influenced by racial considerations, our [courts] are presented with serious practical problems. People come to doubt

the legitimacy of the law—not just the law associated with crack—
but *all* laws. People come to view the courts with suspicion, as institutions that mete out unequal justice, and the moral authority of not
only the federal courts, but all courts, is diminished. I have experienced citizens refusing to serve on juries, and there are reports of juries refusing to convict defendants."[7]

As I recounted in *From Lynch Mobs to the Killing State: Race and the
Death Penalty in America*, the problems of injustice in our criminal
justice system are continuing and pervasive.[8]

It is ironic that the election of a Black man, against the backdrop
of pervasive racial disparity in the criminal justice system, can undermine our greatest goal: achieving a racially progressive society. Brown
University professor Glenn Loury, who has written extensively on the
topic of race and mass incarceration, has made clear that our focus on
celebrating the president's election is misplaced if we fail to see the
massive incarceration of African Americans as a failure of our democratic society to work effectively. Loury mourns the fact that our sense
of democratic values is undermined by the acceptance of mass incarceration as a tolerable condition in an enlightened society. Loury observes plaintively: "Race helps to explain why the United States is
exceptional among the democratic industrial societies in the severity
and extent of its punitive policy and in the paucity of its social-welfare
institutions."[9]

Loury is even more explicit in his condemnation of the growing
problem of mass incarceration when viewed in light of the nation's
enthusiastic election of Barack Obama. He bemoans the fact that
while we can surely celebrate Obama's election, our values as a democratic society are misplaced. He goes further in taking President

Obama to task for his support of Professor Gates, his friend, when the problem of Black suffering in the criminal justice system goes unabated: "It is depressing in the extreme that the President, when it came time for him to extend political capital on the issue of race and the police, did so on behalf of his 'friend' rather than stressing policy reforms that might keep poorly educated, infrequently employed, troubled but still human young black men in America out of prison."[10] Loury was relentless in his criticism of the president for not addressing, in such a public and global forum, the embarrassing American problem of mass incarceration. Ultimately, the essence of his argument, and one shared by many, is to ask, What is the benefit of electing an African American president if, when a teachable moment on the thorny issue of race arises, he does not use his enormous platform to give America a needed lecture on a criminal justice system suffering from the massive incarceration of African American men? Whether fair or not, Loury expected the president, if he is to use political capital on the issue of race, to use it where a systematic opportunity for change is apparent: "If Mr. Obama were going to lose some working-class white votes to the charge of 'elitism,' I'd much rather it have been on countering the proliferation of 'three strikes' laws, or ratcheting down the federal penalties for low-level drug trafficking, or inveighing against the racial disproportion in the administration of the death penalty."[11]

What is largely ignored is how a Black president should handle the issue of racial disparity when he must also put forth a colorless America. President Obama, in an unscripted explanation of the problem of racial profiling, actually was quite emphatic about its historic and prevalent nature. He did, in fact, use the occasion to raise the issue,

Haney Lopez questions whether the election of an African American president will further or retard the effort to address racial disparities. He cautions against an assumption that broad efforts to address universal problems of inequity will be fruitful in reducing the persistent problem of racial bias and mass incarceration. He takes issue with President Obama's claim that a universal approach will lead to the right result in the matters addressed in this book. Lopez observes:

> "An emphasis on universal, as opposed to race-specific programs isn't just good policy," the *New York Times* quotes Barack Obama as saying, "[i]t's good politics." In rejoinder, a stratification analysis makes clear that no division between a universalistic focus on class versus a particularistic emphasis on race is tenable: race and class in the United States inextricably interdigitate such that neither can be engaged without sustained attention to the other. A focus on class as a complement to a close engagement with race would be quite helpful; but a focus on class as a substitute for race, as part of an evasion of race, will prove counterproductive. Class should not be used to obfuscate the interrelated yet distinct issues associated with race, or vice-versa. Whether one privileges class or race, focusing on their interconnection will advance justice, while stressing one to the exclusion of the other will lead to failure along both fronts.[13]

What Professors Loury and Lopez make clear is that progressive intellectuals are not happy with Obama's reluctance to embrace a social contract focusing on racial stratification and believe that he, and only he, is in a position to transform the problem of mass incarceration of African Americans.

The lesson from the arrest of Professor Gates, the intervention by President Obama, and the firestorm of public reaction is a reminder that race still matters. Efforts to put it aside or to assume that the election of an African American president will address the larger problems of racial disparity are not really convincing. The arrest of Professor Gates is a reminder that we have a long way to go to live in a post-racial America. Even more problematic is the fact that our efforts to achieve a post-racial America may obscure rather than eliminate true disparities.

President Obama may have the authority to change national policies on these matters, but he cannot change the heart-felt perceptions of many Americans. Sadly, the issue of racial profiling is not limited to incidents with people like Professor Gates or to African Americans. In Arizona on Friday, April 23, 2010, Governor Jan Brewer signed a pernicious bill that is classic racial profiling. The bill, entitled Senate Bill 1070, gives virtually unlimited discretion to law enforcement officers to question, detain, and ultimately deport individuals who appear to be Mexicans.[14] Moreover, Arizona polls indicate that governor Brewer's signing of the bill has substantially improved her rating among Arizonans.[15]

We have much work to do to change the perceptions held by some police officers that lead to the profiling of far too many African American men. Too many assumptions about misconduct are made based upon race, and too many police officers lack the necessary training to discern the difference between suspicion and simply color. The problem to be addressed is not one of race alone. Many of the officers who are criticized for their wrongful suspicion of African Americans, Latinos, and others are themselves members of these racial groups and still engage in improper behavior.

What the Gates case reminds us of is the need for broad and universal efforts to look at race and police conduct and to come up with concrete, meaningful, and thoughtful responses. The goal is not simply to criticize the police. That is an unproductive exercise in futility. Throughout the country, police work diligently every day trying to prevent crime, arrest those who are responsible, and protect victims from crimes that undermine their dignity and threaten their safety. They work for relatively low pay for the risks that they take, and although in some communities their role is respected and admired, in other communities they are vilified and treated as outcasts.

But just as the police must be respected for their role in law enforcement, it is necessary that we as a society no longer continue to profile African American men. It should not be assumed that anyone wearing a skull cap, baggy pants, and a particular color is a gang member or that Black people driving expensive cars, or living in expensive neighborhoods or in penthouses of luxury buildings don't belong there. These misguided assumptions about Black men need to be addressed in a meaningful way.

If we are to learn anything from the race and class encounters addressed in these pages, it is that each American has the capacity, and indeed the obligation, to find ways to eliminate racial disparities in our society and to create opportunities for police and all citizens to mutually respect each other. Likewise, it is incumbent upon all of us as members of the larger American community to find ways to focus our collective efforts, as a society, on measures dedicated to both the prevention of crimes and the contexts that create them, rather than on punishment.

For far too long we have focused on being tough on crime without the corollary agenda of being smart about preventing crime. We focus on addressing the violence and locking up the offenders while ignoring such societal ills as hunger, poverty, abuse, and neglect. Today, we live in a society where too many African Americans are in the criminal justice system for nonviolent drug offenses and are unable to find employment when they are released. Our responsibility is not only to focus on jobs for the formerly incarcerated, but also on meaningful ways to prevent the crimes, including nonviolent drug offenses, being perpetrated by those who wrongly see those crimes as their only option for survival. Too many young people are dropping out, or being pushed out, of our educational system and then resorting to illegal activities to support themselves. Too many homes are broken, and not enough mentors are available for children who need support and encouragement. Our system is broken. If we don't act quickly, the next generation of children will find themselves in this hopeless trap as well.

If there is good news, it is that the arrest of Professor Gates brought national attention to the issues of racial disparity in the criminal justice system, and reminded us that these issues still must be resolved. The charges were dropped against Professor Gates and he has cooperated with the Cambridge Police Department in developing ways to prevent similar breakdowns from happening in the future. Additionally, although he has two years to bring a lawsuit to vindicate his rights, and time will tell what will happen, his focus has been on moving forward in his life's work and on trying to improve relationships between the

African American community and the police. Professor Gates' good news is a hopeful sign that, with effort and commitment, progress—real progress—can be made when we face the issues head on.

One can't help but think that, in some way, the arrest of the professorial expert on matters of race had no other inevitable end but to teach others about these important issues.

AFTERWORD

Race Matters: The Struggle Continues

This Afterword begins where the arrest of Professor Henry Lewis Gates, Jr. left off. After the arrest of Professor Gates on July 16, 2009, the dismissal of the charges on July 22, 2009, and the subsequent "beer summit" at the White House later that same summer, Robert Haas, the relatively new Commissioner of the Cambridge Police Department, retained the services of former Police Officer Chuck Wexler to conduct an evaluation and write a report designed to identify lessons learned from this incident and its aftermath. In doing so, the Commissioner's goal was to help the Cambridge Police Department improve its operations and relationships with the community, and to provide some guidance to other police departments on how to avoid similar incidents in their communities.

The Wexler Commission worked on its report during the same period that I was researching and drafting the hardcover edition of this book, which was published in early June 2010. My first visits to discuss the book were with Reverend Al Sharpton at the House of Justice on Saturday, June 5, and with Reverend Calvin Butts at Abysinnian Baptist Church on Sunday, June 6, where advance copies sold out after the first service. Later that afternoon, I participated in a book signing and discussion at the home of my colleague and friend Michele Roberts in Washington, DC.

The report by the Wexler Commission was released on June 16. I read it eagerly, and, in a blog posting on the Charles Hamilton Houston Institute for Race and Justice website, dated June 30, provided my response.[1] I found much to admire in the report's thoughtful recommendations for key reforms aimed at improving relationships between the Cambridge community and police department, in the obvious care that went into the investigation, and in the leadership exercised by Police Chief Robert Haas in commissioning the study.

I did, however, express my deep concern for the report's major finding, articulated in its title, "Missed Opportunities: Shared Responsibility," that Sergeant Crowley and Professor Gates were equally at fault and therefore shared the blame for the incident's unfortunate escalation. This finding is reinforced throughout the report, starting with the very first page, which reads: "Sergeant Crowley and Professor Gates each missed opportunities to 'ratchet down' the situation and end it peacefully." Later, the report states that "If, on the other hand, both men had shared responsibility for understanding each other and communicating openly, the outcome could have been better."[2] In one of the appendices, the authors write:

> In psychological terms, if either Sergeant Crowley or Professor Gates had summoned a measure of "ego detachment" and stepped outside of himself for a moment to gain some perspective, he could have begun to react strategically rather than responding to the perceived threat to identity being posed by the other man.[3]

I felt then and I continue to feel now that the argument of "shared responsibility" represented an improper assumption of mutual authority. Police officers and the citizens they serve do not interact on a level playing field. The police officer has authority, control, power, status, and, not incidentally, the presumed legitimate use of force on his side. It is the police officer who has the professional training and responsibility to de-escalate a situation, particularly when, as the report makes clear was true in the Crowley/Gates incident, the officer fully understands that he is not in physical danger, and that the citizen poses no safety threat. The finding in the report that private citizens such as Professor Gates should be held to the same standard of conduct as a police officer is based on improper and deeply flawed reasoning. Indeed, as the next paragraph in the report makes clear, it is police officers—not individual members of the public—who need to develop strategies intended to "dampen" rather than "accelerate" conflict and tension.[4]

Since then, while much has happened, little has actually changed. The proverbial phrase "The more things change, the more they remain the same" certainly applies to the current practice of racial profiling in America. In fact, the growing number of incidents of profiling makes one question whether we are making any headway in addressing the issue. Profiling occurs not only in the criminal justice system but in many other venues; it occurs whenever individuals and groups are targeted and negatively influenced by informal policies and actual procedures that treat them as less than citizens and deny them the most basic and fundamental rights of life, liberty, and equality.

In 2009, Attorney General Eric Holder characterized the United States as "a nation of cowards" when it came to discussing race; for that he was widely criticized.[5] Yet, if nothing else, the examples I discuss in this chapter illustrate how the need for a deeper and more nuanced private and public discussion of race in this country is more pressing than ever. These include the uproar that took place when Shirley Sherrod, a prominent African-American woman with a history of racial cooperation, was attacked and labeled as a racist after the deliberately misleading editing of her remarks aired on television. I also refer to growing complaints from members of the African-American community about their treatment by New York City police as well as the frustration of Latinos who are profiled, punished, and then deported by law enforcement groups in Arizona, Connecticut, and elsewhere. Finally, I examine the plight of a four-year-old Black child in Chicago who was falsely held up as an example of our worst stereotyping—a travesty that highlights how race, class, and crime are presented in a way that exacerbates the public's fear of a Black man, and even a Black child. By highlighting examples of this continuing trend and its impact not just on individuals but on communities, I aim to spark broader discussions and narrow the gap of engagement. My hope is that these conversations can move us closer to a society that accepts differences among groups and individuals of different races, genders, ethnicities, classes, and faiths. Even better, I await a day when we not only "all get along," but actually celebrate the fact that we are all critical parts of the "United" States of America.

THE SHIRLEY SHERROD INCIDENT

On July 20, 2010, Fox News published a news story entitled "Video Shows USDA Official Saying She Didn't Give 'Full Force' of Help to White Farmer."[6] The story led with a bit on how the NAACP had recently accused the Tea Party of racism. The article then attempted to juxtapose the NAACP's stance with a statement about how an Agriculture Department official was shown in a video "regaling an NAACP audience" on how she withheld help from a White farmer in bankruptcy. Fox News also reported that these statements had forced the official to resign. That official was Shirley Sherrod, the Georgia Director of Rural Development and an African-American woman.

In the article, the news agency admitted that the Agriculture Department's announcement about Sherrod's firing came "shortly after FoxNews.com published its initial report." Fox News identified the source of the video clips as coming from BigGovernment.com, a conservative website[7] run by blogger Andrew Breitbert. The video clips came from a speech Sherrod had given at an NAACP Freedom Fund Banquet on March 27 and showed her describing the case of a White farmer who had come to her for help. In the clips, she states, "What he didn't know while he was taking all that time trying to show me he was superior to me was I was trying to decide just how much help I was going to give him. . . . I was struggling with the fact that so many black people have lost their farmland and here I was faced with having to help a white person save their land—so I didn't give him the full force of what I could do. I did enough."[8]

The Department of Agriculture's actions were swift and complete. Within 24 hours of the initial Fox News report, the department had fired Shirley Sherrod, with Agriculture Secretary Tom Vilsack stating, "There is zero tolerance for discrimination at USDA, and I strongly condemn any act of discrimination against any person."[9] Apparently the firing occurred without Sherrod being given the opportunity to explain her side.[10] The press picked up the criticisms of Shirley Sherrod, including one from none other than Benjamin Jealous, president of the NAACP—the same body Sherrod had been addressing in the videos. The *Kansas City Star* reported Jealous saying:

> Racism is about the abuse of power. Sherrod had it in her position at USDA. According to her remarks, she mistreated a white farmer in need of assistance because of his race. We are appalled by her actions, just as we are with abuses of power against farmers of color and female farmers. Her actions were shameful. While she went on to explain in the story that she ultimately realized her mistake, as well as the common predicament of working people of all races, she gave no indication she had attempted to right the wrong she had done to this man.[11]

Some saw Fox News' publishing of the Sherrod video clips as an effort by conservatives to establish "evidence of anti-white racism in President Barack Obama's government and within the NAACP."[12] The news article admitted that the video was "only an excerpt of the speech," acknowledging "the point of the story wasn't entirely clear."[13]

In fact, the point of Sherrod's story—in its entirety—was very clear indeed and very different from the portrait presented by Fox. Once the full video was released within the next 24 hours, it became obvious that Sherrod's statements in the heavily edited video clips were not only taken out of context, but had been wildly distorted. In the full video, Sherrod explained that "poverty, not race, is the key factor in rural development" and that she eventually "worked hard to save the farmer's land." She stated that "working with him made me see that it's really about those who have versus those who haven't. . . . They could be black, they could be white, they could be Hispanic. And it made me realize then that I needed to help poor people—those who don't have access the way others have."[14] In other words, far from discriminating against Whites, she had come to recognize how important it was to help all poor people, regardless of color. Her message, in fact, was the antithesis of its portrayal on Fox News.

Following the release of the full video, the White House issued an apology to Sherrod and admitted that the Department of Agriculture had acted in haste.[15] President Obama personally called Sherrod as well.[16] Secretary Vilsack offered her a new position, stating, "I did not think before I acted and for that reason this poor woman has gone through a very difficult time."[17] The NAACP also retracted its initial harsh statements against Sherrod, with the group's president, Benjamin Todd Jealous, declaring that it had been "snookered" by conservatives.[18] Sherrod accepted the apologies but felt that the government had been hesitant to accept her explanation because of a fear of "conservative media backlash."[19]

A few days after these profuse apologies, Johanna Wald and I wrote an op-ed piece for the *Washington Post*, suggesting that the Sherrod incident was "a metaphor for this country's aborted efforts to address race."[20] The handling of the Sherrod incident by the media, and by key officials within the NAACP and the Obama administration, made it appear as if the United States lacked the attention span to sustain a discussion on race beyond a single news cycle. In fact, the country could barely make it through an entire videotape before rising up to condemn the honesty of the speaker. As Eric Holder understands, this incident once again illustrated how initiating any discussions about race continues to make much of America squirm in discomfort. In our op-ed, we argued that it is structural racism rather than individual racism that perpetuates racial inequality. This structural inequality can be witnessed in all facets of life in America, ranging from the disproportionate numbers of young Black men and women in prison, to the tracking of students of color in low-achievement classes, to the continuing housing and educational racial segregation, to the "opportunity gap" that plagues so many communities of color. However, the fact that individuals working within these structures believe themselves to be free of prejudice is one reason why discussions about race remain so difficult and so uncomfortable for so many of us.

PROFILING IN COMMUNITIES OF COLOR: THE CASES OF NEW YORK, CONNECTICUT, AND ARIZONA

In many respects, the past is prologue for the future. While racial profiling is often viewed as the anticipated reaction to the end of slavery, Jim Crow, segregation, and the epicenter of the civil rights movement, and often characterized as a Southern matter, the late twentieth century and first decade of the twenty-first century have convinced us that it was—indeed remains—far more widespread and without geographic boundaries. A series of events in the northern states raised the issue of racial profiling to the forefront of our consciousness. In New Jersey and New York, we witnessed police stops and harassment of African Americans and Latinos, the astonishing cases of the killing of Amadou Diallo, the sodomizing of Abner Luima, and the killing of

Colin Ferguson and Sean Bell, as well as the tragic shooting death of Pace student Danroy Henry in Westchester, New York, and the wounding of Brandon Cox (my client in a pending civil matter) in 2010. These represent only a few of the incidents that continue to stir up tensions in the African-American community.

In particular, police strategies in New York City have shed a whole new light on the practice of racial profiling. New York City's stop-and-frisk—more formally "Stop, Question, Frisk"[21]—policy has been a major law enforcement tool since the 1990s.[22] It became prominent when the New York City Police Department (NYPD) adopted a "broken windows" strategy, emphasizing the regulation of minor crime as well as crime prevention.[23] Like New York, several other cities rely heavily on the stop-and-frisk approach, but only a few employ the tactic with the same vigor.[24]

In 2010, the NYPD made 601,055 street stops—the most ever made over any 12-month period.[25] In 2009, the number was 575,000.[26] Black and Hispanic individuals constituted more than 85 percent of the people stopped by the police,[27] although their combined populations comprised just over 50 percent of the city's overall racial demography.[28] Proponents of the policy attribute the racial disparity to the disproportionate number of Black and Hispanic men represented among offenders, but legal scholar Jeffrey Fagan found that Blacks and Hispanics "were more likely to be stopped at police discretion, not just in high-crime, high-minority areas, but in districts where crime is minimal and populations are mixed."[29] Fagan's report further found that street stops result in arrests at a rate less than 6 percent, which is lower than if the police instituted random checkpoints.[30]

A CASE STUDY OF BROWNSVILLE, BROOKLYN

On July 11, 2010, the *New York Times* published an article titled "A Few Blocks, 4 Years, 52,000 Police Stops."[31] In it, the authors describe their investigation of police stop-and-frisk activity on "some eight odd blocks of Brownsville, Brooklyn." They paint a recurrent nighttime scene in which "dozens of officers, many fresh out of the police academy, walk in pairs or linger on corners. Others, deeper within the urban grid, navigate a maze of public housing complexes, patrolling the stairwells and hallways."

During the period of January 2006 to March 2010, the NYPD made almost 52,000 stops on the eight blocks of these housing projects. This averages out to almost one stop each year for each of the 14,000 people residing there. Moreover, males aged 15 to 34 comprised 68 percent of the stops over the years despite comprising only 11 percent of the area's population. This averages out to about five stops per person within that demographic each year, though it cannot be determined precisely because the data did not include the names and addresses of the individuals stopped. However, the names of all the individuals stopped, whether arrested or not, were stored in a database that the police say is helpful in solving future crimes. Less than 9 percent of the stops were because the targeted person fit a description; by contrast, almost 26,000 stops were on the grounds of a "furtive movement"—something critics say can mean anything—or on grounds listed as "other." The number of stops resulting in arrest within the eight blocks is less than 1 percent. In 2009, for example, 13,200 people were stopped and only 109 were arrested. And despite the fact that the most urgent purpose of the encounters is said to be the removal of guns from the streets, only 25 guns were recovered from the almost 52,000 stops made over the 50-month period.

Officers routinely stopped people they suspected of carrying guns, stopped and questioned individuals who entered public housing buildings without a key (even when they did not need to use a key because the lock was broken), and ran warrant checks on young people stopped for riding bicycles on the sidewalk.

Deputy Inspector Juanita Holmes, who was formerly in charge of the NYPD officers assigned to the housing projects that largely comprise the eight blocks, contended that crime declined in the neighborhood as a direct result of the aggressive stop-and-frisk policy. She asserted that over the first six months of 2010, violent crime was down in nearly all categories in the five housing complexes. Dennis C. Smith, a professor at the Robert F. Wagner Graduate School of Public Service at New York University, found the approach to be effective throughout the city in the cases of robbery, murder, burglary, and auto theft but determined that there was no citywide impact on assault, rape, or grand larceny.[32]

All but 2 of the 12 current or former officers interviewed reported pressure to make a minimum threshold of stops, which is something police officials firmly deny. Officer Ryan Sheridan is quoted as saying the reason that the arrest rate is so low for the people stopped for entering a building without a key despite the existence of a broken lock is that "90% of the people live" there. But, as the *New York Times* reported, Deputy Inspector Holmes "said she never emphasized numbers and scoffed at the notion that her officers were using broken locks to initiate" stops.

FLOYD, ET AL. V. CITY OF NEW YORK, ET AL.

Floyd, et al. v. City of New York, et al. is a federal class action suit in which plaintiffs, represented by the Center for Constitutional Rights, allege violations of the Fourth and Fourteenth amendments (stop-and-frisks and racial profiling) by the NYPD and City of New York.[33] The lead plaintiff is David Floyd, who was stopped in February 2008, the year the complaint was filed. Floyd contests the appropriateness of the encounter, but Judge Shira Scheindlin found there was reasonable suspicion to stop him.[34] Nevertheless, on August 31, 2011, Judge Scheindlin denied the city's motion to dismiss, saying that there was enough evidence for a jury to consider the plaintiffs' claim that NYPD officers use race as a factor in the decision to stop people on the streets and potentially frisk them. She did, however, note that the racial claims seemed "difficult to discern."

One thing seemed not so difficult to discern: Although New York City has seen a large reduction in crime, Judge Scheindlin pointed out that there is no conclusive evidence that the NYPD's stop-and-frisk policy caused the decline.[35] After all, crime has fallen in many different cities, including ones that did not adopt the stop-and-frisk policy. Further, Judge Scheindlin was critical of the NYPD's contention that it has a training program to teach appropriate arrest procedure and to admonish against racial profiling, noting that many officers did not recall receiving the training.

Part of Judge Scheindlin's decision reads: "This case presents an issue of great public concern. Writ large, that issue is the disproportionate number of African-Americans and Latinos who become entangled in our criminal justice system, as compared to Caucasians."[36]

Just two days after Judge Scheindlin's decision, the Editorial Board of the *New York Times* wrote an article in support of allowing the case to proceed. It was titled "The Truth Behind Stop-and-Frisk." The article raised serious questions concerning the efficacy of the program at reducing crime and concluded that "hundreds of thousands of people, mostly minorities, have been stopped for no legitimate reason—or worse, because of the color of their skin."[37]

According to the website of the Center for Constitutional Rights, on November 7, 2011, the plaintiffs in *Floyd, et al. v. City of New York, et al.* filed a motion for class certification.[38]

ARIZONA AND CONNECTICUT PROFILING OF LATINOS

Two recent high-profile cases of long-term, systemic abuse by law enforcement against Latinos in 2011 and 2012—one in Connecticut and one in Arizona—illustrate just how far we have not come. It seems that, as the nation has become more multiracial, so, unfortunately, has our profiling. Both cases are shocking in the level of abuse hurled at Latinos and at the apparent shamelessness of law enforcement in its discrimination.

In East Haven, Connecticut, Latino residents were routinely followed, harassed, and beaten up by police officers for several years.[39] In addition, the police routinely referred them to the U.S. Immigration and Customs Enforcement (ICE) for deportation, despite vehement denials by ICE that it relies upon racial profiling and only deports serious criminals.

In Arizona, Tom Perez, the assistant attorney general for the Civil Rights Division in the U.S. Department of Justice, announced the results of an investigation into the Maricopa County Sheriff's Office (MCSO).[40] Perez noted that the MCSO engages in a pattern of unconstitutional policing that included racial profiling, unlawfully stopping, detaining and arresting Latinos, and retaliating against those who complained or criticized these actions.

If there is one bright spot in these sordid stories, it is that the state and federal governments are taking strong legal action against these systemic abuses of authority. In announcing the indictments of four East Haven police officers after several years of investigation for terrorizing Latino community members, David B. Fein, U.S. Attorney for Connecticut, said, "No person is above the law."[41] Hopefully, such strong language and action will prevent other egregious examples of abuse and profiling from taking place.

THE CHICAGO EXAMPLE OF THE MEDIA'S USE OF RACIAL STEREOTYPES: HAVE THEY NO SHAME?

The City of Chicago has experienced a number of notable problems with gangs and crimes, but a 2011 newscast illustrated how the media practice of racial profiling could sink to new depths. When Chicago television station WBBM reported on a spree of shootings in Chicago, addressing Black-on-Black crime, it also included an interview (without a parent nearby or parental consent to interview a minor) with a four-year-old African-American child who expressed awareness of the problem in Chicago. When asked what he planned to do, it is reported that he said, "I'm going to get me a gun!" The reporter then ended the story, suggesting that even four-year-olds are part of the Black gang/crime problem in Chicago. In fact, the boy said something else that was *not* reported that night and that completely changed what was officially reported to the network's viewers. Here is what was initially reported, followed by what the four-year-old *actually* said:

> **Reporter:** The male's in good condition while the girl's expected to recover and kids on the street as young as four were there to see it all unfold and had disturbing reactions.
>
> **Boy:** I'm not scared of nothing.
>
> **Reporter:** When you get older are you going to stay away from all these guns?
>
> **Boy:** No.
>
> **Reporter:** No? What are you going to do when you get older?
>
> **Boy:** I'm going to have me a gun!

Anchor Steve Bartelstein ended the story saying, "That was scary indeed," and co-anchor Susan Carlson exclaimed, "Hearing that little boy there, wow!"

Here's what was really said:

> **Reporter:** Boy, you ain't scared of nothing! Damn! When you get older are you going to stay away from all these guns?
>
> **Boy:** No.
>
> **Reporter:** No? What are you going to do when you get older?
>
> **Boy:** I'm going to have me a gun!
>
> **Reporter:** You are? Why do you want to do that?
>
> **Boy:** I'm going to be the police!
>
> **Reporter:** Okay, then you can have one.[42]

The four-year-old child was talking about protecting the city, not becoming a gangbanger. When the media can interview a four-year-old without apparent parental present (the first problem, as questioned by NAACP President Jealous in a clip following the airing of the interview) and carry only his misconstrued incendiary comment, not the full, positive notion of crime prevention, we must ask: Does the media have no shame? And if racial profiling starts with a four-year-old, where does it end?

CONCLUSION

The arrest of Professor Gates on Thursday, July 16, 2009, set into motion a renewed national reflection about issues of race, class, and crime in our society. The fact that the issues raised by this incident and discussed in this book continue to reverberate throughout the country in countless examples is a reminder that, as a people, we are still not able to sustain a civil, thoughtful, reflective, and ultimately powerful conciliatory conversation about race, religion, gender, class, and ethnicity. In some respects, it seems that we are farther apart now than we were in the past. As much as we might wish to believe that we live in a "post-racial" America, in light of the recent cases just described, we must recognize that we have a very long way to go to turn that wish into a reality.

100 Ways to Look at a Black Man[1]

No, this is not an afterthought or a conclusion, as you might expect from an epilogue. Rather, here you will find the voices of countless people who symbolize the past, present, and future of these important issues. While this book focuses essentially on a single confrontation between one Black man and one White police officer, the events of July 16, 2009 are emblematic of a deeper problem that cannot be ignored. The arrest of Henry Louis Gates, Jr., provided a monumental opportunity for examining the issues of race and class in the criminal justice system.

During the course of my representation of Professor Gates, I received an endless stream of emails, text messages, calls, and letters from many people describing police encounters and other events they perceived as racial profiling. Those who reached out to me were not only African American men. They were men and women, diverse in terms of race, religion, and class, and many felt that their complaints had gone unanswered; only a few felt that theirs had been appropriately resolved.

The largest single category of people who contacted me was, however, African American men, many of whom, like Professor Gates, are successful in their professions. They described a range of encounters that had reminded them that their educational and professional achievements did not protect them from being profiled. Their descriptions of these incidents, some involving police and others involving race-laced contact with the general public, showed that race mattered despite their accomplishments.

This concluding chapter is about their stories, as reported to me or as presented in other public documents and forums. Some of the individuals, like Justice Thurgood Marshall, Dr. John Hope Franklin, and Johnnie Cochran, Jr., have passed away. These stories are constant reminders of the complexity of the problem and the lack of simple solutions. Each man's story of an unfortunate experience reveals a system that is fraught with ambiguity and shortcomings. To overcome these shortcomings, we must, at a minimum, accept the responsibility to collectively endeavor to eliminate all forms of discrimination.

The point of this epilogue is not to create some sort of exceptional treatment of African American men who have been successful in their educational pursuits or their positions in business or government. Far from it. The point is to describe how the problem of racial profiling experienced by far too many poor and powerless African American men is not an issue of class, but undeniably an issue of race.

Most of the experiences presented here fall into a number of general categories. The narratives sometimes involve significant historic events; in other cases they reflect recent events. That some of these events have taken place decades apart is clear evidence that racial profiling is an enduring problem in America.

The narratives provide examples of African American men finding themselves pulled over and asked questions about the car they are driving or their reasons for being in a particular neighborhood, or even being asked to submit to a search of their car trunks, while the police themselves provide no articulable suspicion of the men having committed a crime.

The range of profiling issues involves encounters with police, but is not limited to those examples. In other circumstances, African American men complain of attending exclusive events in prominent venues and being handed a claim check by a White person and being asked to bring that person their coat or park their car. African American men report calling the police when they believe that their home has been burglarized only to have the police arrive and suspect the caller as the burglar. In still other cases, African American men are walking from work, are in their business offices, or are heading for their cars, dressed professionally, and are suspected, usually by White women, as potential rapists, robbers, or both. What these stories tell us is that, even after these African American men, like Professor Henry Louis Gates, Jr., have attended college and become doctors, judges, lawyers, scientists, ministers, teachers, public officials, entrepreneurs, or retirees, they are still viewed as criminals or servants by police and the public. These perceptions are largely based upon race, not upon reason. These stories stand out as compelling examples of profiling and present the range of experiences that these individuals, many well-known, have encountered.

The following eight categories encapsulate what the men herein reported to me or to others. First, there are the classic cases of Driving while Black. Second is the related, but distinct category of mistakenly being accused of criminal conduct by law enforcement officials. Police aren't alone in accusing African American men of criminal conduct without justification. The third category includes instances in which African American men are suspected of criminal conduct by members of the public. Another troubling category involves occasions when Whites have demonstrated an unwarranted fear of a Black man. Other men in the epilogue describe occasions in their professional lives when individuals have assumed that they were there to serve them, when the men were actually guests or hosts, and not in service positions. In another category, African American men who have committed no crimes express exasperation and annoyance with being profiled by police. A number of men report that they experienced unwarranted assumptions about their credentials and qualifications. Finally, there are a number of instances where African Americans report that their race is the key factor in how they are viewed.

Some of the stories that you will read below have been shared in public and private forums in the past. However, many of these stories were shared with me through emails, letters, text messages, and phone calls after the arrest of Professor Gates and during the course of writing this book. Most of these stories are presented here for the first time. To the extent possible, I have tried to tell each person's story in a way that conveys their reporting of these incidents to me. I accept full responsibility for any presentation that in any way does not reflect the views of those who spoke to me or wrote me.

DRIVING WHILE BLACK

JUSTICE THURGOOD MARSHALL

Thurgood Marshall was a native of Baltimore, Maryland, and a graduate of Lincoln University in Pennsylvania and Howard Law School in Washington, DC. Marshall served as lead counsel in the seminal civil rights case *Brown v. Board of Education* before being the first African American appointed to the United States Supreme Court, by President Lyndon B. Johnson in 1967.

Justice Marshall often told a story about being stopped in the South after a particularly important case in the fight to end discrimination and to ensure civil rights. He and his passengers were leaving town when they were pulled over by a police officer and accused of driving while intoxicated. Despite telling the police officer that he hadn't had anything to drink, Marshall was detained and driven to the location of the closest magistrate. Marshall recalled that the magistrate hearing the case that night asked Marshall to "Blow in my face." Marshall blew as hard as he could several times. The magistrate said, "That man ain't drunk, I don't smell any liquor on him at all. Case dismissed!"

JUDGE RICHARD **ROBERTS**

Judge Richard Roberts was born in and reared in New York City and earned a double major in black studies and political science at Vassar College as well as a master of international affairs degree from the School for International Training and a JD degree from Columbia Law School. Since 1998, he has been a United States District Judge for the District of Columbia.

In his junior year in 1973, Roberts was enrolled as a visiting undergraduate at Princeton University in New Jersey. During one visit to Detroit, his godmother let him drive her shiny custom Thunderbird to and from a dance late one night. As Roberts drove back alone at about 3 A.M. on one of the city's deserted, six-lane boulevards, a police car turned on its emergency lights and signaled him over. Roberts stopped, rested his hands on the wheel, and expected to wait for the police to run their computer check on the car before coming forward. In a few moments, Roberts saw a sparkle out of the corners of his eyes, one to the left and another to the right. Two revolvers were aimed dead at his head from not 10 feet away, gripped with two hands, locked arms outstretched, triggers cocked. Roberts responded in deliberate slow motion to their barked orders to show his license and registration, leaving one hand high on the wheel while announcing that he was using the other to reach into his pocket for his wallet. Headlines flashed through Roberts' mind about all the Black men in America who had died from police gunshots fired allegedly "after the suspect made a sudden motion causing the officer to fear for his life." Roberts did not want to be another statistic. It was after the officers saw his eye color—listed as hazel on his New York license—that they muttered something about watching out for the speed limits here in Detroit, holstered their guns, and pulled away. Only the next day did Roberts learn that a Detroit cop had been shot the prior week by someone described as a Black man with a big Afro. That's all it took for Roberts to almost lose his life if his motions had been too quick.

N. JEREMI DURU

N. Jeremi Duru was born in Silver Spring, Maryland. He is a graduate of Brown University and Harvard Law School, and he is currently a law professor at Temple University.

Duru relates an experience dating back to when he was a junior at Brown University. Duru said that he was driving with a classmate, Jacques, and returning to the university, when they were pulled over by a police officer who had followed them for three or four miles. The officer ordered them out of the car, told them to put their hands on the hood, and frisked them both. Soon after, a second police cruiser arrived. The second officer put a consent form in front of Jacques, the driver, asking for permission to search the vehicle. Jacques and Jeremi were both frightened by the stop and the request for consent to search the car but decided to sign the form. A K–9 unit with a dog arrived, and a search ensued. The men were there for at least half an hour as the officers searched everything—from dirty napkins stuffed inside empty McDonald's cups to the innards of Jacques' younger brother's remote control car. Finally satisfied that the men were not carrying any contraband, the police allowed them to return to their car and leave. Duru reports that the officers offered no explanation or apology.

LARRY **WATSON**

Larry Watson was born and raised in the Bedford-Stuyvesant section of Brooklyn. Watson graduated from the State University of New York at Oswego (where his majors included secondary education and history) and received a master's degree from Cornell University in Ithaca, New York. Watson is a singer, educator, and civil rights activist.

In 2005, Watson remembers being the first vocalist to perform for the State House General Assembly swearing-in of the commissioner for the Massachusetts Council Against Discrimination. In attendance were the mayor, the governor, and the State Senate. Watson left the event euphoric, feeling that America was changing. That weekend he traveled to Rhode Island and sang at an event held at the estate where Jackie Kennedy had grown up. On his way back to Boston, he dropped off one of his international students in Alston and decided to take a shortcut through the adjoining town of Brookline.

An hour later, Watson was thrown up against a police car with three other police cars watching. The officer who stopped Watson refused to follow through with the assault, so his partners took over, and one policeman in particular volunteered to bring Watson down. Watson was booked for driving with an expired license. The first policeman had no reason for stopping Watson: he had a valid car registration, no broken taillight, no tickets on his plates, he had not run a light, he was not speeding, and obviously the policeman did not know the status of his driver's license. Watson's crime was "driving while Black" through a White neighborhood. As they fingerprinted and booked Watson, he wept in humiliation and fear. He couldn't understand why this was happening to him. He was a prominent singer, a professor, and had just sung at the State House for the governor and the mayor. Then he heard the booking policeman say, "What you cryin' for? You only going to jail—you will be out in the morning."

MICHAEL A. **LAWSON**

Michael A. Lawson was born in Little Rock, Arkansas, and attended Loyola Marymount University in Los Angeles and Harvard Law School. In 1980, he joined the firm Skadden, Arps, Slate, Meagher & Flom LLP as an associate, and he later became a partner.

As a Black male teenager growing up in Los Angeles in the late 1960s and early 1970s, Lawson was taught that his survival depended on a clear understanding that the members of law enforcement—the Los Angeles Police Department in particular—made a regular practice of profiling young Black men. Lawson asserts that if you were a Black

male and you were out on a Friday or Saturday night, you were prepared to be stopped by the police for no other apparent reason than
being Black.

Lawson reports driving with three of his friends through North
Hollywood on their way to a jazz club when they were stopped by the
police (ostensibly because they had a missing taillight). Each was
asked to provide his driver's license. Then the questioning began:
What's your name, boy? Where are you going? Where do you live?
Where do you work? You live a long way from where you work, don't
you? What do you do? How many times have you been arrested? They
were never issued a ticket, but for members of the LAPD, four Black
men in a car was reason enough to stop the car and run their driver's
licenses through the system to see what they could find.

Once while Lawson was in college, he asked out a female classmate
who was very light skinned. After greeting her parents, Lawson
walked her from the front door of her home to the passenger side of
his car and then walked over to the driver's side. As soon as he had
closed the door, an LAPD officer had a flashlight in his face and was
asking his date if she was okay. Lawson feels that, in order for this police officer to reach him that quickly, he had to have been watching
them the entire time. He believes this was done simply to harass
him—a Black man who had the audacity to date someone who just
might be White.

After going to Harvard Law School, Lawson began working at
Skadden, Arps, Slate, Meagher & Flom LLP in New York City as an
associate. During the summers, the firm always had a summer outing
at a country club in Westchester, and it had shuttles to take people
back and forth to Manhattan after it was over. One associate who had

a car—a Mercedes SLC coupe—offered to give Lawson a ride back to Manhattan. The route back to Manhattan took them along the Major Deegan Expressway through the Bronx. As they passed through the Bronx, an NYPD police car pulled them over. The officers told Lawson's friend that she was speeding and asked her a few seemingly unrelated questions. She flirted with them, and eventually they relaxed and let them go with just a warning. After they pulled off, she said that she was certain that she wasn't speeding and wondered why they had been stopped. Lawson told her that, based on the way the officers were acting, he was certain that they were stopped because she had a Black man in the car with her. She insisted that Lawson was just being paranoid. The next day, she came by Lawson's office to tell him that she was bothered by what he had said and had called up an old boyfriend who was an NYPD officer. She said that he told her that one of the unwritten rules in the NYPD was that if you see a Black and White couple in an expensive car in the Bronx, you always stop the car to determine if the couple are drug dealers. She said she was shocked. Lawson was not.

ROBERT JOHNSON, JR.

Robert Johnson, Jr., is a native of Chattanooga, Tennessee, and a graduate of Bowdoin College and Cornell Law School. He is a professor at the University of Massachusetts. He instituted proceedings against the State of Vermont and a Vermont state trooper for racial discrimination.

On the evening of May 23, 2003, Johnson was driving to his house in Vermont in his Honda Civic on Interstate 91N near Thetford, Vermont. He was driving in the right lane (i.e., the slow lane) when he noticed a police car parked on the right-hand side of the road. The posted speed limit for the Interstate was 65 mph, and Johnson noticed that he was traveling at 68 mph. He also noted that at least two other cars passing him on the left were going faster than he was. To Johnson's surprise, the state trooper pulled up behind him and asked him to stop. The trooper informed Johnson that he was traveling at 84 mph. Johnson corrected him, saying he was only doing 68 mph, and he also pointed out that other cars on the road were going at 80 mph. The trooper nevertheless wrote Johnson a speeding ticket, which Johnson challenged. In court, Johnson argued that he was traveling only at 68 mph and stated that he was stopped only because he was Black, as a number of White drivers who were traveling faster than he had been had not pulled been over. The trooper, however, testified that Johnson was driving in the fast lane. A videotape of the stop confirmed Johnson's story. As a result, the speeding ticket was dismissed. Johnson continues to fight his allegation of racial discrimination.

JOHNNIE L. COCHRAN, JR.

Johnnie Cochran was a native of Shreveport, Louisiana, and was an outstanding civil rights and criminal justice attorney during the last half of his career. Cochran represented such well-known clients as O. J. Simpson, Sean "Puff Daddy" Combs, Michael Jackson, Geronimo Pratt, and Ron Settles, a young African American who reportedly died as a result of a suicide hanging in jail after his arrest, but the Southern California city settled Cochran's lawsuit on Settles' behalf for over $700,000 in a wrongful death case. Prior to his success as a civil rights and criminal defense attorney, ironically, Cochran was a prosecutor in Los Angeles, working with Lance Ito (who would later be selected as the judge in the Simpson case) and Gil Garcetti (who was the LA district attorney during the Simpson trial).

In the early 1980s, Cochran, accompanied by his son and daughter, was pulled over while driving his Rolls Royce on the highway. It was a shattering experience for his young children to see police officers draw their guns and ask him to step out of his car. It was particularly disappointing for Cochran because, as a prosecutor, he had fought against racial profiling. In the end, the officers saw his district attorney badge, had no case involving him, and let him go. Cochran would later identify this experience as "Driving While Black" and discuss it in his book *A Lawyer's Life*.[2] Cochran realized that the crime of driving while Black is real—at the time, a Black man driving a Rolls Royce in Los Angeles created suspicion among police, even if there were no reports that the car had been stolen and the driver was, in fact, a successful lawyer who happened to be an African American able to afford the car.

ATTORNEY GENERAL ERIC **HOLDER**

Eric Holder is a native of Queens, New York, and serves as the first African American U.S. attorney general, appointed by President Barack Obama in 2009. He is a graduate of Columbia University and Columbia Law School in New York.

Shortly after the arrest of Professor Gates in July 2009, Holder was interviewed about the matter. In the interview, he described his own encounter with racial profiling with law enforcement officers while he was an undergraduate at Columbia University in the 1970s. Holder said: "I was a young college student driving from New York to Washington [and was] stopped on a highway and told to open the trunk of my car because the police officer told me he wanted to search it for weapons. I remember, as I got back in the car and continued on my journey, how humiliated I felt, how angry I got."[3]

REGGIE TURNER

Reggie Turner was born in Chicago, Illinois. He is a graduate of Stanford University in Palo Alto, California, and of the Georgetown Law Center in Washington, DC, and was my college classmate. He served as an agent for many professional athletes, and recently produced a documentary film, *Before They Die,* about the African Americans who lost their homes and businesses as a result of the 1921 Tulsa race riots.

In the early 1980s, Turner and his wife, Chris (a former DC public defender), with the assistance of two close friends, Dr. Jackie Long and Thomas Myers, had just completed moving their belongings into their first home. To thank the friends for their help, and because they were all starving, they decided to head out for a late-night meal in Turner's brand-new Mercedes-Benz 300. It was around 10 P.M., so they headed to the only diner they knew of that served quality food late at night—the Beverly Hills Café, located on Wilshire Boulevard. As they drove west on Wilshire, they noticed a parked Beverly Hills police cruiser. They kept driving, unconcerned, because they were observing the speed limit, were under the influence of nothing stronger than fatigue and hunger, and were driving a beautiful new car quite appropriate for their surroundings. Yet within 30 seconds of passing the police car, the policemen pulled them over, directly in front of the restaurant, where several patrons seated by the windows turned to watch the action. The police used their loudspeaker to order Turner, Chris, and the two friends to lower their windows and place their hands in a raised position so that they could be seen. Turner was then told by the approaching lead officer to "Exit the vehicle slowly and move to the curb adjacent to the car, keeping your hands up and visible." Only then was he asked for his driver's license and car registration. Turner produced his valid California driver's license from his wallet but informed the officer that his registration was inside the vehicle's glove box. Turner's wife heard the demand so she attempted to hand the papers out of the window to the second officer. The officer pointed his gun at her and told her to "Freeze" and to remain in the car. Stunned and scared, she obeyed. Turner reports that after 10 minutes of calls and radio runs, the lead officer told him that he could lower his hands, as the police had verified his license and car ownership. Turner reports that the officer still wanted the other three to step out of the car, produce identification, and stand next to Turner on the curb in front of the café. As the three produced their licenses, Turner, speaking for the first time, asked why they had been stopped. He was told by the second officer to shut up and not cause any further trouble. When Turner's wife, the public defender, began to speak about their rights, the second officer raised his weapon again and stopped her in midsentence. After reviewing the identification of each person in the car, the group was allowed to enter the vehicle again. The officers continued to question them, asking where they going at that time of night in Beverly Hills, why had they come all the way there to eat (they had driven less than three miles), and where they worked. Turner, in turn, asked them to explain why they had been pulled over. He reports being stunned when an officer informed them that they had been stopped because the police were stopping all "suspicious-looking cars" that night because the Bank of Iran had been broken into earlier that evening. Someone rammed a car into the bank's front entrance, smashing the windows and doors and then speeding off before taking anything.

STUART SIMMS

Stuart Simms was born in Maryland and received his undergraduate degree from Dartmouth College in Hanover, New Hampshire, and his law degree from Harvard Law School. He currently is a partner in the Baltimore-based law firm Brown, Goldstein, and Levy.

In 1992, Simms was the elected prosecutor for Baltimore City. On this particular Saturday, he was returning a ceremonial gown to a store, which he had worn to the installation ceremony for the new president of the University of Maryland, Baltimore City, Freeman Hrabowski. His academic hoods for Dartmouth and Harvard were in the trunk, and he was driving around the block in his blue BMW looking for a place to park. A White police officer flashed his blue lights and stopped him. "Is there a problem, Officer?" Simms asked. "I would like to see your license and registration," the officer said. Simms, however, repeated, "Is there a problem?" But the officer simply said, "Just do as I said." In response, Simms asked, "Will my state's attorney badge do?" The officer just stood there. "Look," he responded, "never mind, I had to stop . . . I mean, . . . Let's just call it a day." He then drove off.

About a year later, Simms was giving some kids from a middle school a tour of the Clarence Mitchell, Jr., Courthouse. As the elected prosecutor, he occasionally gave tours to explain the career possibilities available to students and describe the obligations and functions of his office. As they approached an exhibit concerning Mr. and Mrs. Mitchell, with Simms explaining the importance of Mitchell's life, his contributions to the NAACP and the United States as "the 101st U.S. Senator," a voice shouted: "Hey, you, sir, get away from the poinsettia plants." The comments came from a new deputy sheriff who was White. "No one is permitted to damage the plants." As Simms continued to discuss Mr. Mitchell's achievements, the deputy again shouted, "I told you, get away from the plants." "Officer," Simms replied, "I am certain the intellectual growth of these kids is worth more than these plants. If there is a problem, my office is down the hall." The officer responded: "I don't care who you are, get away from those plants." Simms took a step in the officer's direction and then it struck him—40 pairs of eyes were watching him. Simms took the kids back to his office, where they talked about the confrontation and about defusing such incidents. Simms reports that, later, when the officer realized who Simms was, he came to his office and apologized.

ERNEST J. WILSON III

Ernest J. Wilson was born in Washington, DC, and graduated from Harvard College and the University of California, Berkeley, with a PhD in political economy. He has taught successively at the universities of Pennsylvania, Michigan, and Maryland. Wilson is the dean and Walter H. Annenberg chair at the University of Southern California's Annenberg School for Communication and Journalism and was the elected chairman of the board of the Corporation for Public Broadcasting in 2009.

As a father, the worst racial experiences Wilson has had have not been the insults to him but the continuing injustices meted out to his two sons. Their experiences range from "driving while Black" pull-overs to regular police stops in their own upper-middle-class suburban neighborhood. For Wilson, the most painfully poignant part of this continuing American drama was finally learning that, at a certain point, both sons decided to cease telling him about their profiling experiences with the police. They did it because the harassment was so routine, they knew it would upset Wilson and their mother, and because, in the end, they believed there was little their parents could do to stop it.

FRED JOHNSON

Fred Johnson is a native New Yorker and a graduate of Stanford University in Palo Alto, California. He left a job in television news to go to Los Angeles to write for sitcoms. His credits include *Moesha* and *The Bernie Mac Show*.

Johnson feels profiling happens many times and in many places: He gets "typed" or profiled by the store detective, who follows him from floor to floor; by the waitress, who assumes he won't tip; by the doorman, whose "Can I help you?" doesn't sound helpful; by the stranger, who tenses up if he gets on the same elevator; and by the countless cab drivers, who don't even slow down, let alone stop, for him. In Johnson's opinion, it comes with the territory, like hypertension, colon cancer, and rhythm. But according to him, the hardest profiling to accept or to shake off are the incidents involving the police. He still remembers a June night in 2000, on Interstate 40, along a desolate stretch just east of the California–Arizona border, when a zealous highway patrolman saw two Black men in a loaded-down Suburban and figured "drug bust." When Johnson refused to sign a consent form allowing the officers to search his truck, one officer's suspicions were further aroused. "Why not?" he asked. "Because it's un-American," Johnson replied. Johnson's principled stance was made moot, however, by the extreme agitation a drug-sniffing German shepherd displayed when he approached the rear of the truck. The dog handlers informed him that they now had probable cause and could search without his permission. That's when the fear kicked in: Johnson knew his truck was clean, but the policemen were so eager for a bust that his only hope was that they were not eager—or racist—enough to plant drugs. They were certainly eager enough to remove every single box of odds and ends and thrift store finds; eager enough to open door panels and look in the oddest places for the secret stash that would put Johnson away and earn them cop of the month distinction. It was at that moment, shivering on the side of the road—from fear, not cold—that Johnson realized how powerless and unprotected he was. His fate hung on the police officers' scruples, their honesty, their whims. They released him without incident, but their disappointment was palpable. Johnson was carrying no drugs, possessed no weapons, and his papers were in order. Johnson remained calm and polite and gave them no reason to make this "personal." His only offense was "driving while Black," and, on that night, that wasn't enough to take him down. He hopes there is no next time.

JOHN SILVANUS WILSON, JR.

John Silvanus Wilson, Jr., was raised in the Philadelphia area. He attended Morehouse College in Atlanta, Georgia, and then finished three degrees at Harvard University and began a 16-year career at the Massachusetts Institute of Technology as an officer in two capital campaigns that garnered nearly $3 billion. He recently joined the Obama

Administration, where he serves as the executive director of the White House Initiative on Historically Black Colleges and Universities.

Back in 1984, Wilson spent a year in Princeton, New Jersey, on a research fellowship to complete his Harvard dissertation. He traveled frequently between Cambridge and Princeton, and on this particular trip to Cambridge, he was joined by his fiancée, Carol, who was completing her doctoral work in engineering at MIT; his brother, Lucas, who was completing his doctoral work in economics at the University of Massachusetts at Amherst; and Lucas' wife, Tammy, a Spelman College graduate who was preparing to apply to medical schools. Their plan was to drive from Princeton to Amherst via Cambridge. They pulled off in a packed car and were barely three blocks away from the home Wilson was renting in Princeton when the bright lights of a Princeton squad car flashed them to a halt. Two officers approached and ordered Wilson and his brother out of the front seats. As Wilson exited the driver's seat, he asked, "Why, what's the problem?" No response. The men were ordered to place both hands on the hood of the car with their legs spread. While doing so, Wilson again asked, "Why, what have we done?" The officer said, "Be still and be quiet!" The second officer shined his light on Carol and Tammy and told them not to move. One officer patted Wilson and Lucas down while the other officer had his hand on his gun. Wilson was livid yet scared, but he insisted that they give him an explanation. His brother used body language and whispers to plead with Wilson to remain calm. One officer finally asked, "What are you doing here in Princeton?" Wilson said, "I live here! Is that a crime?" The officer replied, "You have out-of-state plates, you don't look like you live here, and you have a car full of belongings which may or may not be yours." The two brothers had to swallow hard to keep their cool. Wilson demanded the officers' names and badge numbers, but they oozed with confidence and ignored his request. One officer asked where they were going, and Lucas described their trip. The officers then told them to get back in the car and leave, which they did. But they used a good portion of that trip debating whether and how to officially protest what happened. They decided it would be utterly fruitless. It took Wilson a couple of weeks before he could feel comfortable going back to Princeton to finish the year.

HAAZIM RASHED

Haazim Rashed was born in Memphis, Tennessee, and is a graduate of Stanford University in Palo Alto, California.

In the late 1980s, Rashed and his family moved to Woodinville, Washington. At the time, Woodinville was a small suburb of Seattle and had a small African American population. For the first seven years Rashed lived there, it was possible to locate his house simply by asking any of the residents for the Black family in the neighborhood. When they first moved there, Rashed's job had him out of town almost every week, so rather than owning a car and parking it at the airport, he found it more convenient to rent a car at the airport, drive home, return the car to the airport, and fly out again. Since he usually arrived home late on Friday nights, he found it unusual that he was being stopped by the police on a regular basis. The worst weekend occurred when he had rented a white Lincoln Town Car. He was stopped four times. Each time he was given a warning for something or other, but as soon as he gave the officer his address, he was let go. Rashed has no doubt that all of the stops were related to his being in a neighborhood where the police thought he did not belong. As his sons grew up and began to drive, they also reported numerous instances of being stopped, simply because they were Black in a White community. These have been the most irritating and memorable experiences in Rashed's recent years. He does not even deign to mention the questioning looks, the shifting in the elevators, the crossing of the street, and other normal day-to-day occurrences.

VOLTAIRE RICO STERLING

Voltaire Rico Sterling grew up on Chicago's South Side and attended Morehouse College in Atlanta and Harvard Law School. He is an actor and writer in Hollywood as well as an attorney and educator.

In 2009, Sterling had been a resident of Beverly Hills for almost four years. On June 5, 2009, at 4:05 P.M., Sterling was stopped in Beverly Hills for "driving while Black" in broad daylight as he was on his way home from work. Notably, he was modestly dressed—wearing jogging pants and a black "hoodie" sweatshirt—as he had visited the gym prior to stopping by his boss's office: the Beverly Hills Unified School District. As he drove away from the school, he could clearly see in his rearview mirror that he was being followed by a squad car. He could also see that the two officers were White men. Likewise, he is certain that there was no question in their minds about Sterling's race and gender. The police car followed him slowly for a number of blocks. Sterling noted specifically that he was driving within the legal speed limit and that he had not broken any traffic laws. At the intersection of Beverly and Olympic boulevards, as Sterling proceeded through the green light, the police squad car turned on its lights and pulled him over. As a driver who had not committed any traffic violations, Sterling was naturally surprised at being pulled over. He asked the first officer who approached him why he had been stopped. The officer replied that he and his colleague had run the license plate and the vehicle registration had come back expired. Sterling informed the officers that the registration was current—which indeed it was. He also showed his registration to one of the officers. When the current registration card and the current sticker on his license plate proved the invalidity of the officer's claim of expired registration, Sterling asked the officers why they felt compelled to stop him and run his tags. At this point, the same officer asked for Sterling's license and insurance card, asked him where he was coming from, and explained that there had been a rash of violence, robberies, and crime in the area. They told him that he had been stopped because he had out-of-state license plates and that, in their experience, the crimes might have been committed by visitors. Sterling asked whether the officers had stopped him because he was a young Black man. The interrogating officer denied that this was the reason. The other officer, however, stated that there were many reasons why they could have stopped Sterling: (a) Sterling's registration showed up expired (which was false and was shown to be false); (b) Sterling had things hanging from his rearview mirror that obstructed his view (the "things hanging" were a parking permit and an air freshener, neither obstructed the driver's view); and (c) the plastic cover over Sterling's license plate blocked a clear view of his license plate and was illegal. Sterling had recently cleaned the plastic cover and checked it after he was stopped; the license plate was unquestionably visible from a dis-

THE PRESUMPTION OF GUILT

tance of four or five car lengths or more. Sterling explained to the officers that these were mere pretexts for a discriminatory stop. They vehemently denied this, and after about 15 minutes, they let him go. Sterling was livid. He filed a complaint with the Beverly Hills Police Department and was brought in for an interview with a supervising officer, but nothing came of the investigation.

JUDGE REGGIE WALTON

Judge Reggie Walton was raised in Donora, Pennsylvania. He graduated from West Virginia State University and the American University, Washington College of Law. He served as a public defender in the Defender Association of Philadelphia, and an assistant United States attorney in the District of Columbia. Judge Walton also served as the associate director of the Office of National Drug Control Policy in the Executive Office of the President, and as the senior White House advisor for Crime, under President George H. W. Bush. Judge Walton is currently a United States district judge for the District of Columbia and a judge on the United States Foreign Intelligence Surveillance Court.

Judge Walton was stopped by the police on three occasions, all in Western Pennsylvania where he grew up. On the first occasion Walton was wrongfully stopped as a teenager by the police and accused of stealing a package from a delivery truck. Fortunately, the truck driver told the officer that Walton was not the person who took the package. The second stop also occurred when Walton was a teenager. He was wrongfully accused of failing to stop at a stop sign. Judge Walton believes that the reason that he was stopped was because he was giving a white girl a ride to a basketball game. Judge Walton recalls a third stop when he was an assistant United States attorney and was visiting his parents. Walton was driving a new Corvette and firmly believes that he was stopped because of the car he was driving, because there was no other reason for the stop to have been made.

DON WEST

Don West grew up in Brookline, Massachusetts, and has worked as a freelance photographer for the last 28 years.

West recalls two relatively minor incidents of racial profiling by police.

Once, in Detroit in the early 1970s, when he was walking home alone at night, he was stopped by a patrol car and asked for his identification and where he was coming from or going to.

On another occasion, West was driving on the New Jersey Turnpike in the late 1960s with a White woman when he was stopped for no apparent reason by two state cruisers with lights flashing. Both he and his companion were ordered out of the car and told to stand with their arms outstretched on the car and their legs apart while the policemen searched the car, apparently looking for drugs. This incident occurred at about 1 P.M. on a sunny day with the traffic slowing down to watch the spectacle. The policemen found nothing and let them go.

TIM WRIGHT

Tim Wright grew up in Compton, California, and is currently the co-managing partner of the national law firm Gonzalez, Saggio & Harlan.

As a kid growing up in Compton, he remembers one summer planning a bike trip with his friends to go fishing at the pier at Redondo Beach. As they got close to the beach the traffic got a little heavy, so they took a shortcut and rode through some neighborhoods. Suddenly they were surrounded by three or four police cars. The boys were made to get off their bikes and lie facedown on the ground while the officers ran the serial numbers on their bikes, then searched and questioned them. An hour later, they were released but told to return to Compton and warned that if they were ever seen near Redondo Beach again, they would be arrested.

In another event, Wright reports that he picked up two associates at the airport and brought them to his condo in the Hyde Park section of Chicago. After helping them upstairs, he went back down to park his car properly. After doing so, he proceeded to open the door to his building. He then heard someone calling—it was a single policeman calling from his patrol car, asking if he could speak to Wright. Wright said of course and walked over to the officer. At that moment, the officer stepped out of his car and pulled his weapon. Three other police cars arrived simultaneously, and the officers began to question him. Wright reports being accused of rape and being arrested, then handcuffed and taken to a local hospital to be identified by the rape victim. Wright was not confirmed as the rapist. Meanwhile, another officer had gone to Wright's home and noticed pictures and plaques on the wall of Wright with President Clinton and with Mayor Harold Washington of Chicago. The police eventually brought Wright back home and released him.

BRUCE BENNETT

Bruce Bennett was born in Pine Bluff, Arkansas. After completing his JD degree at Georgetown University Law Center, Bennett worked in the City of New York's Washington,

DC, office, advising the mayor, police commissioner, and corporation counsel on criminal justice and police matters on Capitol Hill. He currently works for a Miami, Florida–
based law firm.

Bennett spent a good part of his professional life working to ensure
that police officers have the equipment they need for their work and
safety. A few years ago he moved to Miami, and one Sunday afternoon, on the drive home from church, he and his family found themselves in bumper-to-bumper traffic at a red light in Bal Harbour, a
beachfront community in Miami that has very few African American
residents. Bennett's sons pleaded to stop at a hamburger place. To get
there, Bennett needed to get out of the right lane and over into the left
lane. So Bennett stuck his long, black arm out of the window and
kindly asked the driver of the car next to him, a police car, if he could
get in front of her so that he could turn left. The woman kindly allowed him to do so, but as soon as he got in front of her, she turned
on her flashing lights and asked him to pull over.

Bennett pulled over, and the policewoman asked for his license, registration, and insurance. When he politely asked, "Officer, what is the
problem?" she did not respond. When Bennett asked again, she put
her face within inches of his and yelled at the top of her lungs, "If you
would shut up I will tell you why you were stopped." She continued,
"You should take a clue from your girlfriend, she knows to sit there
and shut up." Bennett's two young sons were terrified and his wife's
hands were trembling. As Bennett handed the officer his insurance
papers, she explained that when Bennett had pulled over in front of
her, his back tires crossed a solid white line (Bennett later went back
to check, and there was no solid white line). She then decided to give

Bennett a ticket, not because he had crossed a solid white line, but because according to her, he had failed to produce the insurance papers
in a timely fashion. Bennett took a day off from work to go to court
and the ticket charges were dismissed. He also reported her to the
captain at the local police station.

Bennett feels that this type of incident happens all over Miami—
African American and Haitian drivers are pulled over for no apparent
reason all day long. The first eight months that Bennett lived in
Miami, he was pulled over five times and his wife three times. His
sons would say to him, "Dad, I thought that you said that you used to
work fighting on behalf of the police? Why are they always trying to
pick a fight with you?"

DOUGLAS McHENRY

Doug McHenry was born in Fort Knox, Kentucky, and received his BA from Stanford
University and his JD from Harvard Law School. He has been a successful film director and producer, with such movies as *New Jack City, House Party,* and *Jason's Lyric,*
among others.

McHenry and his co-producer, George Jackson (also African American), were shooting *Jason's Lyric* in Houston, Texas. Late one night,
they were driven by their assistants to the set to film that morning. En
route, at about 4 A.M. on a week night, several blocks from the set,
McHenry noticed that Jackson's car had been pulled over by the
Houston police. McHenry was surprised to see the police stop Jackson's car but was shocked when the police immediately handcuffed
Jackson, who was the passenger in the car, but did nothing to the
White driver. The police refused to let Jackson explain what they

were doing that morning but instead directed all their questions to the driver. The driver explained that they were shooting a film there and that Mr. Jackson was in fact his boss! When McHenry pulled over to find out what was going on, he and his African American driver were immediately ordered to place their hands on the hood of their car. The police then continued to ask Jackson's White driver all of the questions while refusing to let anyone else participate in the discussion. As the questioning of Jackson's driver continued for several minutes, McHenry showed them his California driver's license and explained that he was the director and Jackson was the producer of the film that was shooting in the neighborhood. Nonetheless, Jackson remained handcuffed for what McHenry recalls as hours. The situation was finally resolved to the embarrassment of the police when it was confirmed that the individuals were lawfully there and Jackson had committed no crimes. McHenry reports that the police later asserted that Jackson's rental car was stolen, which McHenry states was absolutely false. McHenry is still angry that his friend, who subsequently died of a massive heart attack, was placed, as the passenger of the car, in handcuffs while no effort was made to arrest or detain the White driver. The police officers who stopped and placed the handcuffs on Jackson that night: One Black and one White. And the Black cop was clearly the one in charge. As McHenry reflects upon this situation, he sadly recalls that Jackson and his White driver couldn't have been more different. Jackson graduated from Harvard College with honors and was class marshall. He was a millionaire Hollywood producer who achieved success very early in his career. He would later go on to become the last president of Motown Records. McHenry reports that the White driver, a production assistant on the film, had only a high school education and was work-ing for minimum wage. At the time of the incident Jackson was 32 and the White driver was 20.

WARREN BALLENTINE

Warren Ballentine is a native of Chicago, Illinois, and a graduate of Ohio Northern University, Pettit College of Law. He has served as a prosecutor and defense lawyer and is currently the host of a national urban radio program, *The Warren Ballentine Show*, heard weekdays throughout the United States.

Ballentine was in the middle of a murder case and had just completed an hour-and-a-half cross-examination of a police officer in the case. At the end of the day, Ballentine went home to change into more ca-sual clothes and then went back to his office. While he was driving his Buick Cutlass, he was pulled over by a police officer in the same case. The officer, who failed to recognize him as the same lawyer who had crossed-examined him earlier in the trial, told him that he was not wearing his seat belt and told him to step out of his car. Ballentine in-sists that he was wearing his seat belt but stepped out of the car so that the officer could search it nonetheless. The officer asked him if he had drugs in the car. Ballentine said no, and began to question the of-ficer as to the basis for the stop. The officer asked him, "Are you a lawyer or something? I ask the questions." Ballentine then informed the officer that he was the same lawyer who had cross-examined him earlier. Ballentine reports that the officer seemed surprised and em-barrassed and then told Ballentine that he was free to go. He never apologized for the stop, search, or questioning. Ballentine was deeply troubled that the officer pulled him over for no reason but saddened when the officer did not even recognize that he was the same lawyer who had cross-examined him earlier. Ballentine still wonders if, in fact, the officer did recognize him but refused to say so.

DONALD MARVIN JONES

Donald Marvin Jones is a native of Baltimore who graduated from the New York University School of Law. He is currently a professor of law at the University of Miami, teaching constitutional law and criminal procedure. He has written widely on the dangerous intersection of "race and law," and his most recent published book is *Race, Sex, and Suspicion: The Myth of the Black Male.*

Sweet Home Baptist Church in Perrine, Florida, is a welcoming church located in the middle of the Perrine ghetto—an area ravaged by crime. The church nonetheless has numbered among its congregation many of the Black elite. There have been teachers, attorneys, doctors, and at least one black law professor. Jones was on the Trustee Board, which oversaw the financial dealings of the church. One evening, Jones attended a church meeting, which ended at about 10:30 P.M. Tired, he got into his 300ZX Nissan sports car and headed home toward Palmetto Bay, an affluent community in South Florida on the water, about two miles away. Jones was a bit disoriented because he had never driven home from the church in the dark, and soon drove into a park area. He had to double back and get to the main street, passing a group of houses adjacent to the church. Someone called out to him from one of the backyards, but Jones did not pay attention. He found the main street and drove south thinking he'd be home in a minute. But before he could get out of Perrine, he saw blue lights flashing and heard a policeman asking him to stop.

The policeman informed Jones that he had had him under surveillance and that he had observed him "talking to someone." Jones reports that his explanations for being in the area were viewed suspiciously by the police officer, and within seconds a SWAT team arrived, dressed in flak jackets and fatigues and carrying some very big guns. They asked Jones if they could search the car. Jones knew that he had "a right to refuse," but the police were heavily armed, and they were not smiling, so he said yes.

Jones was dressed well—he was in a designer sport coat and slacks and was wearing an expensive watch. He wondered how the officer saw him? As a drug dealer? As someone trying to buy drugs? When Jones told the officer that he was a professor of constitutional law and criminal procedure at the University of Miami, the cloud of suspicion lifted. "Did we do anything wrong?" the officer asked sheepishly. He gave back Jones' faculty ID, and the officers closed the car trunk, got into their vehicles, and drove away. No one ever apologized.

WRONGFULLY SUSPECTED OF CRIMINAL CONDUCT BY LAW ENFORCEMENT OFFICIALS

KAMAU KEMAYO

Kamau Kemayo was born in Chicago, Illinois, and is currently assistant professor and chair of the African American Studies Program at the University of Illinois at Springfield. He received an MA in Afro-American studies from the University of California, Los Angeles, in 1986, and a PhD in American studies from the St. Louis University in 1999.

Kemayo commuted 119.7 miles round trip, each day, from his home to the parking lot closest to the building where his office was and where he taught classes at James Madison University in Harrisonburg, Virginia. He normally got up at 4:30 A.M. for the commute, but if he woke up earlier, he would leave when he was ready and catch a catnap before going in to work—either in a borrowed trailer near his office or in his car, with license plates DR KAMAU. One day in mid-August, Kemayo arrived in Harrisonburg at around 4:40 A.M. He intended to sleep for a few hours in his car; the large parking lot was relatively quiet. He reclined his seat and quickly crashed. Just before dawn, Kemayo was awakened by a bright light shining in his face and an ungentle rapping at his window—a campus cop was rousting him. Shaking off the cobwebs, Kemayo rolled down his window and asked what the officer wanted. The officer asked him, "Do you belong here?" It was not so much a question as an aggressive challenge. A little sleepy, Kemayo asked him what he meant. The officer repeated, "Do you belong here?" Unintimidated but getting angry, Kemayo answered, "As far as I know, I am a resident of this planet." "Here in this lot, right now?" was the cop's question this time. Kemayo asked whether the lot was restricted, knowing well that it wasn't. But the cop again asked Kemayo, "Do you belong here?" Kemayo pointed to his license plates and his parking sticker and also showed the officer his faculty ID. Unimpressed, the officer said again, "I still need to know, do you belong here?" At this point, Kemayo felt that his rage was going to consume him. He told the officer that he had been woken up not to see if he was okay or had lost consciousness in a parked car, or if there was some problem with the vehicle itself, or if there was some domestic problem. Instead, the officer had assumed that a Black man had no right to be on the campus. Kemayo continued, "If you cannot figure out whether or not I belong here after seeing my license plates, which might seem appropriate on a college campus or in a hospital parking lot; after seeing my faculty ID, which might validate my title; after seeing my parking sticker, which should have been enough by itself, then I cannot help you. I suggest you go to Blue Ridge [a community college a few miles to the south] and see if they have any openings in Common Sense 101." He then told the officer that he was going to try to get back to sleep. Kemayo rolled up the window and laid back, putting his forearms over his eyes. The officer rapped at the window again, a bit more lightly this time, but Kemayo ignored him. A few minutes later the officer left, but Kemayo never got back to sleep. After 10 or 15 minutes, he got up and noticed two campus cop cars parked by the corner exit; he went out another exit and never heard from that cop again.

DAVID SMITH

David Smith was born in the Bronx, New York, and completed a degree in engineering at Stanford University in Palo Alto, California.

When Smith was a student at Stanford University in the late 1970s, he was told that he looked like a suspect when a cop stopped him in downtown Menlo Park near Stanford. Smith was riding his bike to work when he was asked to pull over. He thought that perhaps he hadn't signaled; but the stop had nothing to do with his riding. According to the officer, he looked like a bank robber who had robbed the Bank of America across the street from where he was stopped. A bike-riding bank robber? By the time Smith had provided his IDs— driver's license, Stanford student ID, and employee card—a second police vehicle had arrived with a sergeant. Smith was photographed—he was told it was legal and that, if he refused, he would be taken to a police station and photographed there. The police determined that Smith was not the suspect, and then, after waiting for what seemed like an eternity, he was allowed to continue on to work after the delay and the humiliation.

Another time, Smith was in the company of students from UCLA Law School, USC Medical School, and undergrads from Stanford who were majoring in electrical engineering, psychology, economics, and pre-med. They were crossing a side street in Los Angeles, about a block from one of the main streets, when an LAPD cruiser made a U-turn and pulled up to the curb to investigate their "gang activity." They had merely been crossing a street with no traffic or traffic lights. But to the LAPD they were a "gang." The police accused them of stopping traffic and requested their IDs. Smith experienced other indignities during his career as an engineer, in which people have mistaken him for a nontechnical, nonprofessional employee, an HR person, or, the most common, a mailroom person. Once, at a job interview at Apple Computer, when a hiring manager came to the lobby to let him in, she approached each and every other person in the lobby, looking for David Smith, until finally he introduced himself to her as the senior ASIC engineer candidate from Stanford.

BLAIR UNDERWOOD

Blair Underwood was born in Tacoma, Washington, and graduated from Carnegie Mellon School of Drama in Pittsburgh, Pennsylvania. He has been a successful actor on screen and stage for more than 20 years.

In 1987, Underwood was living in a penthouse apartment near MacArthur Park, in downtown Los Angeles, when he returned home after a long day of work on a short-lived TV series called *Downtown*. After parking in the lot in front of his building, he was startled to notice flashing lights coming from a Los Angeles police car.

Underwood was upset that he was being detained by the White police officer. He was tired and simply wanted to go upstairs and get some sleep. While in his own car and parking lot, the interrogation began. "Is this your car?" He answered, "Yes, it is."

He was asked, "Do you have any registration?" and he responded, "Yes, I do." Underwood distinctly remembers that the officer then pulled out a silver revolver and jammed it against his left temple and angrily said, "This is no B***SH**!" Underwood reports that he then took a long, deep breath and quickly reverted to what he describes as the "Black Man's Survival Manual," placing both hands on the steering wheel, so the officer could see that he was not reaching for anything that could escalate the situation. He then proceeded to say, "I am now taking my right hand and reaching for my insurance and registration cards in my glove compartment." After Underwood provided his documents, the officer holstered his revolver.

When Underwood asked the officer why he was stopped and what he had done wrong, the officer for the first time reported that a car that resembled Underwood's had been stolen in the area. Underwood could only grin; the officer had his registration and license and knew the car belonged to him.

To this day, Underwood wonders what to tell his three young African American children to prepare them for when they grow up, knowing that their skin color will be the first thing people notice and assumptions about them will burden them throughout their lives.

CURTIS **VALENTINE**

Curtis Valentine was born in Elizabeth, New Jersey, and completed his BA at Morehouse College in Atlanta, Georgia, and his master's in public policy from the Harvard Kennedy School of Government in Cambridge. He is currently the senior program officer for World Vision.

In his years growing up in New Jersey, studying in Atlanta and Cambridge, traveling throughout the world, and living in the DC metro area, Valentine cannot recall one specific incident of racial profiling but rather a series of interactions with the police that have left him skeptical of their actions. As early as age 15, Valentine remembers being threatened by a police officer who was substituting for his teacher and who said, "I better not catch you outside of this school." Personal and secondhand accounts of police brutality and profiling of friends who have been stopped by police have shaped his perception of the authorities. Living in constant fear of the authorities is both emasculating and stressful; Valentine has overcompensated by steering clear of certain neighborhoods and highways in order to avoid giving the authorities the opportunity to profile him. As a father of a young boy, he loathes thinking that his son, despite his education and character, will also be treated differently by those tasked with protecting him.

JULIAN **BOND**

Julian Bond was born in Nashville, Tennessee. He is a graduate of Morehouse College, and served in the Georgia Legislature and the U.S. Congress. He is a professor at

American University and the University of Virginia. He served as chairman of the National NAACP.

One morning in the early 1990s, Bond was driving with his wife, who is White, from Washington to Philadelphia. At the time he was teaching at Drexel University in the afternoon and the University of Pennsylvania at night. They stopped at a Maryland highway rest stop, and while he waited for his wife to return to their car from the restroom, a White Maryland state trooper approached Bond with his hand on his gun and said, "Come with me."

At the same moment, Bond's wife arrived and they both asked the officer what the problem was and the reason for his request. The policeman told Bond: "You resemble a suspect in a robbery." The officer then made a call on his car radio, seeking to find someone else.

A few moments later, an elderly White woman slowly made her way down the nearby stairs from an upper floor at the rest stop restaurant. As she approached Bond, his wife, and the police officer, the elderly woman blurted out: "I told you, it was a kid."

On that morning, Bond was in his late fifties and dressed in a tweed jacket, dress shirt, and tie, and, he sheepishly admits, his hair had begun to gray and no one would say he was a "kid." The police officer looked at the victim in disgust and simply walked away from the scene. Bond reports that the officer offered neither an explanation nor an apology.

RONALD SULLIVAN

Professor Sullivan is a native of Gary, Indiana, and a graduate of Morehouse College and Harvard Law School. He served as director of the DC Public Defender Service and taught at Yale Law School, before being appointed as the director of the Criminal Justice Institute at Harvard Law School.

Sullivan recalls the day that he received his acceptance letter from Harvard Law School as one of the happiest days of his life. He had worked hard in school for many years and Harvard Law School was the school he dreamed of attending when he finished college. When he received his acceptance letter to Harvard, he got into his car and drove to a local department store where his Mom worked. She was helping customers when he arrived, so he decided to walk around the Men's Department to simply look at clothes. When she had a short break, he excitedly headed toward her section of the store to show her his letter. But, before he could hand her the letter, she told him that the guy who had appeared to Sullivan as another customer was actually an undercover mall security officer. Sullivan shrugged it off, gave his mom his Harvard letter, and she began to cry. She planned to celebrate at dinner after work. Sullivan then headed for the door. At that point the undercover officer came running to the door and stated that he was under suspicion for stealing store merchandise. The guard asked Sullivan to submit to a search and he declined. The guard prevented him from leaving the store and called the local police. Once the police arrived, Sullivan was again asked to submit to a search and he refused, knowing that he had done nothing wrong. After much argument and a begrudging admission from the security officer that he had nothing more than a general hunch that Sullivan had behaved suspiciously, the police let him leave but could not resist telling him that he should feel lucky that they had not called the paddy wagon.

Sullivan was heartbroken. He had just graduated from Morehouse College as its salutatorian and had been announced as a Phi Beta Kappa scholar. His letter of admission from Harvard Law School was still in his hand. Yet the security officer, upon seeing him there in the store, assumed that he was a criminal. Sullivan made up his mind then that he would use his legal training to fight for others who were victims of racial profiling.

ROBIN WASHINGTON

Robin Washington was born in Chicago and is a national award-winning journalist and filmmaker. He is currently the editor of Minnesota's *Duluth News Tribune* as well as a radio commentator for National Public Radio.

Although Washington has experienced bigotry, he has rarely been racially profiled by the police. He thinks that it is partly because he is biracial—the son of a Black and White Jewish couple—and, as Senator Harry Reid inartfully said of President Obama, he's "light-skinned with no Negro dialect" unless he chooses to use one.

Washington's experience took place when he was about 16 years old, and it has dictated how he comports himself in public ever since. In the 1970s, the family's neighborhood, on the near North Side of Chicago, was unsafe; and Robin was viewed by the neighbors as a good kid. One day he was walking through a vacant lot separated from his house by a fence when two police officers approached him. His parents' house was frequently broken into and vandalized, and although he was the one who usually called the police, he had never seen these officers before. "Freeze!" one officer yelled. Washington didn't think the officer was talking to him, so he looked around, still walking toward them, and asked, "What?" "Freeze!" the officer yelled even louder. Angry at being stopped for no reason, Washington started talking back. "Freeze!" the police officer yelled a third time, then crouched, pulled his weapon, and aimed it dead at Washington. The young man did freeze but was absolutely astounded. He remembers trying to talk to them and being patted down by the second cop. After checking him, they let him go. Washington says that it's not his nature to be combative, and ever since this incident he has been extra obedient around cops, no matter what the circumstances. Washington immediately thought of his encounter when he heard of the Gates incident. His reaction? "Yeah, he was right, but he still should have shut up. I'm alive to say that."

ROGER WILKINS

Roger Wilkins is a native of Kansas City, Missouri. He graduated from Michigan Law School and retired as a professor of history and American culture at George Mason University in 2007. He was awarded a Pulitzer Prize in 1972 for his coverage of the Watergate break-in.

In the summer of 1965, Wilkins reports that he was an associate director of the United States Community Relations Service. Accompanied by former Florida governor LeRoy Collins, Wilkins witnessed the Watts riots in Los Angeles. Collins had brought his top aide—a White man named John Perry—and Wilkins to help him assess the situation in Watts, and to determine what action to take, if any. They were to report their observations and recommendations directly to President Johnson. One night, after days of hard community work, Collins gave them the evening off. After dinner, as Wilkins and Perry were driving back to the hotel, Wilkins noticed a car that he could tell from his earlier experiences observing such cars during his days in the civil rights movement, was an unmarked police car. The car was carrying two White police officers in plain clothes, and it was following them.

When they got to their hotel, Perry signaled to take a left turn. At that point, the police siren began to blare. A spotlight was splashed on their heads and the siren kept screaming as Perry completed his slow-motion turn. As he pulled over to the curb, the two men were bathed in the spotlight and ordered by a loudspeaker to "Stop and get out of the car!" As Wilkins got out of the passenger side, he was flabbergasted to see a uniformed officer with a long gun at port arms. "Show me your driver's license!" the man screamed. "I wasn't driving," Wilkins said as he handed the man his Commerce Department identity card. It was laminated and accurate and had a good photograph of him with height and weight listed. Not satisfied, the officer ordered: "Give me your driver's license." Wilkins told him, "What you have is accurate. I work at the U.S. Commerce Department." But, according to Wilkins, the policeman responded, "Well, I work for the Los Angeles Police Department." The officer's partner then interceded, apologized, and said, "*They* make us do these things." When Wilkins told a friend about this encounter, the friend reportedly said: "You're damn lucky you're not dead." Reflecting on this incident, Wilkins says: "In the 44 years since then, I've considered the wisdom of arguing with an armed and angry uniformed White man—and have concluded that there's no wisdom in having such an argument. PERIOD."

WILLIAM JULIUS **WILSON**

William Julius Wilson was born in Deery Township, Pennsylvania. He currently serves as the Lewis P. and Linda L. Geyser University Professor at Harvard University, following his service as the Lucy Flower University Professor and director of the University of Chicago Center for the Study of Urban Equality. He is the author of such works as *The Declining Significance of Race* and, recently, *More than Just Race: Being Black and Poor in the Inner City.*

In 1995, Professor Wilson, who was then married to Beverly Ann Wilson, who is White, lived in the Hyde Park–Kenwood district on the South Side of Chicago, only a couple of blocks away from Barack and Michelle Obama's home. One night while the Wilsons slept, someone tried to burglarize their home. When the house alarm went off, William Wilson hastened downstairs in his pajamas to survey the situation. A Chicago police officer arrived in response to the alarm, and Wilson opened the door to discuss the attempted burglary. The officer seemed surprised to see an African American man in the house. Despite the fact that Wilson was in his pajamas, the officer put his hand on his service revolver while asking in a very loud voice, "Do you live here?"

Beverly, who was walking downstairs, quickly said to the officer, "He's my husband, he lives here." Wilson had put this matter aside for more than a decade, but after learning of Professor Gates' arrest in Cambridge in July, Beverly sent him an e-mail recalling the incident. It is an event that Wilson has forever etched into his mind about how careful African Americans need to be in situations involving law officers.

EARL GILBERT "BUTCH" GRAVES, JR.

Born in Brooklyn, New York, Butch Graves graduated from Yale University and then earned an MBA from Harvard Business School. He currently serves as the president of *Black Enterprise* magazine.

In 1995, Graves was detained and searched by two New York Metro-North police looking for a suspect who did not resemble him in any way except for their race. Later, the police department publicly apologized, and the Metro-North Railroad purchased advertisements featuring a printed apology in three New York newspapers. On July 22, 2009, in response to the arrest of Professor Gates, Graves stated to the media, "There's nothing post-racial about the U.S."

JOE MORGAN

Raised in Oakland, California, Joe Morgan attended Castlemont High School. He is a 10-time Major League Baseball All-Star, two-time World Series Champion, and two-time league Most Valuable Player (MVP). Morgan was inducted into the Baseball Hall of Fame in 1990 as a member of the Cincinnati Reds. He is currently an Emmy-winning commentator for ESPN television and radio.

One day, sometime after Morgan's baseball career was over, he flew to Los Angeles. He got off the plane and was making a phone call when a police officer came up, grabbed him from behind, threw him to the floor, and handcuffed him behind his back. Morgan was arrested because he fit the profile of a Black drug dealer the police were waiting for. Needless to say, Morgan felt extremely humiliated lying on the floor of the airport with his hands behind his back with all the passengers staring at him. Even though a number of people went up to the officers and told them that he was Joe Morgan, the famous baseball player, they still didn't let him go for some time. Morgan demanded an apology. When he didn't receive one, he sued the LAPD and won.

REVEREND MINIARD CULPEPPER

Reverend Miniard Culpepper was born in Boston and completed his BA at Brandeis University and his JD at Suffolk University Law School, both in Massachusetts, and his master's of divinity at Howard University School of Divinity in Washington, DC. He is currently the acting associate general counsel of the United States Department of Housing and Urban Development in DC and pastor at a historic Boston Baptist church.

Culpepper was in the South End of Boston studying for the bar exam in the early 1980s. He was going home from studying one evening when the police pulled up, told him that he looked like the man who had recently robbed someone, and threw him into the backseat of their squad car. Culpepper tried explaining that he was coming from the library, but the policemen weren't interested. Luckily, a friend who went to college with Culpepper was a police officer at the scene. She recognized him and stated that he couldn't possibly have been the robber, but the other officers paid no attention to her. The policemen continued to hold Culpepper in the back of the squad car until the person who was robbed arrived at the scene. The victim told the police that Culpepper was not the robber. Only then did they allow Culpepper to go. Culpepper still can't believe this incident happened to him.

KEITH BOYKIN

Keith Boykin was born in St. Louis, Missouri, and attended college at Dartmouth in New Hampshire and law school at Harvard. He currently works as a television commentator for CNBC and MSNBC. He previously worked in the White House for President Bill Clinton.

On Sunday, July 19, 2009, in the same week in which Professor Gates was arrested, a New York City police officer stopped Boykin in a Harlem subway station and accused him of illegally jumping the turnstiles, which he had not done. Boykin was the only one on the subway platform wearing a red T-shirt that afternoon, but the officer claimed he saw a Black man with a red T-shirt sneak onto the platform. Boykin complained that he was being harassed as the officer demanded to see his subway card. After protesting, Boykin provided the card, which was then swiped to confirm that it had just been used. Immediately after the officer returned the subway card, an unknown Black woman standing nearby spoke up in Boykin's defense, saying: "Do you know who he is? He worked in the White House." The officer then apologized, but the experience convinced Boykin that he would have been treated very differently if he were not an "established" figure. Boykin filed a formal complaint with the New York Police Department that month, but, to his knowledge, as this book goes to press, no action has been taken on the complaint.

M. RICK TURNER

M. Rick Turner was born in Hartford, Connecticut. He served as the dean of the University of Virginia's Office of African American Affairs for 18 years, until 2006. He is the founder of the Saturday Academy, an educational enrichment program for families.

Turner often has been contacted by Black males involved in incidents of racial harassment and racial profiling. One such incident occurred a few years back when he was asked by Black graduate students and Black adult men from the Charlottesville-Albemarle community to

convene a town hall meeting. The purpose of the meeting was to respond to the city police who were randomly stopping Black men to request or demand DNA samples as they searched for a serial rapist who
had been identified as a Black man.

HAFIZ FARID

Hafiz Farid was born in Newark, New Jersey, and is an independent filmmaker, writer,
and producer. He is also the executive director of a not-for-profit organization called
NoCane Inc., which he founded 20 years ago to help at-risk youth in the community.

As Farid grew up in New Jersey, personal incidents of racial profiling
by police occurred almost daily. But the one incident that affected him
more profoundly than any other occurred as an adult, in Montclair,
New Jersey. It began with a visit to his home from a Montclair police
officer requesting to see Farid's 18-year-old son. When Farid inquired
about the reason for the request, he was told that the police wanted his
son to be part of a police lineup in the investigation of an alleged sale
of a controlled dangerous substance. Although the suspect had escaped,
the officer who had witnessed the event from two blocks away asserted
that he saw a Black male with a white T-shirt whom he recognized as
Farid's son. Farid told the officer that he himself would have a hard
time picking out his own son in a crowd from a block or two away because all kids dressed alike—sneakers, jeans, and white T-shirts were almost a uniform of urban youth. After Farid refused to turn his son over
for a lineup, the officer left to prepare a case to arrest the young man.
Farid received a call the next day asking him to bring his son in, and
the teen subsequently was arrested based on the officer's visual account.
Bail was set, and Farid posted the fee and contacted his attorney. Farid
and his son filed formal complaints against the police department and

contacted the prosecutor's office. The case was heard by the grand jury, and fortunately no indictment was returned. Farid's son, who had no history of criminal conduct, narrowly escaped a felony indictment based on the profiling of the young Black male.

On another occasion, Farid and his wife were leaving the home of a dear friend and business partner, Shelly Seidenstein, who lived in the town of Verona, New Jersey. Verona's population is 99 percent White and 1 percent African American. Nannies, drivers, live-in maids, and caretakers of elderly, wealthy, and affluent families dominate the landscape of this small suburban town. As they were about to exit the luxury high-rise building, Farid's wife remembered that she had forgotten her purse. She asked the doorman if he could call upstairs to the Seidensteins. The doorman called and stated, "Ms. Seidenstein, this is Glenn at the front desk. Your gal is here in the lobby; she says that she left her purse upstairs." Farid's wife, a well-educated professional woman with an assertive demeanor and great dignity, quickly exclaimed, "Excuse me! I'm not anybody's gal, I'm Mrs. Farid." The doorman turned red with shame and stuttered a humble apology. In Farid's opinion, the use of the word was a Freudian slip that clearly exposed the perception rooted in slavery that Blacks are servants and slaves, destiny's children forever deemed to be "gals" and "boys" in the minds of those who still suffer from what Einstein called America's worst disease, racism.

BILL FLETCHER, JR.

Bill Fletcher, Jr., was born in New York City and received a bachelor's degree from Harvard College and a master's from Brooklyn College–City University of New York. He is currently the field services and education director for the American Federation of Government Employees.

In the late 1980s, while living in Boston, Fletcher was employed as an organizer for District 65–United Auto Workers. His primary responsibility was serving as the chief negotiator, and one evening he was driving home around 8 P.M. at the end of a series of negotiations. It was dark. Approaching him was a Jeep that suddenly swerved and cut him off. Two White men got out of the car and started to approach him. Not having any idea what was going on, Fletcher threw the car into reverse and prepared to make a run for it, but something stopped him. Fletcher heard one of the men yell something that sounded like " . . . police . . ." so he yelled back, "Police?" They said, "Yes." They showed Fletcher no identification, there were no lights on their vehicle, and there was nothing to indicate that they were police. They looked into Fletcher's car, then one said to the other, "This is not the car," and they returned to their Jeep. Apparently, there had been a robbery in the area. There was no apology. They just left. Fletcher found himself shaking and at the same time remembering the man in Miami in 1980 who fled the police only to be killed . . . for doing nothing.

RONALD E. HAMPTON

Ronald E. Hampton was born in Washington, DC. He has served as a police officer in Washington, DC and other places and is the former executive director of the National Black Police Association.

Hampton had been a Washington Metropolitan Police Department officer for about five years, and on this day he was working the day shift (7:00 A.M.–3:00 P.M.). He had recently purchased a brand-new 1974 Ford Thunderbird. His car had just been detailed and looked great. He pulled out of the police personnel parking garage and headed down to Haines Point to enjoy a very nice summer day. In order to get there, Hampton planned to use the straight route down 9th Street NW going through downtown DC and then drive past the waterfront. Hampton was cautious to drive at the speed limit because his new car generally drew attention. Somewhere between Constitution and Pennsylvania avenues, still on 9th Street, a marked police car with sirens and lights flashing pulled up and motioned him to pull over. Hampton did exactly what the White officer instructed him to do. The White police officer looked over the car several times and asked Hampton for his permit and registration papers. Hampton responded by asking the officer why he had been pulled over and what (if any) was his traffic violation. The officer seemed to be more interested in the car, so Hampton asked him again. After asking the officer the third time about the reason for the stop, Hampton informed him that the General Orders (police department rule books) stated that an officer is required to give the driver certain information during a traffic stop. The officer stopped and asked Hampton if he was a police officer. Hampton told the officer that he was, and the latter responded: "Why didn't you mention that in the beginning?" Hampton asked, "Do you have to be a police officer to be treated with respect and dignity?" The White officer replied while walking back to his patrol car, "I thought you had stolen the car."

KEITH BARNES

Keith Barnes is a native of New Orleans and a graduate of Stanford University in Palo Alto, California. He has worked for a number of businesses since graduating from Stanford.

In 1985, Barnes purchased a Porsche Targa in Mobile, Alabama. He sold the car in 1989. In those four years, he received 11 traffic tickets;

in 10 of those instances, the first question from the cop was "Whose car is this?" On another occasion, Barnes was driving from New Orleans to Mobile in his white 1985 Chevy Impala. He was stopped five times in 1,355 miles because a Black man in a white car was robbing convenience stores along the I–10 corridor in Mississippi. Barnes was wearing a suit during the entire episode. The next morning the news showed a high-speed chase in which the robber was apprehended. Unlike Barnes, the suspect was described as "high-yellow" and driving a white Toyota Corolla.

BILLY WALKER

Billy Walker was born in Dallas and has been a practicing attorney for almost 29 years in Utah, where he is currently head of the office that investigates and prosecutes attorneys for misconduct. He graduated from Stanford University in Palo Alto, California, with a BA in economics and then attended the University of Utah College of Law.

When Walker was in high school, he was riding home with some friends when three police officers pulled them over, placed them up against a wall on a main street in Compton, and held them at gunpoint for about 45 minutes. After they were eventually told that they were free to leave, Walker learned that they were being held on suspicion of robbery because four young adult Hispanics had committed several robberies that day. All of the people with Walker were African American teenagers.

BYRONN BAIN

Byronn Bain is a native of Brooklyn, New York. He received his BA from Columbia University, his MA from New York University, and his JD from Harvard University. Brook-

lyn's own prison activist, a spoken word poet, hip-hop artist, actor, author, and edu-
cator, Bain hosts the talk show *My Two Cents,* which has included guests such as LL
Cool J, Snoop Dogg, Damon Dash, Malik Yoba, Jim Jones, Malik Zulu Shabazz, Ciara,
Omali Yeshitela, Kevin Mohammed, and Ben Chavis.

After hundreds of hours and thousands of pages of legal theory in law
school, Bain finally had his first real lesson in the Law. On Sunday,
October 18, 1999, he was taken from the corner of 96th Street and
Broadway by the NYPD and held overnight in a cell at a precinct in
New York City. While home from school for the weekend, he had
been arrested for a crime he witnessed someone else commit.

Bain, with his cousin and younger brother, left the Latin Quarter
nightclub on the fateful night and headed for a store around the corner for a turkey sandwich that Bain's brother wanted. As they left the
store, armed only with sandwiches and Snapples, the three of them
saw a group of young men standing around a car parked on the corner in front of the store. As music blasted from the wide-open doors
of their car, the men around the car appeared to be arguing with someone in an apartment above the store. The argument escalated when
one of the young men began throwing bottles at the apartment window. Several other people witnessed the altercation and began scat-
tering to avoid the raining shards of glass. Bain, his brother, and his
cousin decided to walk up the street toward the subway to avoid the
chaos that was unfolding. They were halfway up the block when they
looked back and saw the unruly guys jumping in their car, turning off
their music, and getting away from the scene as quickly as possible. As
Bain's group continued to walk toward the subway, about six or seven
bouncers came running down the street yelling, "Where do you BOYS
think you're going?!" The bouncers came at Bain and his family with

outstretched arms to corral them back down the block. Bain answered, "To the 2 train," and insisted that the bouncers had no authority to restrain them. Bain is certain that this pissed off the bouncers. Bain told his brother and cousin to ignore them—the disturbance had occurred an entire block away from the bouncers' "territory," they were clearly beyond the bouncers' jurisdiction, and the bouncers had not bothered to ask anyone among the many witnesses what had happened before they attempted to apprehend Bain and his family. But a crime had been committed, and someone Black was going to be apprehended.

Less than 10 minutes after Bain had walked past the bouncers, he was staring at a badge worn by a police officer. According to Bain, the bouncers then said, "That's them, officer!"

Bain believes that the officers could have asked any of the witnesses and easily cleared up the issue of who had thrown the bottles, but they did not do so. Bain and his family were now being punished for the crime of thwarting the bouncers' unauthorized attempt to apprehend them. They were going to be guilty unless they could prove themselves innocent. Having failed to convince the officer on the scene, Bain and his family were placed up against the wall in a matter of minutes and were frisked down from shirt to socks. Bain reports that the officer told them to shut up and keep facing the wall or he would treat them like they were trying to fight back. Bain and his family members were shoved into the squad car. Bain reports that they were never told that they had a right to remain silent or that they had the right to an attorney, or informed that anything they said could and would be used against them in a court of law.

After their mug shots were taken, they were locked up all night long for no good reason in a filthy cell barely bigger than a bathroom.

It should have mattered that they had no record. But it didn't. What mattered was that they were Black and they were there. That was enough for everyone involved to draw the conclusion that they were guilty until they could be proved innocent.

On Wednesday, February 23, 2000, after four court appearances over five months, the D.A.'s case against Bain, his younger brother, and his cousin was dismissed. No affidavits or other evidence were produced to support the charges against them.

THEODORE SHAW

Theodore Shaw is a native of New York City, a graduate of Wesleyan University in Connecticut and Columbia Law School. He has been a civil rights attorney, and served as director-counsel and president of the NAACP Legal Defense and Education Fund. He presently teaches at Columbia Law School and is involved in private practice in the area of civil rights and equality.

As a young man in New York, Ted Shaw often worked at a neighborhood supermarket, for which he would receive some food items at the end of the day. On one occasion when he was walking home from work, he was stopped by a New York police officer who accused him of being involved in selling and using drugs. Ted was handcuffed and arrested and taken to the police precinct. When he was there the officer seemed convinced that he was a drug addict, and asked him to remove not only his shirt and T-shirt, but also his pants and underwear. Finding no marks or evidence indicating that Ted was a drug user or in any way a lawbreaker, the officer was nonetheless insistent that Ted was a criminal. After searching Ted's bag and finding only food items the officer eventually had to let him go.

As Ted recalls this event more than four decades later, it is clear that it made an indelible mark on him. As a civil rights lawyer and someone committed to justice, he is still troubled by the fact that because of his race, police officers assumed he was a drug dealer and never even considered the fact that he was a young kid working in an urban area, trying to improve not only himself but the quality of life in his community. Ted wonders if the officer who arrested and searched him that day is aware that the person he accused of being a criminal became one of America's most prominent civil rights leaders.

WRONGFULLY SUSPECTED OF CRIMINAL CONDUCT BY MEMBERS OF THE PUBLIC

MAKAU MUTUA

Makau Mutua, born in Kitui, Kenya, is a graduate of Harvard Law School. He is the dean at Buffalo Law School, the State University of New York.

In the mid-1990s, while living in Boston, dressed in a suit, Mutua went to a major department store to shop with his four-year-old son, Lumumba. Virtually all the customers were White. Mutua reports that he noticed a security guard following them around the store. After being followed for about 30 minutes, Mutua stopped and asked the guard, "Are you following us?" to which the latter replied, "I thought you needed my help." Mutua told him, "Bull—, why do you think of all these people here we are the only ones who need your help?" At that point, the guard said in a confessional tone, "Brother, you know how it is—we have to make sure there are no shoplifters." The security guard left without exchanging another word. Mutua was upset and contemplated raising the matter with the store but did not, partly because he didn't want to get the guard in trouble. All the while, Lumumba, his son, had stood there. He finally told his father that the way they had been treated "was not fair." This episode, and many similar ones before and after it, bothers Mutua to this day.

RORY E. VERRETT

Rory E. Verrett is from New Orleans, and graduated from Howard University in Washington, DC, and Harvard Law School. He currently serves as an executive recruiter with Spencer Stuart, one of the world's top search firms.

As an executive recruiter, Verrett is always interviewing people, whether for active searches for clients or for networking purposes. On one such occasion, he was requested by a former client to meet with a female executive, a chief operating officer of a local gas company, about her interest in moving into a nonprofit leadership role. The female executive invited him to a private dining club in Atlanta. After a very productive conversation and lunch, they exchanged cards and agreed to stay in touch. Upon exiting the club, Verrett walked over to the valet and handed him his ticket. The valet looked around the driveway of the building and saw that Verrett's car was parked in front, pointed it out to him, and handed him the keys. Verrett walked over to his car, a 2008 Toyota Prius. As he sat down and thumbed through the 10 or so e-mails that he'd received on his BlackBerry during lunch, another valet ran up to him and yelled, "Get out of this car! This is not your car! You are stealing this car!" Verrett explained that it was his car, but the valet was undeterred and kept yelling, "Get out of this car! You stole this car!" By this time, the first valet had come running over to the car and stated that it was indeed Verrett's. Upset, Verrett asked to see the manager, a Latino gentleman, who apologized profusely and fired the angry valet on the spot.

KWAME REED

Kwame Reed was born in McComb, Mississippi. He is a graduate of Howard University in Washington, DC.

Reed's wife, Rita Arama, is a physician educated in Ghana, the United Kingdom, and the United States. She comes from a very privileged background and for years refused to believe the stories of racism that she was told by African Americans. Here is just one of the early experiences that started to open her eyes. Reed and his wife had just bought a new car, and Reed parked it next to an identical one at the Tysons Corner (Virginia) Mall. The only visible difference was that the other vehicle did not have Howard University School of Law and Yale Divinity School decals or the very visible Black and Gold AIA tags. Later, after Reed started to drive out of the parking lot, a middle-aged White male ran in front of their car emotionally shouting, "Hey!" Rita and Reed were both startled. Suddenly the man calmed down. Reed assumes that he spotted one of the aforementioned distinctions between his car and Reed's. Calmly and with a smile on his face, he walked over to the driver's-side window and engaged in some chitchat about what a lovely machine the car was and how much he loved his own one. As Reed resumed driving away, his wife said, "That was really nice of him." She was not joking. Reed said, "Sweetheart, he thought that I had stolen his car." She did not believe Reed, but as she looked back, she saw the man talking to a police officer who had stopped his cruiser there.

COLVIN **GRANNUM**

Colvin Grannum was born in Brooklyn, New York, and earned a BA from the University of Pennsylvania in 1975 and a JD from Georgetown Law Center in Washington, DC, in 1978. After many years of practicing law, in 1995 he transitioned to the nonprofit management sector by serving as the first chief executive officer of Bridge Street Development Corporation, a church-affiliated community development corporation. In 2001, he assumed the helm of Bedford Stuyvesant Restoration Corporation, the nation's first community development corporation.

Ironically, Grannum has almost no recollection of several profiling incidents that occurred in the last 10 years but can recall vividly incidents from his high school, college, law school, and early professional years. Two of his clearest recollections date back to the late 1980s, when he worked at NYNEX Corporation.

Grannum was meticulous about his work and his appearance, daily wearing three-piece suits and carrying a leather attaché case. One evening, he went to an upscale department store to look for a gift. Upon entering the store, he decided to ask the security guard for directions. As he got within six feet of the guard, a voice crackled from the guard's handheld radio: "Black male, tan trench, carrying attaché case." The guard, who was a Black male, gave Grannum the directions he had requested while looking chagrined. Although Grannum continued on, he was shocked that almost instantly upon entering the store he could be perceived as a potential shoplifter, even though he looked liked a relatively well-heeled corporate lawyer.

A similar incident occurred while he was working in the office one weekend. He decided to take a break and look for a new suit. So he went to a relatively upscale, conservative men's clothier on Fifth Avenue. Grannum just wanted to check their prices. As he rode the escalator to the mezzanine level, where the suits were displayed, he could see salesmen asking customers whether they could assist them as they stepped off the escalator. When Grannum stepped off, no salesman volunteered his assistance. Grannum looked around the suit department; every customer was being assisted except him. All the salesmen were middle-aged White men. All the customers were White. Despite feeling deeply offended and angry, Grannum decided to look at the suits. Many minutes passed before a salesman asked him if he needed assistance, and Grannum reluctantly consented. But several more minutes passed before he was finally approached by a very courteous, eager, young Hispanic male, who Grannum suspects was on his first day as a salesman. Almost instantly, Grannum decided to make a point. He spent close to $1,500 in the store that day. Eventually the other salesmen seemed to get the point. They stood around watching and whispering, and some even lent a hand and congratulated the young man assisting Grannum. Grannum patronized that store several more times and always received respectful service. He doesn't think they remembered him personally, but he believes that his $1,500 spending changed, to a limited extent, their perception of the young Black males who entered the store. He does admit that he has never since had another $1,500 day at that or any other clothing store.

REVEREND BRANDON THOMAS CROWLEY

Reverend Brandon Thomas Crowley was born in Atlanta, Georgia. He is a graduate of Morehouse College. Crowley is the senior pastor of one of the oldest African American churches in New England, the historic Myrtle Baptist Church of West Newton, Massachusetts. He moved from Georgia to Boston to pursue a master's of divinity degree from Harvard Divinity School and, at the age of 23, became the pastor of Myrtle Baptist.

As a first-year Harvard divinity student in 2009, he was walking from the library to his car to head to his apartment in Cambridge. He was dressed in a standard black suit, black topcoat, and black wide-brim derby. While walking down the street, a White woman heard his footsteps behind her and glanced over her shoulder. When she saw that he was Black, she pulled her purse off her right arm, put it under her coat, and held it tight to her chest. Crowley was disturbed by her actions and decided to walk briskly past her, to ease her fear. As he drew closer, she began to run and scream for help. Crowley realized that she had perceived his brisk walking as an attempt to attack her and steal her purse, so he decided to take a detour down a side road. After his quick turn, he heard the sound of a speeding car behind him—a police officer had pulled to the side of the road and was talking to the woman. Apparently, the Cambridge police officer had heard her scream, seen her walking frantically, and stopped to check on her. As Crowley looked back to see what was happening, the woman pointed in his direction. The officer swiftly drove down the dark alley to stop Crowley and began to question him regarding his reason for being in the area. Crowley explained that he was a student walking home from the library and pointed in the direction of his apartment. The policeman followed him to his door before leaving the area.

LEON WILSON

Leon Wilson was born in Bangor, Maine. He was the first African American vice president of the Shawmut Bank of Boston as well as the first senior vice president of color
at the Bank of Boston. Later on, he accepted a position as corporate senior vice president of General Motors Acceptance Corp. He retired as the executive vice president of
Bank of America in 2005. Currently he is the executive vice president of the Nonprofit
Finance Fund, a New York–based national not-for-profit community development financial institution.

Despite Wilson's achievements and economic status, he was accused
a number of times of entering a hotel in New York City to steal a
free breakfast. Ironically, he had been a registered guest of the hotel
on numerous occasions, he frequently ate lunch at the hotel restaurant, and his company often scheduled after-work events and recep-
tions there. In May 2008 three troubling incidents took place. The
first occurred when Wilson went to the hotel for lunch. As the restaurant was not yet open, he sat in the lobby to wait. Shortly afterward,
he got a business call and decided to return to his office. As he departed, the doorman said to him, "We have cameras, and we know
when people come in and steal coffee and danish." Wilson told the
doorman that he had obviously mistaken him for someone else. A
few weeks later, Wilson went to the hotel to meet with a staff member who was a hotel guest. As Wilson waited, the same doorman
came over and warned him against stealing breakfast. Wilson once
more told the doorman that he was mistaken. Although Wilson was
angry, he decided that the doorman was simply a rude idiot and let
the incident pass. On the Thursday before Memorial Day, 2008, Wil-

son registered as a guest at the hotel. At 7 A.M. on Friday, he went down to the lobby to read the newspaper. As Wilson sat there, the same doorman approached him and asked him to leave. He continued with more threatening rhetoric, ultimately indicating that if Wilson did not voluntarily leave the premises, he would get him out of there. The doorman never asked if Wilson was a guest of the hotel. The doorman disappeared for a short while after leaving two men to keep an eye on Wilson. In the meantime, Wilson noticed a young White woman walk in and head to the free breakfast. She got coffee, grabbed a paper, and sat in a chair next to him. Overhearing her phone conversation, Wilson was able to conclude that she was not a guest but was meeting another nonguest there, using the hotel as a connection point. No one from the hotel staff inquired who she was or interrupted her free breakfast. Shortly afterward, Wilson noticed a New York police car pull up in front of the hotel, and two officers entered the lobby. At this point, Wilson became concerned that the matter could escalate out of control. Therefore, he went to the front desk manager and indicated that he was a guest being harassed by the doorman. The desk staff demanded to see Wilson's room key and his picture ID as evidence. They then called the doorman over; he remained belligerent, but the police left without further action. Wilson demanded an apology, but when it did not come, he asked to see the general manager, who said that he needed to look into the issue before commenting. A few days later, Wilson was told by the manager that it was his word against that of a long-term valued employee of the hotel. The hotel never issued any apology. Wilson's company moved its business relationship elsewhere, and Wilson himself has never visited that hotel again. He is convinced that his race was the major factor in this incident.

BENJAMIN F. WILSON

Benjamin F. Wilson was born in Bloomington, Indiana. He graduated from Dartmouth College in Hanover, New Hampshire, in 1973 and from Harvard Law School in 1976. He has been practicing law for 33 years and currently serves as the managing partner and board chairman of a leading national environmental law firm.

Approximately six years ago, Wilson was returning home from a business trip and had a flight change at the Pittsburgh airport. When his connecting flight to Washington appeared to be running late, he asked the airline representative, a middle-aged White woman, if she could provide him with an update on the flight status. She blithely ignored his request, pretending not to hear him. When he calmly asked his question again, she stated, "I will let you know when I get ready." He responded, "That much is clear," and walked away from the counter. She never provided Wilson with any information regarding his flight. After a wait of another 45 minutes, the passengers, including Wilson, began boarding. However, as he approached the departure gate, the same airline representative called security. Several armed guards came to the gate and, at the request of the airline representative, subjected him to a pat down. Wilson had done nothing to warrant such humiliating treatment. Indeed, even his fellow passengers protested, noting that he had done nothing more than ask a simple question regarding the status of the flight. Wilson's frequent flyer card and suit and tie did not enable him to avoid this indignity. All it took was a word from an unprofessional and rude airline representative to identify him as a potential security risk. To her, Wilson was not worthy of respect.

THE UNWARRANTED FEAR OF BLACK MEN

EARL MARTIN **PHALEN**

Earl Martin Phalen was born in Springfield, Massachusetts, and is a graduate of Yale University and Harvard Law School. He is the founder of BELL, an after-school and summer school program for elementary and middle-school students in Boston. He is the founder of Advantage USA and also serves as the chief executive officer of Reach Out and Read.

Phalen reports that various racial incidents during his childhood and young adulthood served to heighten his negative feelings about being Black in our society. One incident in particular remains at the forefront of his mind. He was in his car in Boston looking for his condominium's garage door clicker to open the door and park his car, but he could not find it. Suddenly, a White woman in a Jaguar passed by him and opened the door, so he decided to pull in behind her. She saw that Phalen intended to enter the garage and attempted to physically obstruct him by leaving her car at the edge of the door. After rummaging through his backpack, Phalen located his garage door opener. He held his clicker out of the window so that she could see it, but she still did not move. Finally, he walked toward her car window, clicker in hand. When he did this, she rolled up her car windows, locked her doors, and frantically motioned him away from her. Phalen returned to his car, opened the door with the clicker, and then entered the garage. Meanwhile, the woman parked her car inside the garage and hurriedly went to the elevator. During this entire incident, Phalen felt frustrated, angry, and confused. At first he rationalized that she was obstructing his entrance because she assumed from his initial inability to get into the garage that he did not own a space. But then other emotions began to surface. Phalen could not believe that she would not move even after he displayed proof that he lived there. In her mind, Phalen did not belong. When he exited his car and approached her, after proving to her that she was wrong, she did not acknowledge her mistake or speak to him. When she locked her doors and rolled up her windows, she made him feel as if he were less than human—someone that did not deserve to be communicated with.

JOHN PAYTON

John Payton was born in Los Angeles and is a graduate of Pomona College in California and of Harvard Law School. He was a partner in the law firm of WilmerHale and successfully litigated the Supreme Court cases in 2003 that upheld the affirmative action plan at the University of Michigan Law School. He now serves as director-counsel and president of the NAACP Legal Defense and Education Fund in New York City.

John Payton had been a partner at WilmerHale for more than 20 years. One evening, when leaving the office by means of an elevator that was available only to company employees, he was joined by another staff member, who was White and female. Payton, thinking about several legal matters that he would be addressing the next day, didn't quite notice the woman's apparent discomfort. However, when the secure elevator stopped at one of the parking lots, he was shocked that the woman not only rushed out but hit the electronic device to open her car while running to it and hastening out of the lot. Although Payton thought about making a point of it the next day, he realized it would be unfruitful and ultimately counterproductive. Here he was, an established lawyer of more than 25 years, working at a prominent law firm, and one of his staff members reacted to him in ways that made no sense under the circumstances. It was an event that Payton will never forget.

VINCENT FRY

Vincent Fry was born in Chicago and has a BA in psychology from Morehouse College in Atlanta and a JD from Northwestern University in Chicago. He is currently a political, governmental, and business consultant, counseling clients on strategy, operations, and communications.

On June 6, 2009, Fry's son, Charlie, was born. After his birth, the family decided to go to a small condo they owned in South Palm Beach, Florida. They have owned the place for over eight years and have had the same car during this time. South Palm Beach is a one-mile-long community that is home to many present and former captains of industry and has many wealthy residents. Although a few residents live there year-round, most use it as a winter retreat. Due to the community's small size, everyone knows everyone, including the local police. Because Fry's family did not spend much time there, they did not maintain a telephone or Internet service. In addition, Palm Beach is an island with poor cell phone service—it is common to see winter residents in parking lots using their cell phones to make calls.

One afternoon after arriving, Fry needed to check some e-mails and make some calls, so he did his usual thing: he went out into the parking lot and sat in his car with his cell phone and laptop. Several minutes later a police car pulled up behind him. Fry stepped out of the car with his laptop and walked toward the police car. Fry recognized the officer, and the officer recognized the car and Fry. They greeted each other, the officer gave the all-clear call back to headquarters, and the two began to chat. The officer told Fry that someone in the complex that shares Fry's parking lot called the police and said there was a man who looked suspicious. Over the past eight years, Fry's neighbors have been very kind and the police have been courteous. However, he always remains on guard because encounters like this are not unique.

KEVIN JONES

Kevin Jones was born in Reading, Pennsylvania. He is a corporate real estate attorney in New York City. He received a JD degree from Harvard Law School, a master's in theological studies from the Boston University School of Theology, and a joint master's degree in public affairs and master's in urban & regional planning from the Woodrow Wilson School of Public and International Affairs at Princeton University.

One wintery January night in 2006, Jones returned home to Somerville, Massachusetts, with his family just after midnight after spending the Christmas and winter break in New York. To enter his building from the garage, one had to use a remote to open the garage door and then use the building key to open one of the lobby areas, from which one could access either the stairs or the elevator. Many of the residents in the building, including Jones, were graduate students

his family's items from the car. Choosing the latter, he strolled out of the elevator, shook his head in disgust at the lady (who was now joined by her mother), and continued to his car. Just as Jones opened the car trunk, two officers came running around the corner from their manhunt. Without giving them an opportunity to say much after they screamed, "Hey, do you live here? . . . Show us some ID," Jones immediately entered into a rant—"Yes, I live here, but the real question is why on earth you are bothering me in my own home, and why was this lady so unable to recognize me as her neighbor? She clearly has issues with race, and if either of you fails to see the problem with bothering a man at the trunk of his car in the garage of his home, then you are just as racist as she is!" The woman who called the police screamed, "How can I be racist? Look at me!" Still not going for the easy way out, Jones screamed back, "That comment is about as stupid as this whole situation. I suppose I stole a garage remote to drive my expensive car into this garage and then chased you down with toys in my hands. No, you have issues, and I really don't have the energy or time to explain it to you right now." Despite one officer being visibly upset at Jones' refusal to submit to questioning, the second officer seemed to understand his viewpoint (even if only vaguely) and stepped between the upset officer and Jones. Jones showed the second officer his Harvard ID and excused himself. Now fuming, the upset officer (with one hand on his holster) raised an objection, but Jones didn't bother to turn back until the elevator doors were closing, and counts himself fortunate that the calm officer put both his hands on the chest of the upset officer and said, "Let's go." In the days and months that passed, that neighbor frequently crossed paths with Jones in the common areas of the building, but never once did she attempt an apology. The neighbor's insistence that her internal fears justified putting Jones' life directly in danger was little more than an evaluation that her sense of security was more important than Jones' life. Evaluations like hers serve as the very essence and root of racism.

GARY L. FLOWERS

Flowers, a native of Richmond, Virginia, is an analyst, academic, and activist. He is currently the executive director and CEO of Black Leadership Forum, Inc., an alliance and clearing house based in Washington, DC for 30 Black civil rights and service organizations in the United States.

According to Flowers, living as a Black man in the USA is a full-time job—one is regularly viewed as less intelligent, less patriotic, and more violent. He has a recent story as a reminder. On February 1, 2010, he was invited to deliver a keynote address to the Miami-Dade Chamber of Commerce. After the speech he returned to his upscale hotel in the Coconut Grove section of Miami. Flowers was professionally dressed in a dark suit and tie. He entered the elevator and politely nodded to a 60-something White woman who was presumably going up to her room. They both exited the elevator on the fifth floor, and as the gentleman Flowers was trained to be by his parents in Virginia, he motioned for the lady to proceed ahead of him. After he took a few steps behind her, the woman stopped in the hallway, allowing Flowers to go ahead of her. It was only when Flowers had produced a hotel key and unlocked his door that the woman resumed her path. As he had done hundreds of times before, Flowers shook his head in disbelief and smirked—being a Black man in America is not easy.

THE ASSUMPTION THAT ALL BLACK MEN ARE
OR SHOULD BE IN SERVICE OR SUPPORT POSITIONS

D'ARMY BAILEY

D'Army Bailey is a native of Memphis, Tennessee, and a graduate of Clark University
in Worcester, Massachusetts, and Yale University Law School in New Haven, Connecticut. He practiced law in Tennessee and served as a judge there, and is one of the
founders of the National Civil Rights Museum, which commemorates the site where
Dr. Martin Luther King, Jr., was assassinated in 1968.

A few years back, Bailey went to one of the premier professional golf
events, the Annual Pro Golf Tournament, benefiting St. Jude Children's Research Hospital at Southwind Golf Course in Memphis. He
was then an elected state trial judge. His older brother, Walter, a
lawyer and a Memphis county commissioner of some 30 years, invited Bailey and his longtime friend, also an African American and
then director of personnel for the Memphis City Schools, as his V.I.P.
guests for the tournament. After leaving the tournament in one of
the city's largely White suburbs, Germantown, the men decided to
stop for some take-out barbecue at the Germantown Commissary.
The three men entered the nearly empty restaurant, approached the
order counter, and were greeted by a kindly elderly White woman
who casually asked about the golf tournament: "Y'all been to the golf
tournament?" she asked, to which Bailey replied, "Yes, ma'am." The
lady looked up with what Bailey describes as a patronizing smile and
asked, "Who did you caddy for?" Bailey decided to get his barbecue
elsewhere.

JAMES COLE

James Cole was born in Florence, Alabama. Cole is a graduate of Harvard Law School and a prominent African American lawyer working in Florida.

Cole had flown to Philadelphia with two clients to participate in an arbitration hearing. Cole was dressed in a blue business suit. He rented a van and drove the group to the Philadelphia luxury hotel where they were staying. When they arrived, Cole watched and supervised the doorman unloading the van. When he had finished, the doorman asked Cole's clients: "Will your chauffer be staying as well?" Cole's clients were obviously embarrassed but told the doorman, "This is Mr. Cole. If you will check with your front desk, you will see it is he who has rented the penthouse suite for the week." No apology. Just an embarrassed set of red faces—the doorman's and those of Cole's two White clients.

DENNIS HAYES

Dennis Hayes was born in Indianapolis, Indiana, and graduated from Indiana University–Bloomington and Indiana University School of Law. He recently retired as senior vice president of the NAACP.

As with many African Americans, Hayes has been treated as a suspect because of his race numerous times. One instance happened in a professional setting in Denver, Colorado, in about 1994. Hayes was general counsel of the NAACP and was defending a deposition, along with two or three White co-counsel, in a housing discrimination case. Two or three defense attorneys, White, also participated. The deponent and court reporter were also White. Hayes was the only Black present in the group.

The deposition was being conducted in the Denver Housing Authority. The group had broken for lunch, and almost everyone returned at the same time to resume the deposition. This resulted in a line of six or more returning participants in front of a latched half-door behind which sat a White secretary/doorkeeper, who gave the group permission to admit themselves. One by one the returnees filed in and proceeded to the deposition room. Hayes happened to be last in line. When he reached the doorway, the secretary/doorkeeper jumped up, slammed the half-door shut, and demanded to know who he was and what he wanted. Hayes told her that he was also with the returning deposition group. She motioned him in but not before first seeking and obtaining a confirmatory nod from one of the others that Hayes was indeed with the group.

FELTON JAMES EARLS

Felton James Earls was born in January 1942 in New Orleans and graduated from the Howard University School of Medicine in Washington, DC. A professor of social medicine at Harvard Medical School and professor of human behavior and development at the Harvard School of Public Health, Earls is noted for his pioneering research on violent crime reduction in urban neighborhoods, the causes and pathways of juvenile delinquency, the consequences of children's exposure to community and family violence, and the psychological impacts of the HIV/AIDS pandemic on children in sub-Saharan Africa.

The experiences that have had the most impact on Earls and therefore are the most memorable are instances when he has been misidentified as kitchen help or a taxi driver/messenger. Being mistaken for the kitchen help happened just outside his office at the

Children's Hospital a few decades ago. Earls was not wearing a uniform, as the janitorial or kitchen staff do, but in fact was dressed in casual attire, looking terribly academic, he recalls. A middle-aged White man, probably an academic himself and certainly dressed no better than Earls, signaled to him indicating that he had noticed a problem in the kitchen and had taken care of it himself. But as the responsible or irresponsible agent in this case, his attitude was one of paternalistically telling Earls that he had not performed up to the manager's standards. All Earls remembers is turning to him, bluntly saying that he had used good judgment in taking care of the problem, and walking away.

CHRIS HANDY

Chris Handy grew up in the eastern panhandle of West Virginia and is a graduate of Harvard Law School. Handy now runs a consulting firm that helps companies enhance their business initiatives by leveraging sports properties.

Handy does not wish to add to the list of stories about being mistaken for a store employee when he shops during lunch; for a delivery man when visiting a friend at an Upper East Side condo building; for a server at a black-tie function; or for an athlete everywhere. His narrative describes a scarring experience in corporate America. As a third-year student at Harvard Law School, Handy excitedly traveled to New York City for his circuit of "Interview Week." He had interviews scheduled with seven firms over the course of four days, so he departed for New York with a grid that reminded him of where to be when and with whom to meet. Garbed in a dark suit, power tie, and overcoat and carrying his leather briefcase, Handy entered the lobby of one prestigious firm. Unfortunately, he had not written down the last name of the HR recruiter with whom he was supposed to start the day. So he said to the receptionist, "I'm here for my 10:30 interview with Melissa." The receptionist looked up and down a clipboard with a confused expression and then asked Handy, "Are you sure it's today?" A chill ran through his body: Was he at the right place but using the wrong contact name? With false courage, he assured the receptionist that the interview was that morning. She asked Handy to take a seat in the lobby. While he sat there with nerves on edge, he watched her make several phone calls and could read her lips as she said his name into her headset. Handy sat there another 10 minutes or so while someone came to her desk, and they rifled through papers and folders. After about 20 minutes, the receptionist called Handy and told him that Melissa would be right out to meet him. She said that the confusion arose because the firm's recruiter for attorneys and the firm's personnel manager for "staff" (e.g., maintenance, mailroom, and executive assistants) were both named "Melissa." She failed to say exactly why, during law school Interview Week, her immediate and continued assumption was that a tall man dressed in a business suit and wingtips and carrying a leather briefcase could only be there to interview with the staff recruiter. Stuck between indignity and fear of corporate banishment, Handy reluctantly decided to carry on with the morning round of interviews instead of walking out. His only sense of redemption—and it was admittedly inadequate on all levels—was that he knew that the firm was going to have to buy him lunch. Handy ordered the most expensive items he could and left the office. The rejection letter didn't beat him home, but it was signed by the right "Melissa."

BRUCE A. HUBBARD

Bruce A. Hubbard was born in Chattanooga, Tennessee. Hubbard is a graduate of Rutgers University in New Jersey and Harvard Law School. After working at Davis, Polk & Wardwell for a few years, he launched his own practice, Bruce A. Hubbard, P.C., and has practiced in New York City as a single practitioner in corporate, litigation, and general practice for the last 25 years.

Hubbard recalls working at the Boston law firm of Hale & Dorr, where a number of the people—including lawyers, clients, and staff—often confused him with the mailroom staff, couriers, and doormen. Hubbard also reports the persistent problem, later in his career, of going out to the streets, dressed in the finest suits, and having trouble getting a cab. Frustrated, Hubbard reports that he was moved to write an op-ed piece in the *Times* about his 1977 experience. Hubbard reports that, even recently, after more than three decades of law practice, he has had people give him their car keys in parking lots; ask him about merchandise in stores, assuming that he is a salesperson; and even, while wearing a suit, have people assume that he is a subway staff member and ask him for train directions. At home, he reports that, on occasion, people have asked him if he is a servant or employee as opposed to the owner.

PRINCE CHAMBLISS

Prince Chambliss is a native of Birmingham, Alabama and a graduate of Harvard Law School. He is a partner in one of the largest law firms in Memphis, Tennessee.

Chambliss reports being at home cutting his grass and being approached by neighbors driving by, stopping to ask his price for lawn work. He replies to those who raise this question by saying: "The lady who lives here lets me sleep with her." The neighbors drive off, confused and appearing embarrassed. At his law firm, Chambliss always wears a tie, as he feels that he's treated better when he does so; and it stops the persistent problem he has experienced of being identified as the copy boy, mail boy, or delivery man at his law firm.

FLETCHER WILEY

Fletcher Wiley is a native of Indianapolis, Indiana, and a graduate of the Air Force Academy and Harvard Law School. He is a successful entrepreneur in Boston.

Wiley reports witnessing segregation in Indiana as he grew up. As a result, like many African Americans, he developed a self-preservation routine to ensure that he wasn't harmed physically or psychologically by the newly evolving integrated American society. Although in retrospect there has been some criticism of following the routine, Wiley feels that it allowed African Americans to pick their battles and to expend their human and economic resources more strategically. As a result, Wiley reports that when he has been mistakenly identified as a bellhop, valet attendant, or a server in a restaurant, he laughs at it and moves on.

AMOS JONES

Amos Jones was born in Lexington, Kentucky, and graduated from Emory University in Atlanta, Georgia, Columbia University's Graduate School of Journalism in New York City, and Harvard Law School in Cambridge, Massachusetts. Since 2007, Jones has practiced international trade law with the firm Bryan Cave LLP in Washington, DC.

In 2002, Jones walked to the Avery Fisher Hall in New York City on a cold evening for a specific purpose: he had to hear Beethoven's Violin Concerto. For most of the 1960s, his father was a music teacher in the Cincinnati public schools. Jones had also played the viola relatively seriously since the age of nine, taking private lessons and serving as principal viola for two seasons in the Atlanta-Emory Orchestra and performing as a staff violist during the 2000–2001 season for the Charlotte Philharmonic Orchestra in North Carolina. So the symphony orchestra was a natural outlet for his interests. When he heard that the New York Philharmonic was performing Beethoven's Violin Concerto in D Major (Op. 61), he grabbed three nearby friends, who happened to be White, and they headed for Lincoln Center on the student rush tickets he'd bought earlier that day. Jones wore a black suit. When his group stepped into Avery Fisher Hall's orchestra level, he paused just inside the door and surveyed the auditorium to find their section. Jones was holding his program. A White couple entered behind him several seconds later, and the man reached out and requested Jones' program. Without a second thought, Jones handed it to him. And then, as he turned to walk away, Jones realized that the man had assumed he was the usher. Maybe it was the black suit, or his age. In any case, Jones said with a smile, "Pardon me; I'm not an usher." The man turned red and profusely apologized. Jones was not particularly offended—he felt that Blacks were grossly underrepresented in audiences at the Philharmonic and were found in menial positions everywhere in New York City, America, and the world. For Jones, to Whites with limited racial experiences, Black skin remains an indicia of servitude.

WALTER C. CARRINGTON

Walter C. Carrington is a native of New York City and is a graduate of both Harvard College and Harvard Law School. He has served as ambassador to Senegal and to Nigeria.

Carrington reports that doormen and taxi drivers, not policemen, were the bane of his existence when he lived in Washington and New York. In Manhattan, he frequently experienced discrimination when, though well dressed, he would tell his usually immigrant taxi driver that his destination was Harlem, and an argument would ensue. Also, in up-scale apartment buildings, it was often necessary for White hosts to alert the doorman that they were expecting a Black guest in order to avoid an embarrassing incident. In the late 1970s, when Carrington was acting president of the African American Institute, he was invited by David Rockefeller to attend a dinner he was hosting in honor of a visiting African president. It was being held at the Rockefeller Estate located 25 miles from Carrington's office in Midtown Manhattan. When Carrington drove up to the gated entrance, he was waved through without incident as his name was on the guest list. But the estate was a huge, sprawling, six-square-mile property with many mansions belonging to various family members. After losing his way a few times, Carrington finally spotted a fleet of parked limousines and cars. He asked a White man, who seemed to be in charge of the lot, where the dinner was being held. Assuming that Carrington was somebody's chauffer, the man directed him to the small garage-like building where the "other" drivers were gathered. Deeply embarrassed when Carrington explained that he was one of Mr. Rockefeller's guests, the man personally escorted Carrington to the mansion.

JAMES BRANNON

James Brannon was born in Texarkana, Texas, graduated from North Carolina A and T
State University, and worked for the Liberty Group as an executive in the New England
Division offices.

Brannon, a successful African American entrepreneur in Massachusetts, was attending a formal event at the Westin Hotel in Boston.
Since the parking lot was full, he proceeded to the hotel next door,
the Copley Fairmont, to seek valet parking. After the Westin event
was over, Brannon went to get his car at the Copley Fairmont. While
waiting for it, a White woman ran up to him and asked if he had seen
a woman running through the hotel with a bag. Surprised, he answered no, then asked why she had asked him. Without any hesitation,
she said, "Aren't you the doorman?" Brannon responded by asking,
"How often do you see the doorman wearing a tuxedo?" She apologized for the error.

JAMES LOWRY

James Lowry is a visionary management consultant and entrepreneur who was born
in Chicago and now works there.

Lowry reports an incident that occurred in June 2009, while he was
living in an upscale penthouse on the Chicago Gold Coast that has a
private garage. One Sunday he left the condo to get his 460 Lexus in
order to pick up his wife for church. He noticed a White man standing near the doorman with his bags. The man appeared irritated, but
Lowry did not think much about it. As he pulled up his Lexus in front
of them and waited for his wife, the back door of his car opened—the

doorman put some luggage and other items in the backseat, and the man said angrily, "Dammit, you are late; you are going to make me miss my plane." Needless to say, Lowry told him that he was not his chauffeur and that this was not a car service.

WILLIE J. EPPS, JR.

Willie J. Epps, Jr., was raised in North St. Louis County, Missouri. His parents, who are products of rural and poor Mississippi, were the first generation in their respective families to attend college; they earned PhDs in education. They instilled in Epps the belief that faith, education, and hard work are the keys to success. Consequently, they sent him to some very fine schools at enormous financial sacrifice. Epps graduated from St. Louis Country Day School, Amherst College, and Harvard Law School. Currently, Epps is a partner at a national law firm based in Kansas City, Missouri.

A racial incident that stands out for Epps occurred in St. Louis in 2005. At the time, he was serving as vice president and chief compliance officer at a Fortune 500 company and was at Lambert–St. Louis International Airport attempting to catch a flight back home. Epps was dressed in a dark blue suit and white shirt and was waiting in line with his briefcase to board a Southwest Airlines plane. He was also talking on his cell phone to a dear friend from law school. A White man approached him with his children and wife in tow and asked if the flight to Los Angeles was leaving from Gate E14. Asking his friend on the phone to hold on for a moment, Epps told the man that he was unsure which gate he and his family needed. The man then looked Epps up and down and asked, "You don't work for Southwest Airlines, do you?" Epps replied, "No, sir. I do not." He then stated, "Well, you look good enough to work for Southwest Airlines. With the way you're dressed, you would fit right in!" At that moment, Epps could not help but notice that all the Southwest employees that day were wearing their blue and orange Southwest polo shirts with khaki shorts or slacks.

STEVEN H. WRIGHT

Wright is a native of Buffalo, New York, and attended Boston College Law School. He worked in New York for former mayor David Dinkins, and is currently an executive part-ner at the Boston branch of the national law firm Holland & Knight.

Wright reports that in November 2008, the day after Barack Obama's election, he was wearing a white shirt, blue tailored suit, and a red cor-porate tie, basking in the election glow and waiting for the elevator in the garage (B3 level) of a sports club in Los Angeles, California. He was heading up to the sports club at the lobby level. A White woman (he believed to be an architect or a contractor for the hotel) came into the area with three men. As they all entered the elevator, she held the door and proceeded to talk to the three men about renovating the lobby while Wright waited patiently for her to finish. She continued to hold the elevator door open in this time-consuming fashion for floors B2 and B1 as well, exhibiting no concern or courtesy for Wright's time as they headed to the lobby. When Wright interrupted her and requested that she not delay the elevator, she stated that she thought he was a worker in the garage. Wright admits that he lost a bit of his mind—he told her that she was offensive, presumptive, inappropriate, and biased. He asked her whether his clothing looked like that of a garage worker, when he in fact managed a law firm. He also reminded her that the country had just elected an African American president and that it was people like her who would have to make the biggest adjustment. She was by then contrite. Fuming, Wright nevertheless realized that even with Barack Obama in office, it would still be an uphill struggle for a hard-working professional African American to get a taxi or not be considered part of the working crew at the Ritz.

ANTOINE DEVINE

Devine was born in Milwaukee, Wisconsin. He graduated from Jackson State University and the University of Texas Law School. Devine is a former law firm partner, senior VP of a mutual fund company, and outside general counsel for a major airport, among other things. He is also currently an author and adjunct professor of law.

Devine always dresses well when he is out, partially because he likes to do so, but also so he appears nonthreatening. Devine can't even recall how many times he has been asked for directions to the restroom in department stores, asked if a pair of shoes was in stock at a particular store, and even asked to help someone try shoes on. He was once handed keys while waiting for his BMW M5 at a San Francisco restaurant. On another occasion, while standing near a maitre d' station, he was asked if he could check to see if someone's table was ready. And on numerous occasions while walking around the financial district in San Francisco, White women, on seeing him approach (despite wearing a suit or sport coat), have moved to the other side of the sidewalk and performed the "purse grab." All these experiences occurred in San Francisco, the so-called cradle of equality. There are so few African American professionals working or living there that he has stood out like a sore thumb at every upscale venue, art gallery, theater, et cetera in the city, and rarely felt welcome.

NATHANIEL R. JONES

Judge Nathaniel R. Jones was born on May 12, 1926. He was married to the late Lillian Graham Jones for fifty years, and he is the proud father of five children. He has served as a lawyer, jurist, academic, and public servant. Judge Jones was born in Youngstown, Ohio, several blocks from a federal courthouse that now bears his name. Judge Jones pursued his education at Youngstown State University, receiving his AB in 1951 and his LLB in 1956. During his legal career, Judge Jones directed all of the NAACP's litigation as its general counsel. He also argued cases before the state and federal courts as well as several cases before the United States Supreme Court. On May 17, 1979, President Jimmy Carter nominated him to the United State Court of Appeals for the Sixth Circuit, and he began his service that fall. Judge Jones retired from the Sixth Circuit in 2002 after 23 years of service. He is now senior counsel in the office of the law firm of Blank Rome LLP, in Cincinnati.

When the Junior Chamber of Commerce, known as the JAYCEES, began integrating and he was asked to join, Nathaniel R. Jones accepted the invitation to become the first Black member of his hometown chapter, hoping to be accepted into the mainstream of his city's civic life. Each Christmas season, the group had an annual formal black-tie ball. Determined to be a participating member, Jones attended his first event at a local country club. During the intermission, he stood at the urinal flanked by other White guests, all of them decked out in tuxedos. They silently stared at the wall as they answered nature's call. Then, one of the men suddenly broke the silence with the comment, "Say, Fella, your boys play great music." Jones said nothing. As they broke ranks, he asked, "Is your band local?" Jones merely said, "I'm not a member of the band" as he finished washing his hands and left the man standing aghast as he exited the men's room. Jones' reaction? It must have been the black bow tie. Band members also wore black bow ties. They were also Black.

Over the years, as Jones attended countless numbers of black-tie events, variations of the same condescending comments were uttered. Two of the most recent occurrences also bear mentioning. For entry into its Hall of Fame, one of the most prestigious journals of the legal profession, *The American Lawyer*, selects outstanding members of the Bar to receive its Lifetime Achievement Award. On October 24, 2007, Jones was chosen, along with seven distinguished lawyers, to receive that award. They included, among others, such legal luminaries as former United States Secretary of State James Baker III, and former Ninth Circuit Court of Appeals and the first United States Secretary of Education Shirley Hufstedler. The assembled crowd gave each of these recipients, including Jones, standing ovations as their respective achievements were recited. It was, indeed, a crowning event for each of the recipients to be so honored by their peers.

When the evening concluded, Jones departed from Cipriani's surrounded by his proud family and associates from his law firm, Blank Rome. As he stepped out onto New York City's 42nd Street, he met with an affront that he is certain none of the White award recipients ever encountered. He was approached by a White man who breathlessly pierced the circle of well-wishers surrounding him with a request, "Captain, I need a cab to the Upper West Side." Jones merely said, "You'd better find someone who works here." His family and associates were shocked—a reaction that turned to anger. His response to them was that it happens all of the time. Again, it must have been the black bow tie thing. Or was it?

A few weeks later, in his hometown of Cincinnati, Ohio, Jones attended the Opera Ball with his wife, Lillian, who served on the board of the Cincinnati Opera Association. At one point during the evening, Jones left their table in the beautifully festooned ballroom to visit friends at another table when a guest, from his seated position, signaled to him. He did not recognize him, but given the fact that in his hometown many persons know him by virtue of his being a federal judge, Jones went over to him. As he leaned down to hear what the man had to say, he was met with this request: "I need another red wine." Jones gazed at him for what seemed to him to be an eternity. Suddenly, a female guest at the table recognized him and, observing his frozen stare, jumped to her feet, broke in with a loud "Good evening, Judge Jones. Do you all know Judge Jones? He is . . ." It was then apparent that a monumental goof had taken place. Jones merely moved on. It was that black bow tie thing again. Or was it?

One reason he rejects the black bow tie idea is that there have been occasions when he was not so attired but yet was summoned to provide service. One he often shares, which is typical of the many, occurred in a hotel lobby in New Orleans after he had just finished speaking to several hundred persons at a breakfast meeting on affirmative action. While he was waiting for an elevator to return him to his room to pick up his luggage, a White man rushed over to him and got in his face as he pushed a ticket into his hand yelling, "I'm late, get my car." Backing off, Jones said, "You're talking to the wrong person." A light bulb appeared to go off in the man's head as his eyes bucked. He said, "Oh, my God, Mister. I am so sorry." Jones continued to move over toward another elevator bank, trailed by him. He brushed him off with, "Don't worry about it."

JOHN HOPE FRANKLIN

John Hope Franklin is a graduate of Fisk University and Harvard University. He has served as a professor of history at Brooklyn College, Howard University, the University of Chicago, and Duke University. He received the Presidential Medal of Freedom, and his seminal book *From Slavery to Freedom* is in its ninth edition.

John Hope Franklin could not have been more pleased. He and his friend Judge A. Leon Higginbotham, Jr. were having dinner with others at the Cosmo Club following the decision by President William Clinton to bestow the Presidential Medal of Freedom to both Franklin and Higginbotham. Franklin was happy to go to the Cosmo Club because he had served as its first African American president. As they were preparing for dinner, he recalls being approached by a White woman who gave him a ticket to get her coat. Franklin, dressed in a tuxedo, was a little bemused by being identified as the valet to check coats when he was in fact one of the nation's greatest historians. He politely told the woman that he was not checking coats, but having dinner at the Cosmo Club. It was ironic in that if the woman had looked closely, she would have noticed a photo on the wall of Franklin serving as the club's president. John Hope Franklin would not only go on to recount this story to many of his friends, he would also include it in his memoir entitled *Mirror to America*.

THOMAS A. FARRINGTON

Thomas A. Farrington is an entrepreneur and business executive with more than 30 years of experience in the information technology industry. He received his BS degree in electrical engineering from North Carolina A&T State University and attended the Northeastern University Graduate School of Engineering. Farrington was diagnosed

with prostate cancer in 2000. In 2001 he released his book *Battling the Killer Within.*
In 2003 Mr. Farrington founded the Prostate Health Education Network, a Boston-
based nonprofit organization which focuses on the urgent and unmet prostate education and awareness needs of African American men. In 2005, Mr. Farrington released
his second book, *Battling the Killer Within and Winning.*

Thomas A. Farrington was on his way to an event at the Marriott and
had parked his car after dropping off his wife at the main entrance. Farrington was dressed in a tux and thought he was looking rather dapper.
As he was walking to the elevator, he was shocked when a White
woman stopped and asked him where to park. He was also disappointed
because he obviously wasn't looking as dapper as he had thought. Farrington's first instinct was to respond with a few choice curse words, but
he thought he could do more harm if he played along. He told the lady
to leave her car where it was with the keys in it and he would take care
of it. After she left, Farrington left the car sitting there running.

UNWARRANTED POLICE AGGRAVATION

REVEREND CALVIN BUTTS III

Reverend Calvin Butts III was born in New York City, and attended local schools there.
He received his BA degree from Morehouse College and later was awarded his master of divinity degree in church history from Union Theological Seminary and his PhD
in ministry from Drew University in Madison, New Jersey.

On October 14, 2006, Rev. Butts was on his way home, and stopped
with his wife to pick up some take-out food from a favorite restaurant

in Harlem. He acknowledges double-parking, a routine custom in Harlem, as he went in to pick up the order. When he returned to his car, a White New York police officer had stopped. Rev.Butts immediately apologized and explained that he had just stepped in to pick up his order. As he was about to drive away, the officer walked up and gave him a ticket for $115. Rev. Butts asked the officer why he was writing a ticket after the fact, when he was moving his car before the officer had even begun writing the ticket. The officer then told Butts that the ticket was written because of Butts' "Attitude." This comment surprised Butts, and it created a level of frustration in light of what had just transpired. Butts was later contacted by New York City Mayor Michael Bloomberg and police Commissioner Raymond Kelly, who both apologized, but the officer never said a word about issuing the ticket for "Attitude."

EDDIE JENKINS

Eddie Jenkins was born in Jacksonville, Florida. He attended The College of the Holy Cross and the Suffolk University School of Law. He was a member of the 1972 unde-feated Miami Dolphins football team. He served as an assistant district attorney in Massachusetts and has been a lawyer in private practice.

In the late 1990s, when Jenkins was an assistant district attorney in Massachusetts, he was vacationing on Nantucket Island and drove to the airport to pick up his girlfriend. Her flight was initially delayed and eventually canceled. When Jenkins returned to his car to go home, he saw that the police had set up a sobriety test point nearby. As he entered his car, the police asked for his driver's license and registration. Jenkins provided it and also showed the officers his ADA badge. He had not been drinking, so they let him go. But as he left the airport and returned to his summer home, the police followed him with their bright lights on. They never stopped him, and once he arrived at his home they just drove on and never said another word to him. He was annoyed at being followed after producing his identification but decided to just focus on enjoying what remained of his summer vacation.

JUDGE ARTHUR L. **BURNETT**, **SR.**

Arthur L. Burnett, Sr., was born in Spotsylvania County, Virginia. Burnett is a graduate of New York University Law School and former judge of the Superior Court of the District of Columbia. He is the national executive director of the National African American Drug Policy Coalition.

In July 1952, at the age of 17, Burnett was almost shot by two White officers. He was waiting on the back steps of a Howard Johnson Restaurant after closing time in Fredericksburg, Virginia, when some police officers drove up, jumped out of their cars, and assumed the squat position with guns drawn. When Burnett told them that he worked there, one of the officers said sarcastically: "I bet you do." As Burnett started explaining again, his father arrived to pick him up. The officers then put Burnett in the back of the police car and took him to the home of Mr. Overton, the restaurant owner, with Burnett's father trailing behind in his car. Mr. Overton explained that Burnett was his best employee and had been left at the restaurant to finish cleaning up and to lock up. They then permitted Burnett to leave with his father. Burnett says that he will never forget that experience. He frequently tells young Black boys that had he been profane and started cursing or become disorderly that night, he could have been killed.

PAUL **BUTLER**

Paul Butler was born and raised in Chicago, Illinois. Butler graduated from Yale College and Harvard Law School. He is a former federal prosecutor who is now a chaired professor and the faculty development dean at George Washington University Law School in Washington, DC. His book *Let's Get Free: A Hip-Hop Theory of Justice* relates his experiences on both sides of the law, as a prosecutor and as a victim of racial profiling.

Butler lives in the upper-income, racially integrated area of DC known as the Gold Coast. One evening as he walked near his home, he was stopped by the police and questioned about where he lived. After protesting the interrogation—one does not have to reside in a neighborhood to walk on public streets—he reluctantly showed the police his home. His word, alas, was not good enough; the police requested proof that he lived there. Butler refused to display such proof. The police asked him to go inside the house to demonstrate that it was his, but again he refused. As Butler recalls, there were now five police officers who said they would not leave until Butler entered his house. As they sat on his porch, Butler asked the officers, who were all Black, if they had ever been racially profiled. Each cop said yes but said that it didn't bother them because they knew they hadn't done anything wrong. After an hour of debating both racial profiling in general and specifically why the cops refused to leave Butler's porch, one officer decided to interview Butler's neighbor, who confirmed that Butler lived there. The police then left.

STEVEN **ROGERS**

Steven Rogers is a native of Chicago and a graduate of Williams College and the Harvard Business School. He teaches at Northwestern Graduate School of Business.

Rogers reports that in 1989 he purchased a lampshade manufacturing company in Chicago called Fenchel Lampshade Company and, one year later, purchased another lampshade company in Quincy, Illinois, 300 miles south of Chicago. Once a month he drove six hours from his home in Chicago to Quincy to visit his new company. He was returning home after one visit and was approximately 130 miles from Chicago when he was stopped for speeding by a policeman in a small rural town. It was 10 P.M. Rogers immediately turned the interior light on and put both hands on the top of the steering wheel as he waited for the policeman to approach the car. Rogers was dressed in a blue suit, white shirt, and blue tie. The policeman asked for Rogers' license, registration, and insurance card. Shortly afterward, the policeman informed Rogers that he had an unpaid traffic ticket on record from January 1986 and that he would therefore have to arrest him. Rogers was told that his good behavior entitled him to be handcuffed in the front, instead of the customary behind the back. By the time they arrived at the small police station, it was after 11 P.M. Rogers' efforts to pay the fines using his credit card were denied with the comment, "We cannot accept cards." He asked if he could get a cab to the nearest ATM but was told the town did not have any taxis. Rogers' request to be driven by a policeman into town was also held to be not permissible. His only alternative was to walk several miles into town, but he did not think this was safe. So he called his wife and asked her to come get him in the morning. On informing the policemen that he would wait in the lobby for his wife, he was told that they could not allow him to sleep there, but they could let him sleep in a jail cell. Rogers felt that he had no other option. The policemen then strip-searched him, gave him prison clothes, and locked him in a cell with another prisoner. Rogers' wife and brother arrived at 7 A.M., paid the fines, and he was released. While getting dressed, Rogers asked the policeman about the prisoner in his cell and said that he seemed like a good guy who probably did something stupid. The policeman said, "Yes, he did. He sexually molested three children below the age of 10!" Shocked, Rogers asked, "Why in hell would you put me in the jail cell with a pedophile?" The response was: "You are obviously a businessman with no criminal record, and you behaved so nicely throughout your entire time with us that we thought you would not hurt him!" Rogers continued dressing and left.

CHUCK WALKER

Chuck Walker was born in Anchorage, Alaska and raised in Camarillo, California. Walker is currently deputy director and general counsel for Massachusetts' Division of Professional Licensure under the Department of Consumer Affairs in the Deval Patrick administration. He went to the University of California, Santa Barbara, for his undergraduate degree in political science and then to Boston College Law School for his JD degree.

By December 1986, Walker was in his eighth year as a lawyer and working as general counsel to a cabinet secretary in Massachusetts. He and his wife had just purchased their first home in Sharon, Massachusetts. Eight months before this incident, they became the happy parents of the first of two girls. In mid-December, a major snowstorm hit Sharon. To make matters worse, Walker had to work late and caught the 11:59 P.M. train out of Boston's South Station, which was scheduled to arrive in Sharon at 12:30 A.M. Just before boarding the train, Walker used a phone in the station to call a cab company, only to be told that the last pickup was at midnight. Walker boarded the train, knowing that a 30- to 40-minute walk home in the freezing weather awaited him. The train arrived in Sharon and Walker, wearing his topcoat, suit, and leather boots and carrying his leather briefcase, prepared to trudge home. After walking for about 15 minutes, a Sharon police car coming from the opposite direction passed him, made a U-turn, and then with its lights flashing slowly pulled over in front of him. "Finally," Walker thought, "God has sent a police car to rescue me from this miserable walk." As he began to thank the officer for stopping, he was told to step away from the car window and show his driver's license. Walker incredulously looked at the officer and decided to test his sense of humor: "What's wrong, Officer, was I speeding?" This time the officer told Walker to step behind the rear of the vehicle as he ran a check on his license. Walker was dumbfounded but cooperated in the hope that this abuse would result in his getting a ride home. The five minutes Walker stood in the cold seemed like an eternity. The officer eventually got out of the car and returned his license. Walker told him that he lived a short ride away, that his wife was home with their newborn, and that he was walking home because he had missed the last cab. As the officer walked to enter his vehicle, Walker blurted out, "Officer, may I get a ride home?" The officer responded, "This is not a cab," started his engine, and drove away. Disappointed and angry, Walker continued his walk home in the snow.

DERRICK BELL

Derrick Bell was born in the Hill District of Pittsburgh and received an AB from Duquesne University in 1952 and an LLB from the University of Pittsburgh School of Law in 1957. He was the first African American hired at Harvard Law School and is a prolific scholar.

Professor Bell reports that, on one early Sunday evening five or six years ago, he and his wife, Janet, had just driven back to New York City from a weekend at their country house near Woodstock, New York. It was still light as they drove up to their apartment building on Central Park West. With little traffic around, they double-parked their Audi sedan and, with emergency lights flashing, opened the trunk to unload their bags—a procedure Bell reports is pretty much accepted practice for their building and neighborhood. Immediately, a police car drove up. One of the two White officers in the car without provocation angrily yelled at Bell and Janet to move or get a ticket. Bell politely explained that they had just stopped for a moment to unload their bags before taking the car to a parking garage a few blocks away. The officer ignored his explanation and repeated in an unmistakably confrontational tone, "Move right now." As Bell started to walk toward the officers to argue his case, Janet and the doorman started yelling at him to get back in the car. Both Janet and the doorman, a Latino, instantly understood the possible danger posed by an angry White cop with a gun challenging an African American or Latino male. The doorman pointedly called Bell "Professor Bell" to emphasize to the officer that he was not a vagrant. By that time, a second police car had driven up, and the officer in that car opened his window and asked, "Are you having any trouble?" Although angered by the attitude of the police, Bell decided just to move his car and end the dispute. As he got back in his car and drove around the corner Bell recalled another incident that caused distress. In the early 1960s, when he was a civil rights attorney, he traveled frequently in the Deep South. Bell was flying to Jackson, Mississippi, for a case, but a severe winter storm caused the flight to terminate at Memphis, Tennessee. Passengers to Jackson completed the trip on a crowded train that was very slow and very cold. On arrival, exhausted and shaking with cold, Bell looked for a phone booth to call the local civil rights attorney, Jack Young, to come and pick him up. Bell had not noticed that the phone was in the White waiting room, and as he started to dial, two White policemen ordered him out of the phone booth. They pulled him out, arrested him, and, after a search, placed him in their police car and drove to the police station, where he was fingerprinted, photographed, had his belongings taken, and was placed in a holding cell with several other Black men. Thankfully, Bell was able to call Jack Young, who arrived the next morning and obtained his release. Some days later, a trial judge lectured Bell on the need to abide by Mississippi law and remanded his case to the files. The judge's comments, however, paled in comparison to the lecture Bell received from his then boss, Thurgood Marshall, who made it clear that to achieve what he had sent Bell south to do, at times he needed to carefully fold up his civil rights and put them in a back pocket.

VANCE FORT

Vance Fort was born in Marshall, Texas, and raised in San Francisco. Fort graduated from the University of Pennsylvania Law School. He also served in the Air Force.

Fort recalls an incident after he had joined the United States Air Force and was stationed in Biloxi, Mississippi, for most of the first year. In early 1962, there was an organized effort among the local Black population to desegregate the white-sand beaches of the Gulf Coast. Tensions were high, the police clubbed demonstrators, and many were arrested. One night during this time, Fort, driving a friend's car, was headed for the base when he was pulled over by the police for speeding. The officer approached the car with a shotgun, placed it at Fort's temple, and lectured him about the vileness and villainy of "niggers." The officer then threatened to make the world a better place by blowing his nigger brains out. Fort obviously survived the incident, but he did not continue to his destination for some time after the officer left. The remainder of Fort's four years of military service was dotted by other examples of racial discrimination and confrontation. Fights between Black and White airmen were common, and usually involved the "n" word or other blatant acts of disrespect or discrimination. Fort had his only fistfight during his third year, with a White airman from Texas. The guy did not believe that Negroes and Whites should be stationed together—for him racial integration was inconceivable. Fort was on the amateur boxing team, and he knocked the guy out cold. Both lost a stripe that day.

UNWARRANTED RACE ASSUMPTIONS IN ACADEMIC AND PROFESSIONAL SETTINGS

DR. WALTER LOMAX

Dr. Walter Lomax was born in Philadelphia, Pennsylvania. He has been a medical practitioner in a Philadelphia neighborhood for more than three decades. His practice grew from a private single-physician office to a multi-site group practice consisting of over 20 well-trained physicians.

Lomax recalls one of the many incidents of racist behavior he has encountered. Shortly after he opened his medical office in 1958, he put his name on the list of the Philadelphia County Medical Society (the local branch of the American Medical Association) to make emergency house calls. One night he responded to a request for a house call at 3 A.M. With his black medical bag in hand, he rang the bell. When the White lady who answered the door saw that Lomax was Black, she slammed the door in his face.

WOODROW MYERS, JR.

Woodrow Myers, Jr., was born in Indianapolis, Indiana. Myers has been the director of Genomic Health since April 2006. He holds an AB degree and a business degree from Stanford, and a medical degree from Harvard University.

As a 20-year-old, first-year medical student at Harvard Medical School, Myers couldn't wait to become a part of the action. Instead of spending Friday and Saturday nights studying or partying, he would put on his white uniform and hang out in the emergency room at Massachusetts General Hospital. The trauma cases always tended to pick up after the bars closed, and since in those days age restrictions were rarely enforced, inebriated adolescents were not uncommon. On one of Myers' shifts, a 14-year-old boy had received a long scalp laceration in a fight. Much to Myers' delight, the surgery resident assigned the case to him. The minor trauma room was a large, open space with a dozen or more patients in close proximity. Myers' patient was mostly asleep during the procedure, but when Myers was about halfway through, the kid woke up and screamed, "Nigger, you just betta get away from me."

Myers was the only African American in the room, so everyone stopped in their tracks and time just froze. All eyes were on him to see what would happen next. The hardened 20-year-old from the north-east side of Indianapolis knew that a strong, physical response was re-quired. He knew that showing weakness invited a continuing tirade or maybe even a 14-year-old fist. The young Stanford graduate and cur-rent Harvard medical student quickly surmised that flattening an al-ready inebriated 14-year-old patient would not be an understandable response. So in a voice not quite as loud as the patient's, Myers told him, "If I put down this suture and stop before I'm done sewing you up, I will call your old man again and tell him he needs to get dressed and come down to the hospital and sign you out, and I don't think that's all he'll do with his right hand when he sees you." It was now the patient's turn, and he chose not to reply. Drunk or not, he knew that he was going to be in enough trouble when he got home and that Myers could make it worse. So after what seemed like an eternity, but actually was only a few seconds, the standoff was over. Myers contin-ued to treat the patient, and everyone in the room took a breath and went back to what they were doing. Myers had never spoken to the patient's father, but the teen did not know that.

DR. ERIC PHILLIPS

Dr. Eric Phillips was born in Chicago, Illinois. Phillips is a graduate of Stanford Uni-versity and Meharry School of Medicine. He is employed as a doctor conducting re-search in the area of pharmaceuticals.

Phillips recalls an experience in 1978 when he was assigned to treat patients in a hospital in Nashville, Tennessee. An elderly White pa-tient refused to allow Dr. Phillips to examine him. Even after the nurs-ing staff and fellow physicians confirmed Phillips' status as the physician assigned to assist the patient, he was still unwilling to be treated by Dr. Phillips. Although the hospital was firm in its support for Phillips' assignment to this patient, in the end the patient nevertheless continued to refused treatment from Dr. Phillips.

KEVIN CHAVOUS

Kevin Chavous was born and raised in Indianapolis, Indiana, graduating from Wabash College in Crawfordsville and Howard University School of Law in Washington, DC. He is a national leader in the education reform and parental school choice movement and is a partner at the law firm Sonnenschein Nath and Rosenthal in Washington, DC.

Chavous reports that in the early 1980s, he was a lawyer in a county courthouse in a suburb of Denver. He had appeared in this courthouse before, and on this day was there for a status hearing on a misdemeanor criminal case. All the criminal hearings that day were being heard by the same judge in the same courtroom. The veteran courtroom clerk was a middle-aged White woman who had been working in the same courtroom for many years. On busy days, such as that day, the courtroom clerk allowed the lawyers to sit in the jury box as they waited for their case to be called; the parties, witnesses, and other nonlawyers were supposed to sit in the main seating area. Chavous had been practicing in the Denver area for about a year and had come to know several of his criminal defense lawyer peers. When he entered the courtroom, he immediately went to the jury box and sat down next to a lawyer he knew, whereupon they began to chat. Of the approximately 20 lawyers in the room, Chavous was the only Black lawyer. As he began to talk with his friend, he noticed the White courtroom clerk eyeing him from across the room. Looking directly at Chavous, she slammed a file down on her desk, said "Excuse me" to the person she was assisting, stormed from around her desk, and walked quickly toward him. When she got to Chavous, she loudly said, "Sir, this seating area is for the lawyers! All defendants need to sit over there," and pointed to the general seating area. The courtroom fell silent as she glared at him. Chavous was unprepared for the hostility and so was momentarily speechless. Seizing the moment, his friend stepped in. He said, "Ma'am, this man is a lawyer." Not missing a beat, the clerk snorted, shrugged her shoulders, and said: "These days, one can't know for sure. The defendants dress as well as the lawyers!" With that, she turned and walked away. She never apologized to Chavous. He correctly guessed that she assumed he was not a lawyer, but he had no idea why she assumed he was a criminal defendant. What burned him even more was that his case was the last one called.

The second incident occurred while he was working as in-house counsel for Aetna Life and Casualty. By 1990, Chavous had achieved significant courtroom success for the company, winning several major civil trials. As a result, management wanted to make sure that newly hired lawyers went to court with him from time to time to second chair him at trials. While the lead counsel does most, if not all, of the arguments and witness interrogations, the second chair plays a supportive role, helping with witness logistics, legal arguments, and so on. Late that year, Chavous was the lead counsel for an important jury trial in the DC Superior Court and had a young White lawyer serving as his second. The young lawyer was very inexperienced—being less than a year out of law school, he had never tried a case, had never questioned a witness, and had only just started to conduct his own depositions. During the superior court trial he seconded with Chavous, he did not make any arguments, examine a witness, or speak directly to the court during the legal debates. The jury did not hear him utter one word. As fate would have it, Chavous tried a terrific case, one of his best ever. They won the case, and after the jury verdict Chavous and his young colleague spoke with several jurors. Six of the eight jurors were Black. Three of the Black jurors were excitedly singing Chavous' praises about the way he handled the case. As they all were leaving, one elderly Black juror grabbed Chavous' hand, walked him over to his young, inexperienced White colleague, and whispered to them almost conspiratorially. Pointing at Chavous but looking at the young White lawyer, she said, "He did such a good job for you. He really does deserve a raise or at least a good bonus. I can't tell you how to run your business, but he really did do a good job." She then smiled, squeezed Chavous' hand, and turned to walk away. Chavous' young colleague was totally flummoxed and red as a beet. Initially, he didn't know how to respond, but then he ran after the woman, yelling, "Ma'am, I work for him. He is my boss!" The woman just smiled and kept walking away.

DAVID **WILMOT**

David Wilmot is a native of Ancon, Panama Canal Zone, and a graduate of Georgetown Law Center in Washington, DC. He served for 20 years at Georgetown as the dean of admissions.

In the second year of Wilmot's tenure as the Georgetown Law Center's dean of admissions, he was visited in his office by a delegation of

university placement officers who were attending a recruitment conference hosted by the center. As the delegation was ushered into his
office, he was concluding a staff meeting. Before he could be formally
introduced to the group by his secretary, several members of the delegation proceeded to introduce themselves to one of his assistant directors of admissions (a White male), referring to him by Wilmot's name
while expressing their pleasure in making his acquaintance. Wilmot
immediately departed his office, leaving his young assistant director to
handle the situation. The delegation, embarrassed, apologized for their
mistaken assumption. Wilmot reports other similar incidents while
serving as a dean at Georgetown. He recalls a luncheon hosted by the
law center's Alumni Office at the Four Seasons Hotel in Washington,
where both he and Professor Sam Dash were introduced to the 400-
plus alumni in attendance. At the conclusion of the luncheon and as
Wilmot was trying to retrieve his car from the parking garage, an alumnus who had attended the luncheon approached Wilmot as he was
speaking to Professor Dash, handed Wilmot his ticket, and asked him
to get his car. Wilmot politely took his ticket, indicating to him that as
soon as he was through waiting on Professor Dash, he would retrieve
the car. Shortly thereafter, Wilmot's car arrived. Wilmot and Dash
began to leave when Dash asked him what he intended to do with the
ticket. Wilmot responded, "Keep it so as to inconvenience him in retrieving his car, and hopefully the next Black man he sees dressed up
in a suit will not be mistaken for a parking attendant."

DR. REGINALD MASON

Dr. Reginald Mason was born in Toledo, Ohio. Mason graduated from Stanford University in Palo Alto and the University of California–San Francisco Medical School before doing his residency at George Washington University in Washington, DC. He has worked as a lung specialist for 23 years.

While working at an upscale hospital in Atlanta, Dr. Mason reports being asked to consult on a patient. As he entered the room, wearing a white coat clearly marked "Reginald Mason, MD" and with a stethoscope, the patient directed him to the corner of the room where his used dinner tray was. After Mason politely informed him that he was not with the food-service staff, the patient uttered a quick apology and let Mason start the work of unraveling his complex illness.

JUDGE DAMON KEITH

Judge Damon Keith is a native of Detroit, Michigan, and a graduate of Howard Law School. He practiced law in Detroit before being appointed to the 6th Circuit Court of Appeals by President Jimmy Carter. He is currently a senior judge on that court. Keith was selected by former Chief Justice William Rehnquist to be the National Chairman of the Bicentennial to celebrate 200 years of the U.S. Constitution.

Keith says that there's not a day in his life that in some way, large or small, he's not reminded of the fact that he's Black. One incident occurred while he was attending a meeting at the College of William and Mary in Virginia in 2000. Most of the judges were staying at a beautiful hotel in Williamsburg. Judge Altamery (who sat on the second circuit) and Keith were walking out of the hotel to go to the event when a White man walked up to Keith and said, "Boy, will you park my car?" Judge Altamery, who is White, was infuriated when he heard this said to Keith. But Judge Keith wanted to avoid a confrontation and simply told the man that he didn't work at the hotel. Keith told all the judges about the experience that Judge Altamery and he had just witnessed. Some said he should have taken the keys, driven the car, and then thrown the keys away; others asked why he didn't take an ice pick and puncture the man's tires.

Another time, Keith had flown to Detroit on a 747 plane, and the captain that flew it was Black. Keith was getting off at the same time as the captain, and as the captain walked off in his uniform, some lady stopped him and said, "Boy, my bags are right over there. Will you get them?"

Keith says that these things happen every day, all the time—so how do you minimize or destroy this myth of their just seeing a Black face and making assumptions?

RONALD JESSAMY

Jessamy was born in New York City, and has a twin brother by the name of Howard. He graduated from George Washington University Law School, and served as senior partner in the Washington, DC, law firm of Jessamy, Fort, Ogletree, and Botts. He is now in a solo practice in DC.

In the early 1980s, Attorney Jessamy appeared in U.S. District Court for the District of Columbia one morning for a status hearing on a case in which he was counsel for an automobile accident defendant. The case was assigned to his firm by a large, reputable insurance company. He appeared in court on time, but his opposing counsel was late. In a telephone conversation in the judge's chambers, Jessamy overheard courtroom staff telling the judge that the attorney for the Plaintiff was not there yet. It appears the judge instructed staff to call chambers when the other counsel arrived. The instruction was carried out when opposing counsel entered the courtroom.

When the judge, who was White, took the bench, instead of exchanging the traditional pleasantries with counsel, he immediately turned to Jessamy and in a stern and loud voice asked him why he could not get to court on time. When Jessamy informed the judge that he had been there on time and that it was opposing counsel who had been delayed, the judge still did not apologize. Opposing counsel, who happened to be White, informed the judge that he was the one who was late. Nothing more was said about the lack of timeliness. Just because one of the attorneys was late, the judge automatically assumed it had to be the African American lawyer. Jessamy firmly felt that the judge should have consulted his courtroom staff and feels that the judge's jumping to conclusions was an example of racial stereotyping.

JUDGE LESLIE HARRIS

Judge Leslie Harris was born in Chicago and graduated from Northwestern University (BA in history) in Chicago, Boston University (MA in history), and Boston College (JD). After law school, Harris worked as a program director for the Museum of Afro American History in Boston, as a public defender for the Roxbury Defenders, and as an assistant district attorney in charge of the Juvenile Division for his boss, District Attorney Ralph Martin. Judge Harris now serves as a judge in the Juvenile Court for the Commonwealth of Massachusetts.

Harris has chosen to discuss his close encounter in the courts. Early in his career as a judge, he was asked to sit in one of the suburban courts. On his first day there, he tried to enter the court by the front door, as he had never been to the court and did not know where the judges' entrance was. As he approached the security desk, he identified himself and asked to be directed to the judges' lobby. Harris had his robe over his arm and was prepared to produce ID if needed. The security guard told him in no uncertain terms that he would have to go through the metal detector and be searched. He also added that he did not care who Harris was—he would have to go through with the general population. At about the same time, a Black court officer from Roxbury District Court entered in full uniform and was told he had to go through screening. Harris informed the security guard that he was a court officer who was there to train the court officers at this location. Again the guard stated that he did not care who he was; he had to go through the regular screening. Both Harris and the Black court officer told the guard that they would not go through the screening. Harris then told the guard to inform the court that he had been there but that since he was not allowed in, he was leaving. As Harris approached his car, a court officer ran up to him and asked if he was Judge Harris. Harris informed him that he was and told him why he was leaving. The man begged Harris to stay and said he would address the incident with his superiors. He escorted Harris to the judges' lobby and apologized for his treatment. The next day Harris entered through the same entrance he had used the previous day. The same security guard was on duty. He begged Harris' forgiveness and assured him he did not mean his behavior to be racist. Harris told him that he did not believe him, nor would he tolerate similar conduct toward the general public.

GENERAL RACE MATTERS

EARL GILBERT **GRAVES, SR.**

Earl Gilbert Graves, Sr., was born in Brooklyn, New York, and is a graduate of Morgan
State University in Baltimore. He is the founder of *Black Enterprise* magazine.

As a young boy, Graves went to swim at the Central YMCA in downtown Brooklyn. Once he was ordered to leave the pool after being told
that it was only for White children. Graves went home and told his
mother about the incident, who became angry and returned to the
YMCA and spoke to the manager. After apologizing for the "mistake," the manager allowed Graves to swim in the pool. Graves vividly
remembers the incident to this day and views it as one of the few un-
pleasant experiences he had growing up in Brooklyn.

Years later, as a multimillionaire entrepreneur due to his success in
launching *Black Enterprise* magazine, Graves and his wife planned to
move into a new home and sell their home in Armonk, New York,
which was in a mostly White neighborhood. After it remained on the
market for about a year, Graves was puzzled that the house had not
been purchased, particularly since it had been completely remodeled
and landscaped. One day, a close friend suggested that Graves might
have a better chance of selling the home if he took down all the family pictures that remained. The friend also suggested that neither
Graves nor his family attend the open house events, so White potential buyers wouldn't know who lived there. Graves did exactly that.
The house sold the next weekend for the full asking price.

BOB HERBERT

Bob Herbert was born in Brooklyn, New York, and serves as an award-winning op-ed columnist for the *New York Times*. He received a bachelor of science degree in journalism from the State University of New York (Empire State College) and has garnered many awards as a distinguished journalist.

One weekend morning, Herbert left his apartment on the West Side of Manhattan to go to his office at the *New York Times*. As a taxi was nearby looking for customers, he decided to jump in. As usual, he got into the rear of the taxi and told the cabbie that he wanted to go to his office. The cabbie, an immigrant woman, not only refused to take him to his office but insisted that he exit the taxi. Herbert was stunned. As he sat there in the taxi, the cabbie told him that if he did not get out, she would call the police. Herbert encouraged her to do so, because he could not understand how a taxi available for customers would refuse to take him to his office. When the police officer arrived, Herbert was convinced that things would be settled soon and that the cabbie would have to take him to his office. He was wrong. The officer did not require the cabbie to take him to his office and left Herbert only with the option of filing a complaint with the New York City hackers (taxicab) association. It was a sad moment for Bob Herbert, who understood how it felt to be Black in America, when he had done nothing wrong and a cabbie who did not know who he was refused to carry him to his office.

SAM FULWOOD III

Sam Fulwood III was born in Charlotte, North Carolina, and is a graduate of the University of North Carolina, Chapel Hill. He was an award-winning journalist for the *Los*

Angeles Times in Washington, DC, and the *Plain Dealer* in Cleveland. He is the author of *Waking from the Dream: My Life in the Black Middle Class* (Anchor Books, 1996) and *Full of It: Strong Words and Fresh Thinking for Cleveland* (Gray & Company, 2004).

In 1991, Sam was approached by one of his White female colleagues, who asked him a question about Colin Powell: "Sam, what do Black people think about Colin Powell?" Fulwood reports that he responded by saying: "I don't know what Black people think about Colin Powell. Why?" The woman went on to explain how Powell had done an excellent job in explaining the Iraq War and was quite articulate. She went on to say that most White people wished that all Black people were like Colin Powell. Fulwood was deeply troubled by these comments, and particularly troubled that his White colleague never had a clue that her characterization offended him.

JUDGE A. LEON HIGGINBOTHAM, JR.

Judge Higginbotham, Jr., was born in Trenton, New Jersey, in 1928 and attended Purdue University in 1944 before transferring to Antioch College, from which he graduated. He received his JD degree from Yale Law School and served as chief judge of the 3rd Circuit Court of Appeals before retiring to teach at Harvard Law School and serve as counsel in the New York law firm of Paul Weiss.

At Purdue, Higginbotham was one of about a dozen African American students in a student population of more than 6,000 students. The African American students were required to sleep in a separate building, segregated and without heat. When Higginbotham complained, he reports that he was told to accept the conditions or leave. He left, graduated from Antioch College and Yale Law School, and

became a venerable federal judge, a civil rights advocate, and a respected teacher and scholar.

OLIVER HILL

Oliver Hill was born in Richmond, Virginia, and graduated from Howard University
with a BA and Howard Law School with a JD degree. Hill was one of the key lawyers who
argued the *Brown v. Board of Education* civil rights case, and he practiced law in Virginia for over 60 years. He lived to be 100 years old.

Hill recalls the impact of segregation as a child—attending separate
schools for Blacks in Richmond and even having to practice at different times for the all-colored basketball team in high school. He
recalls arguing cases in the Supreme Court as a civil rights lawyer
while not being able either to use the public restrooms or to eat there.
He and the other African American lawyers would have to go to the
segregated dining rooms during breaks or at the end of the day. Winning cases before the United States Supreme Court that were designed to end segregation in public places was among his most
cherished accomplishments.

ROBERT RICHARDSON

Robert Richardson was born in Kansas City, Missouri. He was educated there, and
completed his undergraduate studies and law school at Georgetown University in
Washington, DC, following two tours of duty in Vietnam.

The incident he would like to relate comes from his military training to be an intelligence agent in civilian clothes. After returning
from Vietnam in 1968, Richardson was sent to Fort Holabird,
Maryland, for intelligence officer training. At that time, the mili-

tary needed men of color as agents to collect intelligence on possible civilian uprisings. The final examination consisted of field training, during which students were sent to various towns to perform intelligence functions. Richardson was sent to White Plains, New York, where he was given instructions to report to a public place from which to be picked up and taken to a safe house. As part of the exercise, the identities of the agents were unknown, and no photographs were provided. He was given explicit instructions on what to wear and what to say so that he would be picked up. He followed instructions, went to White Plains, and waited for several hours without being contacted. He returned to New York City for his backup pickup, but he was not picked up there either. During the critique of the exercise, Richardson found out that both pickup agents had observed him but did not contact him, as they did not expect to see a Black intelligence agent.

LOU GOSSETT, JR.

Lou Gossett, Jr., an Oscar-winning actor, was born on May 27, 1936 in Brooklyn, New York. He won an Oscar for his supporting role in *An Officer and a Gentleman*. Gossett is the founder of Eracism Foundation Inc., a nonprofit public benefit corporation, and has decided to commit his life to fighting racism, violence, and ignorance.

Lou Gossett reports that, after winning an Oscar for his supporting role in the acclaimed movie *An Officer and a Gentleman*, he was offered many African American roles that he describes as being derogatory, and believes that he was blacklisted in Hollywood for refusing to accept those roles. Other African Americans accepted the money and toe lucrative roles, but Gossett's pride prevented him from doing the same. It is why he firmly believes that he is still denied important roles today.

JOHN MATHEWS II

John Mathews II was born and raised in California. He graduated from the University
of California, Los Angeles, in 2003 and from Harvard Law School in 2007. He is currently an associate at Latham & Watkins LLP in Washington, DC.

When Mathews was a freshman at UCLA in 1999, he was having
lunch in the dining hall with some friends from the dorms, all of whom
were Black males. They had just settled down to recap the week's events
and devour lunch when a White female student approached their table
from across the room and asked, "So what sport do you guys play?"
There was an assumption that if there was a group of Black male students at UCLA, they must be there on athletic scholarships because of
the high admission criteria for "regular students." Although this was the
first time Mathews had encountered such a stereotype in college, it
wasn't the last. Each of them replied with the most nonstereotypical
sport they could think of—badminton, lacrosse, golf, and table tennis—and then continued with their conversation. Today, one of the
friends is an associate at Ivie, McNeill & Wyatt in Los Angeles; another is a lab researcher for AMGEN in Southern California; and the
third friend is director of media relations at Time Warner Cable Inc.

CHARLES COBB, JR.

Charles Cobb is a native of Washington, D.C., and attended Stanford University. He is
a celebrated journalist and was active in the Student Nonviolent Coordinating Committee as a young adult.

The year was 1962. Cobb got off a bus that was taking him to Houston, Texas, in order to meet and introduce himself to students who

were sit-in protesters in Jackson, Mississippi. After meeting them, Cobb decided to stay in Mississippi and join the voter registration campaign that SNCC—the Student Nonviolent Coordinating Committee—was launching in the Mississippi Delta. He went with two students from Jackson's movement up to the Delta, to a small town in the heartland of the state's cotton country in Sunflower County, where the White Citizens Council was born. They had been in town for just a couple of days when, while they were walking down a dirt road, a car stopped in front of them. Out jumped a White man holding a pistol. He waved it at them while saying, "I know you all ain't from here and you're here to cause trouble. I'm here to tell you to get out of town." Well, he was the mayor! He was also the town constable, the justice of the peace, owned the town's hardware store, broadcasted agricultural news on the local radio station, and headed the local White Citizens Council. Pointing his pistol at them, he ordered Cobb and his colleagues into his car and took them to his hardware store. There he accused them of being communists—New York City communists—and told them again to get out of town. The leader of Cobb's group, Charles McLaurin, told the mayor that they were all Mississippians and were in town to encourage and help people to get registered to vote. "The U.S. Constitution gives us the right to do this," McLaurin told him. The mayor's response: "That law ain't got here yet."

KEVIN J. ARMSTRONG

Armstrong was born in Washington, DC and currently resides in New York. Armstrong is a corporate lawyer specializing in broker-dealer investment management in hedge-fund transactions and regulation.

It is often heard that Blacks have a hard time getting a taxi in New York. Armstrong has a personal story of such an incident that was too bold and obvious to let go without legal recourse. It was a weekend afternoon and he had just finished shopping at a store near Columbus Circle in Manhattan with his young son and sister. They headed to a row of taxis waiting out front for passengers. When his sister reached for the door of the first taxi in line, the driver locked the door and waved her off. Armstrong thought that strange but tried the other door nonetheless. The driver said, "No." Armstrong walked away and within minutes the driver had opened the door for a White woman. Before the taxi could leave, Armstrong approached the driver to inquire why he was rejected. He said, "I do not drive Blacks because Blacks do not tip." The passenger, offended at the exchange of conversation, got out of the taxi and left, but the driver continued his rant. Armstrong filed a complaint with the New York Taxi and Limousine Commission and represented himself at the trial. Under questioning, the taxi driver repeated his comments about "not picking up Blacks" in front of the judge. The Judge told him that the logs showed he was not off duty at that time and that the law states that he could not reject a passenger based on race. He was therefore found guilty on all charges and issued a sentence of $550 in fines and a 15-day suspension. So in some cases, the system does work to help remedy such situations. However, we're still a long way from ending such incidents. Armstrong hopes that in a small way, the taxi driver will think differently next time.

HOWARD MANLY

Howard Manly was born in San Bernadino, California, in 1958, and was raised in Washington, DC. He has been a journalist for the last 30 years, most recently as executive editor of the *Bay State Banner,* Boston's Black-owned weekly newspaper.

The incident occurred on September 6, 2008, during a panel discussion titled "Race, Religion, Age and Gender in the 2008 Election," hosted by the Charles Hamilton Institute on Race and Justice. About 900 people had crammed into the Martha's Vineyard Performing Arts Center to hear the distinguished panel discuss their views on the Obama phenomenon, the possibility of Hillary Clinton as vice president, and the concept of "change" in the context of America's often jittery racial history. During the discussion, Manly talked about Boston's communities of color and how Obama's campaign had forced a community newspaper to cover a presidential election on a regular basis. Manly told the crowd that he published photographs of Obama, especially of him surrounded by American flags or American soldiers, usually on the front page, as often as he could. One of his missions was to close the gap between the perception of African American patriotism and its reality, not only among Whites but among Blacks as well. In the next day's *Vineyard Gazette,* a front-page story on the panel appeared by senior writer, Mike Seccombe. In that story, Seccombe summarized Manly's inclination for placing Obama on the *Banner's* front page: "Whether this is for propaganda or circulation reasons, he left unclear." The use of the word "propaganda" touched a nerve. Manly believes that equating news judgment with deliberate efforts to manipulate the truth in some sinister way is just plain wrong. Manly believed that by using the word "propaganda" Seccombe implied that publishing photographs of an African American presidential candidate was somehow designed to further the cause of African Americans at the expense of all Americans—that a desire for better schools, a vibrant economy, and adequate health care were only minority issues. For Manly, the ultimate reason why he featured Obama on the *Banner*'s front page was simple: the candidate was "one helluva story," arguably the most important story on race since the 1954 U.S. Supreme Court decision in *Brown v. Board of Education* that ended legal segregation.

VERNON JORDAN

Vernon Jordon was born in Atlanta, Georgia. Jordan is a graduate of Depauw University and Howard Law School. He is a senior managing director at Lazard, Freres and Co., and counsel to the law firm of Akin, Gump, Strauss, Hauer & Feld.

In 1955 Vernon Jordan was a sophomore at Depauw University. He received a notice that he would be interviewed for a job at a banking company in Atlanta. He put on his best suit, went to the headquarters, and introduced himself to the receptionist. When he gave his name as Vernon Jordan and said he hoped to get the internship, the receptionist seemed startled. She called a supervisor. A supervisor came and had the same sense of being startled by Mr. Jordan's presence. The supervisor finally had the nerve to say, "They didn't tell us." Jordan responded, "They didn't tell you what?" Embarrassed, the supervisor said, "They didn't tell us you were colored, uh you know, you can't work here. It's just impossible. You just can't." This 1955 example of segregation in the South and being evaluated on your race and not on the basis of your talent is the opening story of Vernon Jordan's best selling book, *Vernon Can Read.*[4]

SPIKE LEE

Spike Lee was born in Atlanta, Georgia. He was raised in Brooklyn, New York, and graduated from Morehouse College. He is an award-winning film producer, director, and entrepreneur.

Spike Lee is one of the country's most successful filmmakers of any race. However, when he tried to auction his debut feature film, *She's Gotta Have It*, in August 1986, he found few takers. It was obvious that as an African American film no one was interested. The film was ultimately independently financed for $175,000, and despite the criticisms of it, Spike was able to gross more than 8 million dollars at the box office. Lee believes it was racism that prevented him from greater access to revenue. The doubters were wrong, as he's become a multimillion-dollar director and producer of many great films, including *Malcolm X, Do the Right Thing, 4 Little Girls, Inside Man*, and *The Original Kings of Comedy*.

These are just a small collection of the stories I was sent by my fellow African Americans in the course of writing this book. These are experiences that they themselves went through; their children and grandchildren are currently going through or will eventually endure similar incidents. Despite all our advancements and achievements, we live in a society where people are not judged on the content of their character but rather on the color of their skin. So I ask again, "How far have we come?" Evidently, not far enough. The opportunities to make change await.

ACKNOWLEDGEMENTS

On July 16, 2009, I had just completed a summer Harvard Law School faculty lecture series and was on my way to New York to hear President Barack Obama give his address before the NAACP at their 100th anniversary convention. I received a call from Ms. Joanne Kendall, assistant to Professor Henry Louis Gates, Jr., who said "Professor Ogletree, Professor Gates has been arrested." That began a journey of hours, days, and now months of looking into the arrest of Professor Gates, why it happened, and what needed to be done.

As a result of this incident, I was contacted by many people expressing their shock and disbelief at his arrest and stating their stories. Ultimately, a number of people asked me if I would be willing to write something about the Gates arrest and its larger implications. I was happy to do so.

This book would not have been possible without the enormous support and help of my executive assistant, Darrick Northington, who worked tirelessly over many nights and weeks to make sure all of the information was available for the book. My scheduler, Jean O'Friel-Quigley, was an inspiration in joining this effort even though her hands were full with many other challenging things, including her then-pending wedding. One of my first student assistants, Sydney Walker, a future lawyer who has worked for me during summers since she was a freshman in high school, joined the team late in the process, but was instrumental as always. As usual I received incredible inspiration from colleagues and friends who took the time to leave comments and feedback on themes that I had and convinced me to change some ideas that were a part of earlier versions of the book. Professor Randy Hertz of New York University Law School and Eric Miller of St. Louis University Law School were quick and decisive in their ideas and very helpful suggestions. A number of my former research assistants who are now either doing clerkships or working in the public or private sector responded to the call when we needed to locate a source or check an idea to make sure it was appropriate. I give great thanks to my former students Shahira Ali, Russell Capone, Jennifer Lane, Jay Osha, Portia Pedro, Rob Smith, and Whitney Washington.

I was very pleased with the work of a number of current law students who spent a number of hours looking at some of the areas that were obscure and unique and provided some helpful suggestions throughout the process. I am thankful to Brittany Gail Brewer, Shaylyn Cochran, Kayla Z. X. Southworth, Roohia Sidhu Klein, Jonathan Tshiamala, and the coordinator of this group who also helped on a number of other projects, Ben Sedrish.

I am most grateful for the tireless efforts of my family members, particularly my wife, Pam Ogletree, and daughter, Rashida Ogletree. They both pushed me endlessly to make sure that I was clear and concise about my arguments and were consistently critical and helpful in my reaching a theme that was persuasive and powerful. I also want to thank my daughter-in-law Rachelle Ogletree and my brother Richard Ogletree, burdened with obligations beyond measure, who still took the time to notice a word, phrase, or concept that seemed out of place and offered their very helpful and timely suggestions.

Of course, this book would not have been possible without the enthusiastic and relentless support of my agents, John Taylor "Ike"

Williams and Katherine Flynn. I also want to offer my heartfelt gratitude to my editor, Airíe Stuart, who emailed, called, and frequently sat down with me to hear the ideas for this book, and was tireless in her efforts to support every point or argument made in the book. I owe a debt of gratitude to her. I can't even begin to describe how wonderful, patient, and thoughtful Alan Bradshaw was in the final stages of editing this book. Alan always exhibited unimagined calmness during the very hectic days of final edits. He always had the best idea about a word or phrase, and was always willing to put in the extra effort, nights and weekends, when it was needed most. As always, the team at Palgrave has been nothing short of superb in editing the book and supporting the work of this humble author. For this paperback edition, I'd like to thank Laura Lancaster, Emily Carleton, Lorraine Jonemann, Michelle Fitzgerald, and Carla Benton. Once again, I'd like to thank Darrick Northington, as well as Johanna Wald, Brittany Gail Brewer, David Harris, Etienne Toussaint, and my intern, Alesha Garvin. I'm also very pleased that several of my students assisted in the research effort for the afterword—James Baker, Jr., Candace Moss, Luke Murumba, Adrienne R. W. Bradley, Mondaire Jones, and Crystal Redd.

I am also grateful to the more than 100 African-American men, who, having experienced one encounter or another with police or other citizens, responded to my request to retell their stories in a way that the world could see that the arrest of Henry Louis Gates, Jr., was not an isolated event. It is hoped that this book will be a reminder that we still have a long way to go in addressing the issue of racial disparities in this country, and that collectively and with great determination and spirit we can achieve that goal.

Sincerely,
Charles J. Ogletree, Jr.

NOTES

CHAPTER 1

1. Abby Goodnough, "Sergeant Who Arrested Professor Defends Actions," *New York Times*, July 23, 2009. Available at http://www.nytimes.com/2009/07/24/us/24gates.html?_ r=1.Courtney A. Coursey, "A Night in the Life of Harvard Police Officers," *The Harvard Crimson*, November 9, 1996. Available at http://www.thecrimson.com/article/1996/11/9/ a-night-in-the-life-of/.

2. Abby Goodnough, "Professor Jailed; Officer is Accused of Bias," *New York Times*, A13, July 21, 2009.

3. Don Van Natta, Jr. and Abby Goodnough, "After Call to Police, Two Cambridge Worlds Collide in an Unlikely Meeting," *New York Times*, A13, July 27, 2009.

4. Professor Gates is one of the very few tenured faculty members at Harvard to be honored with the "University Professor" distinction. See Harvard University, *General Information: Harvard University Professors*. Available at: http://harvard.edu/about/university_professors .php (listing 22 current University Professors and describing University Professorships as "chairs intended for individuals of distinction . . . working on the frontiers of knowledge, and in such a way as to cross the conventional boundaries of the specialties").

5. Queenie Wong, "Ten Things You Didn't Know About Henry Louis Gates, Jr.," *U.S. News and World Report*, July 24, 2009. Available at http://www.usnews.com/articles/news/national/ 2009/07/24/10-things-you-didnt-know-about-henry-louis-gates-jr.html.

6. "Henry Louis Gates, Jr.," available at http://www.fas.harvard.edu/~amciv/faculty/gates.shtml.

7. Jonathan Saltzman, "Sergeant at Eye of Storm Says He Won't Apologize," *Boston Globe*, July 23, 2009. Available at http://www.boston.com/news/local/massachusetts/articles/2009/ 07/23/officer_at_eye_of_storm_says_he_wont_apologize/.

8. Sarah J. Howland, "Republicans in the 'People's Republic of Cambridge,'" *The Harvard Crimson*, November 2, 2008. Available at http://www.thecrimson.com/article/2008/11/2/ republicans-in-the-peoples-republic-of/.

9. However, Crowley's Mother has said that her son "attended racially diverse Cambridge public schools." "They grew up with black kids," she said. See Saltzman, *supra*, note 7.

10. "Cambridge Rindge and Latin School" brochure, page 4. Available at http://www.cpsd.us/ web/PubInfo/CRLS_VIEWBOOK_0607.pdf.

11. From author's interview, December 29, 2009.

12. "Friends and Police Rally Behind Sgt. James Crowley," *Associated Press*, July 24, 2009. Available at http://www.dailynewstribune.com/news/x1543600223/Friends-and-police-rally-behind-Sgt-James-Crowley-who-arrested-Harvard-professor.

13. "Charges Dropped Against Top Black Scholar," *CBS/Associated Press*, July 21, 2009. Available at http://www.cbsnews.com/stories/2009/07/21/national/main5177232.shtml.

14. See *e.g.*, Rev. Irene Monroe, "Living While Black in Cambridge," *L.A. Progressive*, July 22, 2009. Available at http://www.laprogressive.com/rankism/henry-louis-gates-in-cambridge/ (describing Area IV as "the city's known and expected troubled spot" and "an area plagued with all the problems of urban blight and very [few] resources to ameliorate them"); Stephanie M. Skier, "Recent Shootings Stun Cambridge," *The Harvard Crimson*, June 28, 2002. Available at http://www.thecrimson.harvard.edu/article/2002/6/28/recent-shootings-stun-cambridge-dramatic-increases/ (citing Area IV resident: "[T]hese problems of violence, guns and drugs are the same that have plagued the neighborhood since the 1960s . . .").

15. Area IV is also predominately comprised of poor and working class citizens. *See* Rev. Irene Monroe, "Living While Black in Cambridge," *L.A. Progressive,* July 22, 2009. Available at http://www.laprogressive.com/rankism/henry-louis-gates-in-cambridge/ (describing Area IV as "a predominately black poor and working-class enclave" and noting that "[a]s a densely populated area, its average household income was $34,306, according to the 2005 city census. On the other hand, Harvard Square had an average household income of $79,533 in that same year").

16. Justia U.S. Laws, Section 53, Penalty for certain offenses, http://law.justia.com/massachusetts/codes/gl-pt4-toc/272–53.html (accessed April 16, 2010).

17. *Id.*

18. PDF full texts of the Sergeant Crowley and Officer Figueroa (following) reports are available at http://www.cnnac360.files.wordpress.com/2009/07/20120754.pdf.

19. *Boston Globe,* "Transcript of the 911 Call in the Gates Case," Boston.com, http://www.boston.com/news/local/breaking_news/2009/07/transcript_of_t_1.html (accessed November 23, 2009).

20. *Boston Globe,* "Transcript of Police Radio Transmission," Boston.com, http:/www.boston.com/news/local/breaking_news/2009/07/transcript_of_p.html (accessed November, 23, 2009).

21. See Justia U.S. Laws, *supra,* note 16.

22. See *Boston Globe,* "Transcript," *supra,* note 20.

23. Peter F. Zhu, "Renowned African-American Professor Gates Arrested for Disorderly Conduct," *The Harvard Crimson,* July 20, 2009. Available at http://www.thecrimson.com/article/2009/7/20/renowned-af-am-professor-gates-arrested-for/.

24. John Payton, "Wrongful Arrest: Can You Trust the Police? The 'Skip' Gates Incident," The Defenders Online, July 21, 2009, http://www.thedefendersonline.com/2009/07/21/can-you-trust-the-police-the-%E2%80%98skip%E2%80%99-gates-incident/ (accessed April 16, 2010).

25. David Edwards and Steven Webster, "Fox News Analyst: Gates Arrest Was Improper," The Raw Story, July 28, 2009, http://rawstory.com/08/news/2009/07/28/fox-legal-analyst-gates-arrest-was-improper/ (accessed April 16, 2010).

26. John Banzhaf, "Why Gates Should Sue, Not Socialize: Most Effective 'Teachable Moment' Is Court Order," July 30, 2009, PR-inside.com, http://www.pr-inside.com/why-gates-should-sue-not-socialize-r1415279.htm (accessed April 16, 2010).

27. Bonnie Rochman, "The Gates Case: When Disorderly Conduct Is a Cop's Judgment Call," *Time,* July 25, 2009, http://www.time.com/time/nation/article/0,8599,1912777,00.html (accessed April 16, 2010).

28. *Id.*

29. See Payton, "Wrongful Arrest," *supra,* note 24.

30. See Rochman, "The Gates Case," *supra,* note 27.

31. *Id.*

32. Massachusetts District Court, Criminal Model Jury Instructions, 2009 Edition, Public Order Offenses Number 7.160, http://www.mass.gov/courts/courtsandjudges/courts/district court/jury-instructions/criminal/ (accessed April 16, 2010).

CHAPTER 2

1. Video of President Obama's address can be viewed on the Associated Press channel on YouTube: http://www.youtube.com/user/associatedpress?blend=2&ob=4#p/search/62/LZYsW_PxWAM.

2. Henry Louis Gates, Jr., *Colored People: A Memoir* (New York: Knopf, 1994), 30–31.

3. *Id.* at 33.
4. *Id.* at 34.
5. *Id.* at 35.
6. Barack Obama, *Dreams from My Father: A Story of Race and Inheritance* (New York: Three Rivers Press 1995, 2004), 50.
7. *Id.*
8. *Id.*
9. *Id.* at 76.
10. See Jodi Kantor's article in the *New York Times*, "In Law School, Obama Found Political Voice," http://query.nytimes.com/gst/fullpage.html?res=9906E4DF143FF93BA15752C0A9 619C8B63&sec=&spon=&pagewanted=2 (accessed March 31, 2010).
11. "Remarks by the President to the NAACP Centennial Convention," http://www.white-house.gov/blog/2009/07?page=3 (accessed March 22, 2010).
12. *Id.*
13. President Barack Obama, Health Care Press Conference, July 22, 2009. Available at http://www.whitehouse.gov/blog/The-Presidents-Press-Conference-Full-Video/.
14. *Id.*
15. *Id.*
16. Glenn Beck, "Glenn Beck: Gates-gate Keeps Getting Worse for Obama," *The Glenn Beck Program,* July 28, 2009, http://www.glennbeck.com/content/articles/article/198/28519/.
17. For a list of companies that have pulled their sponsorship of Glenn Beck's show, please see: http://colorofchange.org/beck/more/companies.html.
18. "CNN Watch: 2 Black Co-Workers Defend Sgt Crowley in Gates Arrest," CNN television interview, July 28, 2009, http://www.youtube.com/watch?v=CSaDdXNmYys.
19. *Id.*
20. "Barack Obama—2004 Democratic National Convention Keynote Address," http:// C-SPAN television broadcast, July 27, 2004, http://www.americanrhetoric.com/speeches/ convention2004/barackobama2004dnc.htm.
21. Senator Barack Obama, "A More Perfect Union," CNN television broadcast, March 18, 2008, http://my.barackobama.com/page/content/hisownwords.
22. *Id.*
23. Janny Scott, "Obama Chooses Reconciliation over Rancor," *New York Times*, March 19, 2008, http://www.nytimes.com/2008/03/19/us/politics/19assess.html?scp=&pagewanted= print.
24. Transcript, "Obama's Remarks on Wright," April 29, 2008, *New York Times,* http://www. nytimes.com/2008/04/29/us/politics/29text-obama.html?pagewanted=all.
25. Paul Steinhauser, "Poll: Did Obama's Reaction to Gates-Arrest Hurt Him?" CNNPolitics .com, August 4, 2009, http://www.cnn.com/2009/POLITICS/08/04/obama.gates.poll/ index.html[0]. (PDF results available on website.)
26. CNN Opinion Research Corporation, "CNN Opinion Research Poll" at 11, August 4, 2009, http://i.cdn.turner.com/cnn/2009/images/08/04/rel11a.x.pdf.
27. "30% Give Obama Good Marks for Handling of Gates Incident," Rasmussen Reports, July 30, 2009, http://www.rasmussenreports.com/public_content/politics/obama_administration/ july_2009/30_give_obama_good_marks_for_handling_of_gates_incident.
28. "Obama Remarks at Friday Briefing," *Time,* July 24, 2009, http://thepage.time.com/obama-remarks-at-friday-briefing/.
29. Colbert I. King, "Cold Beer and Cold Comfort for Rights," *Washington Post,* August 1, 2009, http://www.washingtonpost.com/wpdyn/content/article/2009/07/31/AR2009073102864. html. Accessed January 25, 2010.
30. *Id.*

CHAPTER 3

1. For more information on Meyer's arrest, please see, Sasha Issenberg, "Student at Kerry Event is Tasered," *Boston Globe,* September 19, 2007, http://www.boston.com/news/nation/washington/articles/2007/09/19/student_at_a_kerry_event_is_tasered/ (accessed April 26, 2010), and Monica Hesse, "Aiming to Agitate, Florida Student Got a Shock," *Washington Post,* September 19, 2007, http://www.washingtonpost.com/wp-dyn/content/article/2007/09/18/AR2007091802115.html (accessed April 26, 2010).

2. Hector Tobar and Richard Lee Colvin, "Witnesses Depict Relentless Beating," *Los Angeles Times,* March 7, 1991, http://articles.latimes.com/1991–03–07/local/me–3174_1_police-officers (accessed April 26, 2010). Doug Linder provides a thorough summary of the events following the beating of Rodney King and the race riots that occurred after the police officers were acquitted. Doug Linder, *The Trials of Los Angeles Police Officers in Connection with the Beating of Rodney King,* http://www.law.umkc.edu/faculty/projects/FTrials/lapd/lapd account.html (accessed April 20, 2010).

3. See Linder, *The Trials of Los Angeles Police Officers, supra,* note 2.

4. *Id.*

5. *Id.*

6. *Id.*

7. Seth Mydans, "The Police Verdict; Los Angeles Policemen Acquitted in Taped Beating," *New York Times,* April 30, 1992, http://www.nytimes.com/books/98/02/08/home/rodney-verdict.html (accessed April 26, 2010), and David Savage and Jim Newton, "Justices Uphold Lenient Sentences in King Beating," *Los Angeles Times,* June 14, 1996, http://articles.latimes.com/1996–06–14/news/mn–14959_1_sentencing-guidelines (accessed April 26, 2010).

8. For more information on the events of the LA Riots, please see, Don Hazen, ed., *Inside the L.A. Riots: What Really Happened—and Why It Will Happen Again* (Institute for Alternative Journalism, 1992); Los Angeles Times, *Understanding the Riots: Los Angeles Before and After the Rodney King Case* (Los Angeles: Los Angeles Times, 1992); Webster Commission, *The City in Crisis: A Report by the Special Advisor to the Board of Police Commissioners on the Civil Disorder in Los Angeles* (Los Angeles: Institute for Government and Public Affairs, UCLA, 1992); Seth Mydans, "After the Riots; 4 Held in Attack at Riots' Outset," *New York Times,* May 13, 1992, http://www.nytimes.com/1992/05/13/us/after-the-riots–4-held-in-attack-at-riots-outset.html (accessed April 26, 2010).

9. See Linder, *The Trials of Los Angeles Police Officers, supra,* note 2.

10. *Id.*

11. Andrea Ford and John H. Lee, "Slain Girl Was Not Stealing Juice, Police Say," *Los Angeles Times,* March 19, 1991, Metro, and "A Senseless and Tragic Killing; New Tension for Korean-American and African-American Communities," *Los Angeles Times,* March 20, 1991, Metro.

12. "Merchant Charged in Girl's Fatal Shooting," *Los Angeles Times,* March 22, 1991, Metro.

13. *Id.*

14. Robert Gooding-Williams, *Reading Rodney King* (London: Routledge, Inc., 1993), 45.

15. Charles Ogletree et al., *Beyond the Rodney King Story: An Investigation of Police Conduct in Minority Communities* (Boston: Northeastern University Press, 1995).

16. Leonard Levitt, *NYPD Confidential: Power and Corruption in the Country's Greatest Police Force* (New York: Thomas Dunne Books, 2009), Chapter 7, and Al Sharpton with Karen Hunter, *Al on America* (New York: Dafina Books, 2002), 232–37.

17. Amy Waldman, "Describing a 'Hard-Fought Year,' 4 Men in Turnpike Shooting File a Lawsuit," *New York Times,* April 23, 1999, http://www.nytimes.com/1999/04/23/nyregion/

describing-a-hard-fought-year–4-men-in-turnpike-shooting-file-a-lawsuit.html (accessed April 26, 2010), and Iver Peterson and David M. Halbfinger, "New Jersey Agrees to Pay $13 Million in Profiling Suit," *New York Times,* February 3, 2001, http://www.nytimes.com/2001/02/03/nyregion/new-jersey-agrees-to-pay–13-million-in-profiling-suit.html?pagewanted=1 (accessed April 26, 2010).

18.   See Levitt, *NYPD Confidential, supra,* note 16.

19.   William K. Rashbaum, "50 Bullets, One Dead, and Many Questions," *New York Times,* December 11, 2006, http://www.nytimes.com/2006/12/11/nyregion/11shoot.html (accessed April 26, 2010), and Michael Wilson, "Judge Acquits Detectives in 50-Shot Killing of Bell," *New York Times,* April 26, 2008, http://www.nytimes.com/2008/04/26/nyregion/26bell.html?_r=1 (accessed April 26, 2010).

20.   Bay Area Rapid Transit, "BART Reaches $1.5 Million Settlement for Daughter of Oscar Grant," BART, January 27, 2010, http://www.bart.gov/news/articles/2010/news20100127b.aspx (accessed April 26, 2010).

21.   The Pew Center on the States, *One in 100: Behind Bars in America* (2008), http://www.pewcenteronthestates.org/uploadedFiles/8015PCTS_Prison08_FINAL_2–1–1_FORWEB.pdf (accessed April 27, 2010), 6–7.

22.   U.S. Department of Justice, Bureau of Justice Statistics, *Prevalence of Imprisonment in the U.S. Population 1974–2001* (2003), http://bjs.ojp.usdoj.gov/content/pub/pdf/piusp01.pdf (accessed April 27, 2010), 1.

23.   The Sentencing Project, *Racial Disparities in the Criminal Justice System* (2009), http://www.sentencingproject.org/doc/publications/rd_mmhousetestimonyonRD.pdf (accessed April 27, 2010), 1.

24.   The Sentencing Project, *Reducing Racial Disparity in the Criminal Justice System: A Manual for Practitioners and Policymakers* (2008), http://www.sentencingproject.org/doc/publications/rd_reducingracialdisparity.pdf. (accessed April 27, 2010), 2.

CHAPTER 4

1.   Copyright 1922 by the Harvard Glee Club.

2.   Dr. Counter found conclusive evidence that Matt Henson (like Robert Peary, who was also on the expedition that discovered the North Pole) had Eskimo (Inuit) descendants, who live in Greenland to this day.

3.   Each of the individuals discussed in this chapter was interviewed by Professor Ogletree in the fall of 2009, and their comments were recorded.

4.   Interview with Professor Charles Ogletree.

5.   Drew Gilpin Faust, "Letter from Drew Faust Regarding HUPD Relations with University Community," August 2008, http://www.president.harvard.edu/speeches/faust/080826_hupd.php (accessed April 21, 2010).

6.   "Harvard to Create Safety Advisory Committee and Safety Ombudsman Function," *Harvard Gazette,* August 28, 2009, http://news.harvard.edu/gazette/story/2009/08/marti/.

7.   *Id.*

CHAPTER 5

1.   Testimony of Robert L. Wilkins, concerning "The Traffic Stops Statistics Study Act of 1999," before the Committee on the Judiciary Subcommittee on the Constitution, Federalism and Property Rights, United States Senate, March 30, 2000, pg. 2.

2.   *Id.*

3.   *Id.*

4.   *Id.*

5.   *Id.*

6.   *Wilkins v. Maryland State Police,* Civil Action No. CCB–93–468 Maryland Federal District Court (1993).

7.   Testimony of Robert L. Wilkins, *supra,* note 1, p. 4.

8.   *Id.,* 2. Settlement Agreement, *Wilkins v. Maryland State Police,* Civ. No. MJG–93–468 at 7 (D.MD. 1994). Available at www.clearinghouse.net/chDocs/public/PN-MD–003–0002. pdf.

9.   Testimony of Robert L. Wilkins, *supra,* note 1.

10. *Id.*

11. *Id.*

12. Maryland Judiciary, Reported in the Court of Special Appeals of Maryland, No. 1476, September Term, 2008: *Maryland Department of State Police v. Maryland State Conference of NAACP Branches,* http://mdcourts.gov/opinions/cosa/2010/1476s08.pdf (accessed April 21, 2010).

13. Charles M. Blow, "Welcome to the Club," *New York Times,* July 24, 2009, http://www.ny times.com/2009/07/25/opinion/25blow.html?scp=1&sq=charles%20m.%20blow%20gates& st=cse.

14. New York City Civilian Complaint Review Board, *Status Report January–June 2009* at 8, http://www.nyc.gov/html/ccrb/pdf/ccrbsemi2009_Jan_June.pdf.

15. Ian Ayres and Jonathan Borowsky, "A Study of Racially Disparate Outcomes in the Los Angeles Police Department" (October 2008), www.aclu-sc.org/documents/view/47.

16. *Id.*

17. Marc Mauer, "Two-Tiered Justice: Race, Class and Crime Policy," in *The Integration Debate: Competing Futures for American Cities,* ed. Chester Hartman & Gregory D. Squires (New York: Routledge, 2009), 169.

18. Charles Ogletree, personal interview with Robert Wilkins.

CHAPTER 6

1.   Mike Seccombe, "Panel Tackles Issues of Race," Martha's Vineyard Gazette Online, August 14, 2009, http://www.mvgazette.com/article.php?22482 (accessed April 20, 2010).

2.   Marc Mauer, "Two-Tiered Justice: Race, Class and Crime Policy," in *The Integration Debate: Competing Futures for American Cities,* ed. Chester Hartman and Gregory D. Squires (New York: Routledge Press, 2009), 169.

3.   Children's Defense Fund, "America's Cradle to Prison Pipeline," http://www.childrens defense.org/child-research-data-publications/data/cradle-prison-pipeline-report–2007-full- highres.pdf (accessed April 20, 2010).

4.   *Batson v. Kentucky,* 476 U.S. In reversing Batson's conviction, Justice Powell observed, "More than a century ago, the Court decided that the State denies a black defendant equal protection of the laws when it puts him on trial before a jury from which members of his race have been purposefully excluded."

5.   *Id.*

6.   *Miller-El v. Dretke,* 545 U.S. 231.

7.   Statement of Judge Reggie B. Walton Before the Sub Committee on Crime and Drugs, Committee on the Judiciary, United States Senate, April 29, 2009. Available at http://www.us courts.gov/Press_Releases/2009/JudgeWaltonTestimony.pdf.

8.   Charles J. Ogletree, Jr., "Making Race Matter in Death Matters," in Charles J. Ogletree, Jr. and Austin Sarat, eds., *From Lynch Mobs to the Killing State: Race and the Death Penalty in America* (New York: New York University Press, 2006).

9. Glenn Loury, *Race, Incarceration, American Values* (Cambridge, MA: MIT Press, 2008), 11.

10. Glenn Loury, "Obama, Gates and the American Black Man," *New York Times,* July 26, 2009, http://www.nytimes.com/2009/07/26/opinion/26loury.html?_r=1&pagewanted=print (accessed April 20, 2010).

11. *Id.*

12. "Obama Criticizes Cambridge Police in Gates Case," *Boston Globe,* July 23, 2009, http://www.boston.com/news/local/breaking_news/2009/07/obama_critiiciz.html (accessed April 20, 2010).

13. Ian Haney Lopez, "Post Racial Racism: Racial Stratification and Mass Incarceration in the Age of Obama," *California Law Review* 210 (2010), 101.

14. "Fact Sheet for S.B. 1070," Arizona State Senate, Forty-ninth Legislature, Second Regular Session, http://www.azleg.gov/legtext/49leg/2r/summary/s.1070pshs.doc.htm; Senate Bill 1070, State of Arizona, Senate, Forty-ninth Legislature, Second Regular Session, 2010, http://www.courthousenews.com/2010/04/16/AzSB1070.pdf.

15. Ginger Rough, "Arizona Immigration Law Boosts Gov. Brewer's Rating," *Arizona Republic,* April 29, 2010, http://www.azcentral.com/arizonarepublic/news/articles/2010/04/29/20100429arizona-immigration-law-brewer-ratings-improve.html.

AFTERWORD

1. "Professor Charles J. Ogletree, Jr. Response to the Cambridge Review Committee Report," Charles Hamilton Houston Institute for Race & Justice, June 30, 2010, available at http://www.charleshamiltonhouston.org/News/Item.aspx?id=100107.

2. Cambridge Review Committee, "Missed Opportunities, Shared Responsibilities: Final Report of the Cambridge Review Committee," June 15, 2010, available at http://www.cambridgema.gov/CityOfCambridge_Content/documents/Cambridge%20Review_FINAL.pdf.

3. *Id.,* appendix D, p. 59.

4. Cambridge Review Committee, "Missed Opportunities, Shared Responsibilities: Final Report of the Cambridge Review Committee."

5. Charles J. Ogletree and Johanna Wald, "After Shirley Sherrod, We All Need to Slow Down and Listen," *Washington Post,* July 25, 2010, available at http://www.washingtonpost.com/wp-dyn/content/article/2010/07/23/AR2010072304583.html.

6. "Video Shows USDA Official Saying She Didn't Give 'Full Force' of Help to White Farmer," Fox News, July 20, 2010, available at http://www.foxnews.com/politics/2010/07/19/clip-shows-usda-official-admitting-withheld-help-white-farmer/. Unattributed quotes come from this report.

7. *Id.*

8. *Id.*

9. *Id.*

10. Kevin Connolly, "White House Sorry for Shirley Sherrod 'Racism' Firing," BBC News, July 21, 2010, available at http://www.bbc.co.uk/news/world-us-canada-10716237.

11. Yael T. Abouhalkah, "NAACP Condemns USDA Official's Racist Remarks," *The Kansas City Star,* 2010, available at: http://voices.kansascity.com/entries/naacp-condemns-usda-officials-racist-remarks/#storylink=cpy.

12. "Video Shows USDA Official Saying She Didn't Give 'Full Force' of Help to White Farmer."

13. *Id.*

14. Connolly, "White House Sorry for Shirley Sherrod 'Racism' Firing."

15. *Id.*

16. *Id.*

17. *Id.*

18.   *Id.*
19.   *Id.*
20.   Ogletree and Wald, "After Shirley Sherrod."
21.   Ray Rivera, Al Baker, and Janet Roberts, "A Few Blocks, 4 Years, 52,000 Police Stops," *New York Times,* July 11, 2010, available at http://www.nytimes.com/2010/07/12/nyregion/12frisk.html.
22.   Editorial, "The Truth Behind Stop-and-Frisk," *New York Times,* September 2, 2011, available at http://www.nytimes.com/2011/09/03/opinion/the-truth-behind-stop-and-frisk.html?_r=1.
23.   *Id.*
24.   Rivera, Baker, and Roberts, "A Few Blocks, 4 Years, 52,000 Police Stops."
25.   Al Baker, "Judge Declines to Dismiss Case Alleging Racial Profiling by City Police in Street Stops," *New York Times,* August 31, 2011, available at http://www.nytimes.com/2011/09/01/nyregion/racial-profiling-case-against-new-york-police-is-allowed-to-proceed.html.
26.   *Id.*
27.   *Id.*
28.   "State and County QuickFacts: New York (City), New York," U.S. Census Bureau, available at http://quickfacts.census.gov/qfd/states/36/3651000.html.
29.   Editorial, "The Truth Behind Stop-and-Frisk."
30.   *Id.*
31.   Rivera, Baker, and Roberts, "A Few Blocks, 4 Years, 52,000 Police Stops." Unattributed quotes come from this report.
32.   Dennis C. Smith and Robert Purtell, "An Empirical Assessment of NYPD's 'Operation Impact': A Targeted Zone Crime Reduction Strategy," New York University Robert F. Wagner School of Public Service, June 27, 2007, available at wagner.nyu.edu/news/impactzoning.doc.
33.   Description, *Floyd, et al. v. City of New York, et al.,* Center for Constitutional Rights, available at http://ccrjustice.org/ourcases/current-cases/floyd-et-al.
34.   Editorial, "The Truth Behind Stop-and-Frisk."
35.   *Id.*
36.   Al Baker, "Judge Declines to Dismiss Case Alleging Racial Profiling by City Police in Street Stops," *New York Times,* August 31, 2011, available at http://www.nytimes.com/2011/09/01/nyregion/racial-profiling-case-against-new-york-police-is-allowed-to-proceed.html?_r=1.
37.   Editorial, "The Truth Behind Stop-and-Frisk."
38.   Status, *Floyd, et al. v. City of New York, et al.,* Center for Constitutional Rights, available at http://ccrjustice.org/ourcases/current-cases/floyd-et-al.
39.   Seth Freed Wessler, "How East Haven, Conn., Became Synonymous With Racial Profiling," ColorLines: News for Action, February 2, 2012, available at http://colorlines.com/archives/2012/02/on_sunday_afternoon_about_ten.html.
40.   "Feds Say Arpaio Violated Civil Rights," Yahoo News/*Associated Press,* December 15, 2011, available at http://news.yahoo.com/apnewsbreak-feds-arpaio-violated-civil-rights-164947314.html.
41.   James Lu, "FBI Arrests Four East Haven Police Department Officers," Federal Criminal Defense Lawyers, from release by *Yale Daily News,* January 25, 2012, available at http://federalcrimesblog.com/2012/01/25/fbi-arrests-four-east-haven-police-department-officers/.
42.   Bob Butler, "TV Station Takes Four-Year-Old Child's Quote Out of Context," Maynard Institute, July 27, 2011, available at http://mije.org/health/tv-station-takes-four-year-old-childs-quote-context (accessed on February 3, 2012).

EPILOGUE

1. This title is adapted from Henry Louis Gates' book *Thirteen Ways of Looking at a Black Man* (New York: Vintage Books, 1997). Professor Gates profiled African American men who in one way or another had some impact on society. His chapters cover James Baldwin, Albert Murray, Bill T. Jones, and Colin Powell. He also looks at the O.J. Simpson case and interviews Louis Farrakhan, Harry Belafonte, and Anatole Broyard.
2. Johnnie Cochran, *A Lawyer's Life,* with David Fisher (New York: St. Martin's Press, 2002), 207–208.
3. "Holder: Race is Tough Issue," *Rueters,* July 29, 2009, http://blogs.reuters.com/frontrow/ 2009/07/29/holder-race-is-tough-issue/ (accessed April 22, 2010).
4. Vernon E. Jordan Jr., with Anette Gordon-Reed, *Vernon Can Read* (Public Affairs: New York, 2001).

INDEX

American Civil Liberties
    Union (ACLU), 106,
    109–10
Arama, Rita, 200
Armstrong, Kevin J., 257–8

Bailey, D'Army, 214
Bailey, Walter, 214
Bain, Byronn, 194–7
Ballentine, Warren, 173–4
Banzhaf III, John, 36–8
Barnes, Keith, 193–4
Batson v. Kentucky, 119,
    272n4
Beck, Glenn, 53–4
"beer summit," 60–2, 129
Bell, Derrick, 46, 237–9
Bell, Janet, 237–8
Bell, Sean, 74–5, 137
Bennett, Bruce, 169–71
Biden, Joe, 62
BigGovernment.com, 133
Blow, Charles M., 110
Bok, Derek, 81
Bolden, Victor, 79–80, 83–91,
    98, 101
Bond, Julian, 180–1
Boykin, Keith, 188–9
Bradley, Tom, 68–9, 72
Brannon, James, 223
Breitbert, Andrew, 133
Breyer, Justice Stephen, 119
Brown v. Board of Education,
    111, 149, 254, 260
Brownsville, Brooklyn, 138–9
Burnett, Sr., Arthur L., 233
Bush, George H. W., 72, 167
Bush, George W., 66
Butler, Paul, 234
Butts III, Calvin, 129, 231–2

Cambridge Police, 10–2, 15,
    22, 26, 33–6, 39–41, 51,
    55, 59–61, 80, 82–8, 93,
    95, 126, 129–30, 203

Carrington, Walter C., 222
Carter, Jimmy, 227, 247
Chambliss, Prince, 219–20
Charles Hamilton Houston
    Institute for Race and
    Justice, 117, 130–1,
    259
Chavous, Kevin, 243–5
Christopher, Warren, 72
Clinton, Bill, 72, 169, 188,
    230
Clinton, Hillary, 259
Cobb, Jr., Charles, 256–7
Cochran, Jr., Johnnie L., 73–
    4, 146, 155–6
Cole, James, 215
Colley, Drake, 87–9, 95
Collins, LeRoy, 184
Combs, Sean "Puff Daddy,"
    155
Counter, S. Allen, 79–82, 98,
    101
Cox, Brandon, 137
Crowley, Brandon Thomas,
    203
Crowley, James:
    arrest of Gates, 9–13, 18–
        41
    background and childhood
        of, 15, 17
    police report of, 20–34, 36,
        38–9
Crowley/Gates affair:
    911 call transcription of,
        26–30
    "beer summit" and, 60–3,
        129
    details of, 9–13, 18–41
    media coverage of, 34–9
    Obama's response to, 12,
        41, 50–5, 59–62, 120–1
    police report of, 20–34, 36,
        38–9
    public opinion and, 59–60,
        116, 120–1

Wexler Commission and,
    129–30
Culpepper, Miniard, 188

Dash, Sam, 246
Deleon, Angela, 61
Denny, Reginald, 69–70
Dershowitz, Alan, 82–3, 96
Dershowitz, Elon, 82–3
Devine, Antoine, 226
Diallo, Amadou, 74, 136
driving while black, 74, 101,
    148–175
Du, Billy Heung Ki, 70
Du, Soon Ja, 70–1
Du Bois, W.E.B., 48, 98
Dunham, Stanley Ann, 43,
    45–7
Duru, N. Jeremi, 150–1

Earls, Felton James, 216–17
East Haven, Connecticut,
    141–2
Edelman, Marian Wright,
    118
Elghannaz, Driss, 19
Epps, Jr., Willie J., 224–5

Fagan, Jeffrey, 137
"Fair Harvard"
    commencement hymn,
    77–80
Farid, Hafiz, 190–1
Farrington, Thomas A., 230–
    1
Faust, Drew Gilpin, 95
Fein, David B., 142
Ferguson, Colin, 137
Figueroa, Carlos, 23–5
First Amendment, 19, 36, 61
Fletcher, Jr., Bill, 191–2
Flowers, Gary L., 213
Floyd, David, 139–41
*Floyd, et al. v. City of New
    York, et al.*, 139–41

Fort, Vance, 239–40
Fossey, Dian, 68
Fox News, 36, 53, 56, 132–5
Franklin, John Hope, 146, 230
Fry, Vincent, 209–10
Fulwood III, Sam, 252–3

Garcetti, Gil, 156
Gates, Daryl, 68
Gates, Elizabeth, 61
Gates, Jr., Henry Louis "Skip":
    arrest of, 9–13, 18–41, 144–5, 148, 156, 186–7, 189
    background and childhood of, 15–7, 43–5
    Colored People, 16, 44
    father of, 61
    first meeting with Obama, 41–3
    mother of, 43–5, 47
    Thirteen Ways of Looking at a Black Man, 274n1
    See also Crowley/Gates affair
Gates, Sr., Henry Louis, 61
Gates, Maggie, 61
Gates, Paul, 43, 61
Gates, Pauline Augusta Coleman, 43–5, 47
Gossett, Jr., Lou, 255
Grannum, Colvin, 201–2
Grant, Oscar, 75
Graves, Jr., Earl Gilbert "Butch," 186–7
Graves, Sr., Earl Gilbert, 251
Greenidge, Sr., George, 17

Haas, Robert, 129–30
Hamer, Fannie Lou, 46
Hampton, Ronald E., 192–3
Handy, Chris, 217–8
Hardman, Della Brown, 42
Harlins, Latasha, 70–1
Harris, Leslie, 249–50
Harvard, John, 77
Harvard Law School Black Law Students

Association (HBLSA), 102
Harvard University Police Department (HUPD), 95–6
Hayes, Dennis, 215–16
health care, 12, 41, 51–3, 60, 62, 260
Henry, Danroy, 137
Henson, Matthew, 81
Herbert, Bob, 252
Heymann, Phil, 87
Higginbotham, Jr., A. Leon, 253–4
Hill, Oliver, 254
Holder, Eric, 131, 135, 156–7
Holliday, George, 67
Holmes, Juanita, 139
Hooks, Benjamin, 72
Horne, Lena, 46
Hrabowski, Freeman, 159
Hubbard, Bruce A., 219
Hughes, V. W., 103–4
Hutchins, Glenn, 61

Immigration and Customs Enforcement (ICE), U.S., 141
innocence, presumption of, 9–13, 18, 65
Ito, Lance, 155–6

Jackson, George, 171–3
Jackson, Mahalia, 46
Jackson, Michael, 155
Jarrett, Valerie, 41
Jealous, Benjamin Todd, 134–5, 144
Jenkins, Eddie, 232–3
Jessamy, Ronald, 248–9
Jim Crow laws, 49
Johnson, Fred, 161–2
Johnson, Lyndon B., 149, 184
Johnson, Jr., Robert, 154–5
Jones, Amos, 220–1
Jones, Donald Marvin, 174–5
Jones, Jr., James M., 79–80, 85, 87, 98, 101, 179
Jones, Kevin, 210–13

Jones, Nathaniel R., 227–9
Jordan, Vernon, 260

Karlin, Joyce, 71
Keats, Ezra, 91
Keith, Damon, 247–8
Kemayo, Kamau, 175–7
Kennedy, Jackie, 151
Kennedy, John F., 58
Kerry, John, 55, 66
King, Colbert, 60–1
King, Kelly, 54–5
King, Jr., Martin Luther, 45–6, 48, 86, 116, 214
King, Rodney, 12–3, 65–75, 102, 115
Koon, Stacey, 72

Lashley, Leon, 25, 54
Lawson, Michael A., 152–4
Lee, Spike, 42, 261
Lee, Tonya Lewis, 42
Lincoln, Abraham, 49, 58
Lomax, Walter, 240–1
Long, Jackie, 157
Lopez, Ian Haney, 122–3
Los Angeles Police Department (LAPD), 67–8, 71–2, 110, 152–3, 178–9, 185, 187
Louima, Abner, 73
Loury, Glenn, 120–3
Lowry, James, 223–4
Luima, Abner, 136

Manly, Howard, 258–60
Maricopa County Sheriff's Office (MCSO), Arizona, 141–2
Marshall, Justice Thurgood, 46, 86, 119, 146, 148–9, 239
Martin, Ralph, 249
Maryland Court of Special Appeals, 108–9, 112
Mason, Reginald, 246–7
Mathews II, John, 256
Mauer, Marc, 111, 118
McHenry, Douglas, 171–3
McLaurin, Charles, 257

media coverage of
    Crowley/Gates affair,
    34–9
Mehserle, Johannes, 75
Meyer, Andrew, 66
Miller-El v. Dretke, 119
Moore, Amanda, 19, 32
Morgan, Joe, 187
Morton, Rory, 79–80, 82–3,
    96–8, 101
Murphy, Wendy, 27
Mutua, Makau, 198–9
Myers, Thomas, 141
Myers, Jr., Woodrow, 241–2

911 call transcription of
    Crowley/Gates incident,
    26–30
NAACP, 35, 47–50, 72, 89,
    109, 133–5, 144, 160,
    181, 197, 208, 215, 227
Napolitano, Andrew, 36
Neufeld, Peter, 73

Obama, Barack, 134–5, 156,
    162, 183, 225–6, 259–
    60
    "beer summit" of, 60–2,
        129
    Democratic National
        Convention address
        (2004), 41, 55–6, 59
    *Dreams from My Father: A
        Story of Race and
        Inheritance,* 45, 55
    election of, 46–7, 111,
        115–7, 120–4, 225
    first meeting with Gates,
        41–3
    keynote address at 2009
        NAACP convention,
        47–50
    parents of, 43, 45–7, 55
    response to Lynn Sweet's
        question about Gates'
        arrest, 12, 41, 51–5, 59
    speech on race at
        Philadelphia
        Constitution Center
        (2008), 57–9

Obama, Michelle, 42, 56, 92,
    186
Ogletree, Charles:
    background of, 11
    *Beyond the Rodney King
        Story,* coauthored by,
        73
    as counsel to Gates, 11, 61
    *From Lynch Mobs to the
        Killing State,* 120
    meeting with Crowley, 61–
        2
    mentor to Obama, 41–2
Ogletree, Richard, 42

Parks, Rosa, 46
Patrick, Deval, 236
Paultre, Nicole, 74
Payton, John, 35–7, 208–9
Perez, Tom, 141–2
Perry, John, 184–5
Phalen, Earl Martin, 207–8
Phillips, Eric, 242–3
Poitier, Sidney, 46
post-racial society, 115–27,
    144, 187
Powell, Colin, 253
Powell, Laurence, 72
Powell, Justice Lewis, 119,
    272n4
Pratt, Geronimo, 155
Prince, Walter, 35, 40
public opinion, 59–60, 115–7

racial profiling, 12–3, 52–3,
    59–62, 79–90, 101–2,
    106–15, 121–27, 129–
    46, 156, 168, 180, 183,
    189–90, 234
Rangel, Charles, 75
Rashed, Haazim, 164–5
Reed, Kwame, 200–1
Reid, Harry, 183
Richardson, Robert, 254–5
Riley, Bud, 31, 34
Rivers, Eugene, 117
Roberts, Michele, 130
Roberts, Richard, 149–50
Robinson, Michelle, 41
Rochman, Bonnie, 37–8

Rogers, Steven, 234–6

Scheck, Barry, 73
Scheindlin, Shira, 140
Seidenstein, Shelly, 191
Sentencing Project, The, 75–
    6, 111, 118
Settles, Ron, 155
Shane, Jon, 37
Sharpton, Al, 74, 129
Shaw, Theodore, 197–8
Sheridan, Ryan, 139
Sherrod, Shirley, 132–5
Simms, Stuart, 159–60
Simpson, O. J., 155–6
Smith, David, 177–8
Smith, Dennis C., 139
Souter, Justice David, 119
South Central LA, 70–1
South Side of Chicago, 92–3,
    165, 186
Sterling, Louis, 79–80, 92–5,
    98, 101
Sterling, Voltaire Rico, 165–
    7
"Stop, Question, Frisk," 137,
    140
Sullenberger, Chesley, 81
Sullivan, Ronald, 181–3
Sweet, Lynn, 51–2

Taylor, Andrea, 42
Tea Party, 133
Ten Point Coalition, 117
Tucker, Chris, 42
Turner, Chris, 157–8
Turner, M. Rick, 189–90
Turner, Reggie, 157–9

Underwood, Blair, 178–80

Valentine, Curtis, 180
Verrett, Rory E., 199–200
Vilsack, Tom, 133, 135

Wald, Johanna, 135
Walker, Billy, 178
Walker, Chuck, 236–7
Walton, Reggie, 119, 167–8
Washington, Denzel, 81

Washington, Harold, 169
Washington, Robin, 183–4
Watson, Larry, 151–2
WBBM (Chicago radio
    station), 142–4
Weisberg, Stanley, 69
West, Don, 168
Wexler, Chuck, 129
Wexler Commission, 129–30
Whalen, Lucia, 18, 21, 24,
    26–30

White, Terry, 69
Wiley, Fletcher, 220
Wilkins, Sr., G. R., 105–7
Wilkins, Norman Scott, 105–
    6
Wilkins, Robert, 102–14
Wilkins, Roger, 184–5
Wilmot, David, 245–6
Wilson, Benjamin F., 206–7
Wilson, Beverly Ann, 186
Wilson III, Ernest J., 160–1

Wilson, Jr., John Silvanus,
    162–4
Wilson, Leon, 204–6
Wilson, William Julius, 185–
    6
Wright, Jeremiah, 56–9
Wright, Steven H., 225–6
Wright, Tim, 168–9

Young, Jack, 239